Forcible Displacement Throughout the Ages

International Humanitarian Law Series

VOLUME 36

The International Humanitarian Law Series is a series of monographs and edited volumes which aims to promote scholarly analysis and discussion of both the theory and practice of the international legal regulation of armed conflict.
The series explores substantive issues of International Humanitarian Law including,

- protection for victims of armed conflict and regulation of the means and methods of warfare
- questions of application of the various legal regimes for the conduct of armed conflict
- issues relating to the implementation of International Humanitarian Law obligations
- national and international approaches to the enforcement of the law and
- the interactions between International Humanitarian Law and other related areas of international law such as Human Rights, Refugee Law, Arms Control and Disarmament Law, and International Criminal Law.

The titles published in this series are listed at brill.nl/ihul

Forcible Displacement Throughout the Ages

Towards an International Convention for the Prevention and Punishment of the Crime of Forcible Displacement

by

Grant Dawson and Sonia Farber

MARTINUS
NIJHOFF
PUBLISHERS

LEIDEN • BOSTON
2012

Library of Congress Cataloging-in-Publication Data

Dawson, Grant (Grant Mathew)
Forcible displacement throughout the ages : towards an international convention for the prevention and punishment of the crime of forcible displacement / by Grant Dawson and Sonia Farber.
p. cm. -- (International humanitarian law series ; 36)
Includes index.
ISBN 978-90-04-22054-6 (hardback : alk. paper) -- ISBN 978-90-04-22055-3 (e-book) 1. Forced migration. 2. International criminal law. 3. Refugees--Civil rights. 4. Internally displaced persons--Civil rights. I. Farber, Sonia. II. Title.
KZ6530.G73 2012
342.08--dc23

2012023808

ISSN 1389-6776
ISBN 978 9004 22054 6 (hardback)
ISBN 978 9004 22055 3 (e-book)

Printed on acid-free paper.

We note with sadness the passing of two esteemed members of our Editorial Advisory Board – Antonio Cassese (01 January 1937 - 21 October 2011) and Leslie C Green (06 November 1920 - 27 November 2011). Antonio and Leslie were outstanding scholars and enthusiastic supporters of the IHL Series and both will be sorely missed.

This book is dedicated to the victims of the Plains Wars, 1851-1890 CE.

Aut viam inveniam aut faciam.

Table of Contents

About the Authors

Grant Dawson

Juris Doctor, Georgetown University Law Center, Washington, DC, USA; Bachelor of Arts, Columbia College, New York City, New York, USA; Legal Officer, United Nations International Criminal Tribunal for the former Yugoslavia (ICTY), The Hague, The Netherlands. The views expressed herein are those of the author alone and do not necessarily reflect the views of the ICTY or the United Nations in general.

Sonia Farber

Juris Doctor, University of California, Berkeley School of Law, Specialisation in International Law, Berkeley, California, USA; Bachelor of Arts, Claremont McKenna College, Claremont, California, USA; currently an associate in the International Dispute Resolution Group at Debevoise & Plimpton, LLP, New York City, New York, USA; former Intern in the Office of the President, United Nations International Criminal Tribunal for the former Yugoslavia (ICTY), The Hague, The Netherlands. The views expressed herein are those of the author alone and do not reflect the views of Debevoise & Plimpton.

Foreword

by the Right Honourable Lord Bonomy[1]

The impact of the United Nations International Criminal Tribunal for the former Yugoslavia (ICTY) is justifiably described as "ground-breaking". Just how fundamental and extensive are the achievements of the ICTY can initially be illustrated by setting them in context. Initial post World War II activity in negotiating international humanitarian and human rights treaties and instruments was followed by a long period of relative inactivity. Prior to United Nations Security Council Resolution No. 827 of 25 May 1993, the international criminal law landscape largely had lain fallow for 40 years through the period of the Cold War. Developments thereafter were rapid, resulting in the establishment of other tribunals and encouraging completion of negotiations on the Rome Treaty and the establishment of the International Criminal Court (ICC).

If all that the ICTY had done was act as a catalyst for these other developments, then that alone would merit celebration as a lasting legacy. However, the influence of the work of the ICTY as an institution, bringing indictments against 161 accused, including ongoing proceedings against 35 persons, materially influencing the development of substantive international criminal law and international criminal procedure, and reaching out to the countries of the former Yugoslavia to build and strengthen judicial capacity in the field of war crimes and crimes against humanity, has been extraordinary.

And yet for all that these major institutional achievements will have a lasting impact that deserves recognition, perhaps it is the impact of the ICTY on the expansion of worldwide interest in ways of combating the most serious international crimes that deserves greatest recognition.

Although in the early 1990s there was considerable public interest in the subject (the Coalition for the ICC alone comprised over 2,000 non-governmental organisations), when compared with the situation now, that was just the start. The highly visible and prominent work of active international criminal justice institutions such as the ICTY captured the interest of more and more people in influencing the development of institutions and mechanisms for securing peace

1 Lord Bonomy interrupted his service as a Judge of the Supreme Courts of Scotland to replace Judge May in the *Slobodan Milošević* trial at the ICTY. He thereafter presided in the *Milutinović et al.* multi-accused trial, was the Pre-Trial Judge in the *Karadžić* case, and sat in a number of interlocutory appeals.

and justice in areas of conflict, an increasingly urgent task. It is shocking to note that between 1945 and 2008 there were 313 armed conflicts in various parts of the world, resulting in close to 100 million deaths. A quick survey of the conflict zones of the world since 2008 simply confirms that there is no let up.

Against that background, the on-going growth and interest in this field is greatly to be welcomed. Those who campaigned and strove for international judicial action against crimes against humanity have since 1993 been able to turn their attention to participating actively in the work of a number of different international criminal tribunals. The young lawyers and interns from all over the world who offer their skills to the ICTY, often in crucial stages of their careers and studies, have taken time out to play their part, during which they have refined their knowledge of law and procedure and expanded their interest in this field of worthy endeavour. In my stint of just over five years in The Hague, my Trial Chamber was supported by many of these young professionals. They were all united in their enthusiastic dedication to the work of the ICTY. That unity of purpose made for a uniquely positive, determined, and productive team spirit.

It has been a feature of major cases in the various tribunals that day and daily they raise engaging questions of law and procedure that have not previously arisen for formal adjudication. There literally is never a dull moment. Much of the work goes largely unnoticed by the general public. Even the dedicated student has great difficulty keeping up to date with developments. There is therefore enormous scope for study, research, and writing reflecting there developments in the field and bringing them to the wider public notice. Such writing has added value when it is the product of those directly involved in the field, whether as lawyers or judges.

The authors bring a unique combination of historical knowledge, keen intellect, inventive minds, and their experience at the cutting edge of developments in international criminal jurisprudence to bear on the subject of forcible displacement (known in its most high-profile form as "ethnic cleansing"), which has been with us almost as long as the hills, but in a number of guises that have not till now been given the attention they deserve. There is a story to tell, a problem to be analysed and fully understood, and, if possible, a solution to be found. All feature here. Seldom does one complete a chapter of a law book, looking forward to the opportunity to open the next to discover how the story unfolds. Would that it were more often so. There is enormous scope for similar works combining academic study, historical perspective, and practical experience, not only to record developments that have occurred so far, but also to point us in the direction of developments to which we should aspire. We are simply short term occupants of a staging post on the developing path towards a fully functioning international criminal justice system. This work is a major step along that path.

Iain Bonomy,
Edinburgh

Acknowledgements

Very few books of this kind can be written in isolation and without the benefit of the assistance and input of many others. This book is no exception. The authors would like to acknowledge the many discussions about the crime of forcible displacement that they have had with their colleagues at the United Nations International Criminal Tribunals for the former Yugoslavia and Rwanda. Joakim Dungel shared with us his experiences while working for the Appeals Chamber of the Special Court for Sierra Leone. We wish to thank anthropologist Nora Farber for her invaluable assistance with chapter one of this book, which was greatly improved by her expertise. We are indebted to Kate Jastram of University of California Berkeley, whose classes on refugee law and international humanitarian law provided a useful knowledge base for the writing of this book. The librarians of the University of California Berkeley and Seattle Public Libraries were also very helpful during our research.

Grant would like to express his sincere gratitude to his father for teaching him that there are things bigger than one's self in this world; to his mother for teaching him his ABCs; and to his wife for her loving support during the writing of this book.

Sonia would like to thank her mother and father for their unwavering support, patience, and humor; she would also like to express her deepest gratitude to her sister for always being there and for willingly discussing the ideas and themes contained in this book.

Introduction

> *And so, the profound irony is that our noblest achievement—morality—has evolutionary ties to our basest behavior—warfare. The sense of community required by the former was provided by the latter.*[1]

Forcible displacement transforms cultures and can even lead to their destruction. Forcible displacement wears many linguistic guises: expulsion, transfer, deportation, migration, dislocation—illegal, involuntary, forced, coerced, and unlawful. Despite these various monikers, the objective, and too often the result, is still the same: the removal of a group of people, which often leads to their destruction and distinctive way of life. Although humans have been displacing each other for thousands of years, we have only recently begun to codify the legal contours of this phenomenon and, indeed, this crime. And we have barely scratched the surface of serious efforts at curbing the displacement of peoples before it occurs. This book strives to lay the foundation for a comprehensive and lasting effort to erect positive legal structures for the prevention of forcible displacement, the implementation of which will require the work of the entire global community.

This book was inspired by the authors' experiences, both at the United Nations International Criminal Tribunal for the former Yugoslavia (ICTY) and elsewhere, with the crime of forcible displacement and with refugee law in general. Working in the field of international criminal law on cases involving forcible displacement can be an experience riddled with confusion and doubt. The conflicts in the Balkans during the dissolution of the Socialist Federative Republic of Yugoslavia in the 1990s were ones of persecutory forcible displacement of one group of people by another. To be sure, tens of thousands were unlawfully detained, killed, raped, and tortured; but, often these were but means to reach the objective: to remove a group of people from a piece of land so another group could use it. That is often what forcible displacement boiled down to in the former Yugoslavia and throughout human history. Other conflicts, like the genocide in Rwanda in 1994, were more pointedly aimed at extinguishing the living existences of a particular group of people, and this will be examined in this book as well, as it relates to forcible displacement. But the displacement of groups does not only happen in war: it also happens during peacetime. And this has often occurred when a government finds that it is in the utilitarian "public interest" to remove a group of people from their homes. Whereas the forcible displacement of people during wartime is mostly regulated by international humanitarian law,

1 Frans de Waal, Primates and Philosophers 55 (2006).

displacement during peacetime is subject to the body of human rights law that has sprung up in modern form since the end of World War II.

In addition to the relevant international humanitarian law and human rights law regimes, a new body of law, international criminal law, has now entered the fray. Since the rebirth of international criminal law in the 1990s, more and more attention has been paid to the crime of forcible displacement. After the watershed events following World War II—where the vanquished were tried at Nuremburg[2] and Tokyo[3] instead of being summarily executed—and the hiatus of the Cold War, the world again focused upon the international dimensions of crimes that were so serious and destructive that they deserved the attention not only of governments, but also of the world community. The United Nations Security Council unanimously created the world's first truly international criminal tribunal, the ICTY, which has made great strides in advancing the contours of the crime of forcible displacement. The Tribunal also set the stage for the new International Criminal Court, which has the potential to provide legal continuity to both international and domestic prosecutions for the crime through the jurisdictional principle of complementarity. But one must be careful not to overzealously codify age-old and complex human phenomena into modern legal constructs, for the attempt to create general legal systems from the experience of multifaceted sociological events can entail the inductive hazards of reasoning from the specific to the general. A theoretical model detached from reality can be useless or even harmful, and it is therefore important to balance the inductive with the deductive when defining forcible displacement so as not to offend the "law of common sense".

This book will attempt to take a nonmyopic view of the human phenomenon of forcible displacement in order to understand it in its true form, freed from preconceived notions. In the face of heart-rending stories from victims of the crime, a body of law has begun to emerge in international tribunals that may not reflect the reality of the actual situations on the ground. Not only has this body of law approached the phenomenon of forcible displacement inconsistently, but it has also at times overlaid Procrustean legal constructs upon difficult fact patterns that evade legal formalism. Any undertaking to comprehensively consider forcible displacement involves being willing to wrestle with the infinite complexities of the facts of a case and devising a legal system of dealing with it that is not inconsistent with the "real world".

It would be impossible to systematically catalogue all the instances of humans displacing one another. One reason for this is that most of our histori-

2 *See generally* Whitney R. Harris, Tyranny on Trial, The Trial of the Major German War Criminals at the End of World War II at Nuremberg, Germany, 1945-1946 (1999); Telford Taylor, The Anatomy of the Nuremberg Trials (1992).

3 *See generally* Beyond Victor's Justice? The Tokyo War Crimes Revisited (Yuki Tanaka, Tim McCormack, & Gerry Simpson, eds.) (2011); Tim Maga, Judgement at Tokyo, The Japanese War Crime Trials (2001).

cal information comes from written records, and written language dates back only 5,500 years.[4] Before that, all we have is archaeological evidence, which is not well-suited to reliably describing the forcible displacement of a group of people far into the past, due to the natural decay of the evidence. The second reason why such a task would be impossible is the sheer scale of the wrongs we have visited upon each other throughout our history. In the twentieth century alone, hundreds of millions of people were subjected to forcible displacement both during war and during relative peace. The situations of concern today are manifold: Afghanistan, Algeria, Bosnia and Herzegovina, Central African Republic, Columbia, Cote d'Ivoire, the Democratic Republic of the Congo, Georgia, Iraq, Kenya, Myanmar, Nepal, Somalia, Sri Lanka, Sudan, and Uganda. And there are more.[5] There are also language barriers to a comprehensive cataloguing of every recorded forcible displacement: it would require the ability to access records from hundreds of languages, both modern and ancient. Set against these limitations, we have tried to excise a sampling of forcible displacements from different parts of the world and from a variety of time frames, in order to obtain a cross-section with which to work.

When one speaks of forcible displacement, the prodigious body of refugee law immediately comes to mind as a relevant source from which to derive conclusions. However, refugee law, by definition, deals with the legal rights of persons and the legal obligations of states *after* a displacement has already taken place. This observation in no way is intended to demean or reduce the necessity of refugee law. After World War II, the plight of millions of persons displaced from their homes and the destruction of states' infrastructure inspired the need for the 1951 Convention Relating to the Status of Refugees (Refugee Convention). And the Refugee Convention is still a seminal legal document that is as relevant today, if not more, than when it was first brought into being. However, it is not a preventive document: it protects those who have already been subjected to displacement, rather than aspiring to prevent people from being displaced in the first place. This is where the need for the next step arises: an international instrument—as well as the implementation of such an instrument—that places a positive obligation upon state actors—and non-state actors, where appropriate—to prevent the forcible displacement of human populations. Such an instrument would be based upon the premise that it is inherently destructive to groups of people and their ways of life to be forcibly uprooted from their homes and sent to someplace else. Moreover, uniform criminal definitions for violations of such fundamental norms must be agreed to and put into practice, be it by domestic or international criminal courts with jurisdiction over internationally-defined

4 David Whitehouse, *Earliest Writing Found*, BBC News, http://news.bbc.co.uk/2/hi/science/nature/334517.stm.

5 UNHCR Statistical Online Population Database, United Nations High Commissioner for Refugees (UNHCR) (19 March 2010), http://www.unhcr.org/pages/4a013eb06.html.

crimes or by the system of state responsibility that has been functioning in the realm of human rights law for decades.

The international community must continue to face the critical problem of the world's displaced people and take definitive, forward-looking action, not only to ameliorate their present struggles, but also to protect more people from future harm. This book is an attempt to confront this situation, with a view to the past, an assessment of the present, and a hope for the future.

Chapter one sets the stage for the rest of the book. It draws upon past research in the fields of archeology and paleoanthropology and recent strides in genetics, in order to give a sense of perspective to our place in Earth's long history. We were once not such a domineering presence on the planet, and a look at our origins may reveal that our existence with each other may not have always been so self-destructive.

Chapter two undertakes to briefly review several literary and historical examples of forcible displacement, some of which bear marked similarities to the transfers we see carried out in our own era. The phenomenon of forcible displacement has not changed much through the centuries; both the motivations of the perpetrators and the effects upon the victims remain the same. Surveying incidents of forcible displacement from our real and imagined past can serve as a utile starting point and integral component to establishing a more comprehensive and effective framework in which to analyse displacement in its contemporary form and to accurately assess its legal aspects.

The modern legal underpinnings of the definition of the crime are then discussed in chapter three. States and the international community as a whole have been grappling with proactive legislation to try to cope with forcible displacement for some time, and it is crucial to have a firm grasp of these efforts in order to intelligibly ground sound conclusions. It is for this reason that the law in this area is discussed in this chapter.

In chapter four, the experience of the international tribunals is explored, as the tribunals have sought to define the elements of the crime of forcible displacement in the specific cases that have been brought before them from areas of recent armed conflict. In this context, the treatment of forcible displacement as a crime that attracts individual criminal responsibility is considered, as well as whether there is justification for a cross-border requirement as a constituent element of the crime. In this regard, the forcible displacement of people historically precedes the geopolitical assignation of borders, which are often irrelevant and unperceived by perpetrators and victims alike during the course of a displacement. While "deportation" has been in use as a term for the forcible displacement of populations for some time, "forcible transfer" is a more recently coined term and is used in a legal, technical sense, as opposed to the traditional, historical term "*deportatio*". Regardless of the phraseology, intra-state displacements can be just as destructive to people's lives as extra-state ones.

Chapter five examines the growing body of scholarly literature on forcible displacement. An analysis of the scholarly work reveals the divergent approaches to the legal issues presented by forcible displacement and the voids that must be filled by the further development of international humanitarian, criminal, and human rights law. This chapter therefore provides the context in which the remainder of the chapters proceed, especially the consolidated reformulation of the legal precepts that are advanced in the final chapter of the book.

Chapter six adds development-induced displacement to the discourse. Finding the right legal framework within which to address development-induced displacement has been a confounding puzzle for scholars and practitioners alike, many of whom have considered development-induced displacement as a purely domestic issue. Recently, entities in the United Nations, among others, have begun the process of addressing development-induced displacement within the rubric of human rights law. This is an important development in the international community's attempts to tackle forcible displacement in a comprehensive fashion.

Chapter seven considers the situation of displacement in Colombia, a country that has been embroiled in a protracted armed conflict for decades. The internal strife in Colombia is paradigmatic of the complexities of modern armed conflict. As such, it provides a useful lens through which to both identify weaknesses in the current applicable law on forcible displacement and consider the real-life challenges of prosecuting individuals for perpetration of forcible displacement.

Finally, in chapter eight, a new convention is submitted for the reader's consideration, along with an explanatory commentary. As the previous chapters demonstrate, there is an acute need for a legal scheme that comprehensively addresses both state and individual responsibility for forcible displacement. The majority of the positive law relating to forcible displacement deals with ameliorating the deleterious effects of the crime, rather than focusing upon preventing it from occurring in the first place. International criminal law has tried to fill this gap for the last couple of decades; and, the treatment of forcible displacement as an international crime, for which individuals can be punished, is an important arrow in the quiver of those who wish to deter violations of the fundamental human rights of people to live where they choose and to do so undisturbed and in peace. Although the developments in the area of international criminal law are welcome, they comprise an intermediary stage in the evolution of the law on displacement, and criminal law is only part of a comprehensive and effective solution to the complex reality of the situation. The time has come for more affirmative and bold action by states and the international community as a whole to eliminate the potential for the displacement of peoples—*before* those displacements occur.

Chapter One

The Origins of Humanity, Agriculture, and Intra-human Armed Conflict

The whole world, in essence, is peopled by the offspring of immigrants and asylum seekers.[1]

We are not the descendents of Neanderthals. Yet, the notion that we are is surprisingly persistent in modern day culture. The neatly linear image of modern day humans evolving from apes, to an early, hairy semi-erect hominid, to a slouching Neanderthal, and then to a modern-looking human—is simply incorrect.

Humans have been searching for their biological and evolutionary origins for some time, mainly through the scientific fields of archaeology and paleoanthropology. Through these disciplines, we have discovered that, about six to seven million years ago, an important evolutionary event occurred on Earth on the east coast of Africa near the equator: the common ancestor of humans and apes underwent a mutation, an evolutionary fork in the road. One path continued on to all the modern-day apes (*e.g.*, chimpanzees, gorillas, orangutans), and the second evolutionary fork went the way of the hominids. The last common ancestor that has been found that humans share with chimpanzees was only recently discovered. In 2009 paleoanthropologists revealed the discovery of "Ardi", a 4.4 million year old skeleton and a member of the newly designated species *Ardipithecus ramidus*.[2] The next major event in our evolution occurred between three and four million years ago, when our ancestors began to walk upright: the genus of this ancestor was *Australopithecus afarensis*.[3] Approximately two and a half million years later, through the twists and turns of evolution, the genus *Homo* finally made its appearance; these hominids used tools and thus started to transform the world around them. Whereas australopithecines stayed at home, hominids

---

1 Peter Heather, Empires and Barbarians: Migration, Development and the Birth of Europe 2 (2009).

2 *See* Michael D. Lemonick and Andrea Dorfman, *Ardi is a New Piece for the Evolution Puzzle*, 1 October 2009, http://www.time.com/time/health/article/0,8599,1927200,00.html; Jamie Shreeve, *Oldest Skeleton of Human Ancestor Found*, National Geographic News, 1 October 2009, http://news.nationalgeographic.com/news/2009/10/091001-oldest-human-skeleton-ardi-missing-link-chimps-ardipithecus-ramidus.html.

3 Australopithecus afarensis is approximately 3.8 to 3 million years old, according to the best estimations of scholars. *See* Ian Tattersall, Becoming Human: Evolution and Human Uniqueness 113 (1999); Ian Tattersall, *Once We Were Not Alone*, Scientific American 58 (Jan. 2000).

ventured forth into other parts of Africa and then on into Asia and Europe. At least four distinct species of hominids coexisted in the same small area of Africa: *Homo habilis, Homo rudolfensis, Paranthropus boisei,* and *Homo ergaster.* Then, between 600,000 and 200,000 years ago, *Homo heidelbergensis* appeared, and travelled to Europe and China. Finally, between 200,000 and 30,000 years ago, *Homo neanderthalensis,* a group of hominids, evolved from *Homo heidelbergensis,* probably in the highlands of Kenya and Tanzania. They were lighter on their feet and swifter in their thoughts than those who came before them.[4]

This is roughly the point to which archaeology and paleoanthropology have taken us. Newly discovered fossil remains are still dramatically increasing our knowledge of our sub-species' collective evolutionary past, most notably with the discovery of a new species of hominid—*Australopithecus sediba*. The almost two million year old fossil remains were found in Malapa Cave in South Africa and belong to an individual whose species probably descended from *Australopithecus africanus* and may be an ancestor of *Homo erectus* or even *Homo sapiens*.[5]

Such wondrous archaeological discoveries will continue, but recently the field of genetics has entered the search for our biological origins, and geneticists have made stunning strides in revealing our origins. Other scientific disciplines have simply not been able to come this close to understanding our origins because of limitations such as *lacunae* in the ancient fossilised record. For example, studies of mitochondrial DNA and Y chromosomes have revealed that all modern humans are the direct descendants of a single group of humans numbering about 86,000 thousand individuals who lived in East Africa between 100,000 to 200,000 years ago. We share the same genetic material with this group of humans, although we continue to evolve. People from this group of *Homo sapiens sapiens* left their evolutionary birthplace in Africa and migrated, over a period of tens of thousands of years, to the Middle East, Europe, Asia, Australia, Oceania, and the Americas.[6]

As humans began to spread out across the globe, their interactions with others like themselves may give us clues to the nature of humanity. For example, are we an inherently aggressive species, or do we possess a proclivity for peaceful relations with each other? Some humans left Africa around 100,000 years

---

4 Ian Tattersall, *Once We Were Not Alone*, SCIENTIFIC AMERICAN 56-62 (Jan. 2000); JONATHAN KINGDON, SELF-MADE MAN: HUMAN EVOLUTION FROM EDEN TO EXTINCTION? (1993).

5 Lee R. Berger, Darryl J. de Ruiter, Steven E. Churchill, Peter Schmid, Kristian J. Carlson, Paul H. G. M. Dirks, & Job M. Kibii, *Australopithecus sediba: A New Species of Homo-Like Australopith from South Africa*, SCIENCE, vol. 328, at 195-204 (9 April 2010); Celia Dugger & John Wilford, *New Hominid Species Discovered in South Africa*, THE NEW YORK TIMES (8 April 2010).

6 STEVE OLSON, MAPPING HUMAN HISTORY, GENES, RACE, AND OUR COMMON ORIGINS 24-28 (2002) (citing Lynn Jorde, Michael Bamshad, and Alan Rogers, *Using Mitochondrial and Nuclear DNA Markers to Reconstruct Human Evolution*, BioEssays 20, 126-36 (1998); Carsten Wiuf and Jotun Hein, *On the Number of Ancestors to a DNA Sequence*, Genetics 147, 1459-68 (1997).

ago, and likely ran into their distant Neanderthal cousins at Skhul, in what is now modern day Israel. These humans stayed there until 80,000 years ago, when they either died out or went back to Africa. The Neanderthals remained. Then, 45,000 years ago, the humans reappeared out of Africa and again may have co-existed with the Neanderthals living in the area. If they in fact did co-exist, the fact that no evidence has been found that the humans and the Neanderthals fought each other could be a remarkable discovery when one considers that the humans at that time were significantly more technologically advanced than the Neanderthals with regards to tool-making. Moreover, Neanderthals even co-existed with humans until at least 30,000 years ago.[7] It is possible that there may have been violence between the two groups, but we have no evidence of it. Nor do we know whether there was competition between the two species for resources, such as hunting and foraging territory.

We now jump ahead to possibly the most important event in human culture: the development of agriculture by modern humans around 10,000 years ago. Before the development of farming, humans lived by hunting or scavenging and by gathering fruits, vegetables, and nuts in their natural environment: in other words, they "lived off the land" and did not cultivate their food. This meant that groups of humans had to be fairly mobile and follow the sources of their sustenance, rather than residing in a single location for the entire year. It also meant that human populations could only grow to a size that was as sustainable as uncultivated food sources would allow. And the land simply did not produce enough food for large, dense populations of humans to exist. The result was that humans lived in small, mobile groups and led a nomadic existence. The fact that we evolved into a species under such conditions and lived like this for hundreds of thousands of years is a significant observation when political scientists are trying to ascertain whether there is some kind of "natural state of humanity" and what the character of that state might be.

With the development of agriculture, however, the food supply increased immensely. Moreover, farming requires a group of people to live in one place for large portions of the year, in order to plant, cultivate, and then harvest their crops. Both these factors fundamentally altered the way that humans associated with each other and the manner in which they organised their cultures because now they were able to support much larger populations, which tended to remain in one place for the majority of the year.[8] By 4,000 years ago, agriculture had spread to all parts of the world.[9] With the advent of stable food crops and a com-

---

7 Steve Olson, Mapping Human History, Genes, Race, and Our Common Origins 73-75, 84 (2002).

8 *See* Jared M. Diamond, Guns, Germs and Steel: A Short History of Everybody for the Last 13,000 Years (1998) (suggesting that Eurasia's geography was conducive to farming and the domestication of animals and thus increased the population density of European cultures)

9 *See* Steve Olson, Mapping Human History, Genes, Race, and Our Common Origins 92-98 (2002).

mitment to farming a particular area of land, people did not move about from place to place as much, led less nomadic lives, and started to form more sedentary societies. People could also now begin to amass more material possessions than they previously did: a farmer needs certain tools to cultivate his or her land and, having invested in planting crops, is not inclined to abandon his or her land easily. Whereas before one's possessions were essentially what one could carry or store for a time, now people could collect food and possessions in a single place.

John Keegan has noted that agriculture "make[s] for war."[10] Indeed, just as there is no evidence of humans killing Neanderthals, there is also no evidence of humans committing mass killings of other humans until the invention of agriculture. Agriculture resulted in humans vastly increasing their numbers and living much more closely together. We do not know, however, whether agriculture was the cause or the effect. Perhaps humans began to multiply for reasons not related to the increase of food, and the land could no longer support the larger groups: agriculture would then have been a solution. Or perhaps, as described above, agriculture was invented and then resulted in larger populations. What is relatively certain is that a dramatic increase in population was made possible by agriculture and allowed people to live in much closer proximity to each other. With the advent of agriculture, humans—who had evolved as small, mobile groups of family clans roaming across the African grasslands, hunting and scavenging game and collecting fruits and nuts in a variety of different places throughout the year—now found themselves competing with each other as they never had before.

The view that humans are an inherently aggressive species—and will always kill and displace each other—may therefore not be as unassailable as some may think. The archeological record of our early origins does not bear out such a portrait of us as a species. We did not evolve to exist closely packed together in cities, but rather to live, work, and love in small groups while roaming freely over vast expanses of grasslands in a temperate climate. The English political philosopher Thomas Hobbes described the "life of man" as "solitary, poor, nasty, brutish, and short".[11] This may have indeed been the case in seventeenth century England, but it has no relevance to our evolutionary origins. Frans de Waal has recently challenged the modern incarnation of Hobbes' view of the world—known as Veneer Theory—and attempted to prove through empirical studies of our closest evolutionary relatives, the great apes, that human morality is not a psycho-cultural

---

10 John Keegan, A History of Warfare 122 (1993) ("Once man invests expectations of a regular return on his seasonal efforts in a particular place—lambing, herding, planting, reaping—he rapidly develops the sense of rights and ownership. Toward those who trespass on the places where he invests his time and effort he must equally rapidly develop the sense of hostility of the user and occupier for the usurper and interloper. Fixed expectations make for fixed responses. Pastoralism, and agriculture even more so, make for war.").

11 Thomas Hobbes, Leviathan, Chapter 13 (1651).

overlay on top of an intrinsically bad nature, but rather the product of millions of years of natural selection upon mammalian sociality.[12]

It may be that some day we will discover that our long and bloody history over the last 5,000 years is the tragic by-product of very specific "choices" in our collective past, such as the "decision" to settle down in one place to start to raise crops. Nevertheless, with the proliferation of humans on the planet and their reorganisation into communities with comparatively high population densities, the contest for resources was set into motion. A consideration of our evolutionary origins as a species may also place into better perspective the notion that individuals or societies are somehow entitled to particular geopolitical territories, *i.e.*, that a group of people "sprung" from the land upon which they live. The concept of land-ownership is well-entrenched in the vast majority of cultures across the planet, but it must be kept in mind that it is a political, legal, and economic construct without any basis in the natural world. As a species, we are all genetically descended from a small group of humans who originated from a small section of Eastern Africa—we did not independently spring into existence in several places, but rather from a single place, and then proceeded to spread across the globe during a process that took tens of thousands of years. As a species, we are all immigrants, and keeping this in mind might assist us in not wronging our neighbours over a piece of land.

12 Frans de Waal, Primates and Philosophers 1-58 (2006).

Chapter Two

Examples of Forcible Displacement

I grow daily to honour facts more and more, and theory less and less.[1]

Recorded history reveals a millennia-old practice of forcible displacement, likely beginning soon after the arrival of agriculture and the ensuing permanent settlement of human populations. The first instance of mass forcible displacement for which historians have found written evidence occurred under the rule of the Assyrian King, Tiglath-Pileser III (745-727 BCE), who replaced large portions of the populations of Assyrian-conquered lands with individuals from elsewhere.[2] Forcible displacement was also carried out in antiquity by the Babylonians and the Greeks. In the Middle Ages, the Romans sought to expel Jews and Muslims from their territories. The displacement of local peoples was a regular feature of Europe's colonial conquests of the 19th and 20th centuries.[3] Yet, as noted by the Special Rapporteurs for the Sub-Commission on Prevention of Discrimination and Protection of Minorities, "the practice and official rationale for forcing the transfer of populations have not changed significantly in the course of history, nor have the consequences."[4] This chapter proceeds from the hypothesis that the misdeeds of our ancestors may mirror those of more contemporary perpetrators and that, by studying the former, we may generate further understanding of the latter.

The examples in this chapter have been selected with two purposes in mind. First, they represent a range of history and geography, beginning hundreds—and sometimes thousands—of years ago. Second, each incident demonstrates the variety of forms that forcible displacement can take and the divergent motiva-

1 Excerpt of a letter from Thomas Carlyle to Ralph Waldo Emerson, 29 April 1836.

2 TOMASZ KAMUSELLA, THE DYNAMICS OF THE POLICIES OF ETHNIC CLEANSING IN SILESIA IN THE NINETEENTH AND TWENTIETH CENTURIES, OPEN SOCIETY INSTITUTE 1 (1999).

3 For a brief but informative discussion on the history of forcible displacement and ethnic cleansing, see Andrew Bell-Fialkoff, *A Brief History of Ethnic Cleansing*, FOREIGN AFFAIRS, Vol. 72, No. 3 110 (Summer 1993).

4 The Human Rights Dimensions of Population Transfer, Including the Implantation of Settlers, Preliminary report prepared by A.S. Al-Khasawneh and R. Hatano, Commission on Human Rights, Sub-Commission on Prevention of Discrimination and Protection of Minorities, Forty-fifth session, ¶ 30 (E/CN.4/Sub.2/1993/17 (6 Jul. 1993).

tions behind that displacement. Despite the various justifications and the specific means by which a displacement has been effected, the lesson remains the same: the coercive transfer of individuals from their homes, whether for ethnic, religious, territorial, economic, or political reasons, violates a fundamental human right to remain in one's home.

1. The Sack of Troy: A Mytho-Historic Account

It may at first seem out of place to include a literary example of forcible displacement in a book of this kind. However, much of the world's literature, although technically works of fiction, derives from actual historical events. And even stories that are not based upon historical realities often reflect the values of the culture that produced them. In the words of Ralph Waldo Emerson, the 19th century transcendentalist philosopher, "[t]he use of literature is to afford us a platform whence we may command a view of our present life, a purchase by which we may move it."[5] In this way, literature can be a cipher for the world around us. The events in the *Aeneid* and the *Iliad* did not in fact take place in a historical sense; however, there was indeed a city of Troy, and it was the target of warfare over an extended period of time.[6] It should be stressed, however, that the inclusion of nonfactual accounts of displacement is by no means intended to diminish the real-world suffering of people who have fallen prey to the actual crime, either past or present.

The mytho-historic account of the Trojan War is a thrice bloody tale. Agamemnon's sacrifice of his daughter, the sack of Troy by the Achaeans, and Agamemnon's own assassination upon his return home at the hands of his wife, Clytemnestra—is one of the oldest dramas of humanity. It is not a work of literature that can be entirely confined to the Western tradition, but rather is a primary epic that in many ways depicts a conflict between East and West.

The story of the fall of Troy and its surrounding tales is told in numerous places in ancient literature. There is no one source that tells of the entire war from beginning to end. Most works depict an episode in the saga, which stretched across decades when one includes the full lead-up to the conflict and its aftermath. Moreover, there were many derivative stories that did not form part of the main story line. In this chapter, only the central plot of the ancient epic is set forth in order to analyse the forcible displacement following the sack of Troy. Some of the main sources include the following: the *Iliad* and *Odyssey* of Homer, composed between 1,000 and 700 BCE; the *Cyclic Epics* in 800 and 700

5 Ralph Waldo Emerson, *Circles*, Essays: First Series 408, *in* Ralph Waldo Emerson, Essays and Lectures: Nature; Addresses, and Lectures; Essays: First and Second Series; Representative Men; English Traits; The Conduct of Life (1983) (first published in 1841).

6 For further reading on the historical city of Troy, see John Gibson Warry, Warfare in the Classical World 29 (1998) (describing the "ruined city" of Priam's Troy that appears to have been "destroyed by fire and violence").

BCE, of which only fragments survive and of which a summary can be found in the *Chrestomathy* of Proclus; the dramas of Aeschylus, Sophocles, and Euripides in the 5th century BCE; Apollodorus' *Epitome* in the 2nd century BCE; and the *Aeneid* of Virgil (published after his death in 19 BCE), especially Book II, which depicts the sack of Troy in potent detail. There are many different versions of the various events that portray the Trojan War, and thus no authoritative account. For the purposes of this book, the fall of the city of Troy is of the most immediate relevance because it ends in the forcible displacement of a civilian population.

The Achaeans had laid siege to Troy for ten years before they finally succeeded in piercing its formidable walls. But what led to this epic struggle between East and West? It all began at the wedding of Peleus and the goddess Thetis, at which Eris, the goddess of strife and sister of Ares, appeared uninvited. Unhappy at being excluded when all the other Olympians had been invited, Eris cast a golden apple—the Apple of Discord—upon the banquet table, upon which was written "For the Fairest". Athena, Hera, and Aphrodite each claimed the prize for herself and sought out Alexandros, otherwise known as "Paris", to choose which of them deserved the apple. The bribing began immediately: Hera promised Paris political power; Athena, prowess in combat. But Aphrodite, the goddess of love, told Paris she would secure for him Helen—the most beautiful woman in the world and the daughter of Zeus and Leda—, if he would declare her the most beautiful. Paris was unable to turn down Aphrodite's offer, and Helen was whisked away across the Aegean Sea to Troy to be his consort.

Now Paris was the son of Priam, the King of the city of Troy, and Helen was the wife of Menelaus, the King of Sparta: problems immediately arose. Menelaus sought the assistance of his brother Agamemnon, the Ruler of Mycenae, who saw a golden opportunity to use the wounded honour of his brother as a pretext to unite the Achaeans in a campaign against Troy, which was rich in gold and other treasures that it had amassed through tariffs on trade through the Aegean Sea.

When fleet-footed Achilleus of Larissa, in Thessaly, heard of the Achaeans preparing to set sail for what would be the most formidable military action in his lifetime, he decided to add his forces to those of his fellow Greeks. Achilleus was the son of King Peleus and the goddess Thetis and was reputed to be the most adept soldier in the world. He was admonished by his immortal mother about the choice he had before him: he would lead a long and peaceful life if he stayed at home, but would live in obscurity, and no one would ever take note of his name in the ages to come. However, if he chose to fight in the war, he would perish in battle, but also earn eternal glory in combat. Achilleus chose the latter.

The Achaean forces assembled at Aulis and readied to set sail, but the winds were not favourable for travel across the sea to the east. Agamemnon therefore prepared to sacrifice his daughter, Iphigenia, in order to satisfy the gods. In some versions she is killed, and in others a deer is sacrificed in her stead. Nevertheless, the winds eventually filled the sails of the black ships, and the Achaeans journeyed to Troy. Once the Achaeans beached their ships upon the Trojan coast, a brief battle took place, as the Trojan forces tried to repel the invaders. Unsuccessful, they retreated into the city, and the Achaeans were unable to breach the thick city walls.

A rather lackluster siege ensued for the next nine years, with the Achaeans spending more time raiding the cities along the Trojan coast for supplies than they did trying to breach the walls of Troy. In fact, it was only a partial siege, because the city was never encircled, thus allowing Troy constant reinforcements from and trade with its allies to the east. A "siege town" sprung up upon the beach around the black ships. In the tenth year of the war, the Achaean army was ready to abandon their campaign against the city of Troy: they were weary of war and wanted to return to their homes, their families. Their leaders convinced them to stay, and the fighting recommenced. Menelaus fought Paris for the fair hand of Helen. Achilleus secured his place in legend by defeating Troy's champion and protector, Hector, breaker of horses, who was another son of King Priam. Soon thereafter, Achilleus managed to breach the walls of Troy, but then was slain by Paris, who was later slain by Philoctetes.

Finally, Odysseus devised a plan to overcome the walls of Troy once and for all—not with force, but with guile. The Achaeans constructed a tremendous wooden horse upon the beach of Troy. The Achaeans then embarked upon their ships and left. When the Trojans learned of this, they rushed down to the sea in disbelief, scarcely believing that their attackers had finally relented and gone home. A debate ensued among the Trojans about what to do, with some thinking that the wooden horse was a trick and others thinking that it was the Achaeans' propitiation to the gods for their unjust siege of Troy. During the debate, an Achaean soldier/spy named Sinon was seized from his hiding place in some nearby bushes, and the deceit of Odysseus began to unfold. Sinon spun a tale for the Trojans, about how the Greeks had foregone their siege of Troy. Knowing that the horse was a sacred animal to the Trojans, they had built the wooden horse as an offering to Apollo, the patron god of the city, in order to appease him and ease their journey back to their homes in the West. Against the advice of his daughter Cassandra and the priest Laocoön—*timeo Danaos et dona ferentis*[7]—, Priam took pity upon the abandoned Sinon, believed his string of lies, and ordered the horse to be hauled past the walls and into the city. The people of the city rejoiced in their good fortune and celebrated long into the night amidst their newest monument—the Trojan Horse.

Later that night, Sinon crept his way through the streets of Troy, while the people slept off their revelries. Keeping out of sight of the guards at the city gate, he made it to the horse and released a secret trap door in its belly. Led by Odysseus, the Achaeans lowered themselves down upon ropes, made quick work of the guards at the gate, and raised the gates of Troy from within. Meanwhile, the Achaeans had not in fact set sail for home, but rather had concealed their ships behind a small island off the coast, called Tenedos. Once given the prearranged signal, they beached their ships back upon the shore and quietly slithered across the plain of Troy to the city. Odysseus' trap had been sprung, and the dec-

7 Publius Vergilius Maro, Aeneid, Book 2, Line 49.

ade-long ambition of the Achaeans had finally been achieved. The Achaeans fell upon the inhabitants of the city—civilian and soldier alike. Some men were slain in their beds as they slept off the night's festivities. Others donned their armour and defended their city and their families. A young Trojan named Aeneus led a small contingent to the palace of King Priam, in order to do what he could under the circumstances. But he and his companions were soon overwhelmed. Although Aeneus was ready to fight to the death, he was persuaded to return home in order to get his family to safety. He managed to escape with his father and son, but his wife during the escape was lost to the fires of Troy, which raged throughout the city.

The son of the slain Achilleus, Neoptolemus, led an assault into the heart of the city, where King Priam and his family had sought refuge upon a sacred altar of the gods. Priam's guards barred shut the heavy doors of the sacred place, but the Achaeans rent them asunder. Neoptolemus slew Priam right upon the sacred altar, and Locrian Aias raped Cassandra, a priestess of Athena, as she desperately clung to her patron goddess' statue in a temple. Over the course of the night and morning, all the men were killed, be they soldier or civilian. Menelaus found Helen and intended to kill her, but then relented and took her back to Sparta as his wife once again. The rest of the women and children were taken captive and carried off as slaves, except for the son of Hector, Astyanax, who was cast from the walls of Troy to his death. The wealth of the city was divided up among the Achaeans, and whatever was left was put to the torch in a great conflagration that razed Troy to its foundations.

The story of the fall of Troy, by today's legal standards, would be a straightforward example of the commission of grave breaches of the Geneva Conventions, war crimes, crimes against humanity, and genocide. The conflict was an international armed conflict: the Achaean forces could be considered an international coalition of different city states, which had joined forces in order to invade a foreign, sovereign neighbour, Troy. In the final battle, not only were soldiers killed, but also men who either were civilians or were soldiers who were not taking an active part in the hostilities (*hors de combat*). Protected persons were the targets as well, such as women, children, and religious figures. The underlying offences that would fall under grave breaches of the Geneva Conventions include willful killing; willfully causing great suffering or serious injury to body and health; extensive destruction and appropriation of property not justified by military necessity carried out unlawfully and wantonly; and unlawful deportation or transfer or unlawful confinement of civilians. In respect of violations of the laws or customs of war, otherwise known as "war crimes", the underlying offences could be classified as murder; the wanton destruction of cities, towns or villages, or devastation not justified by military necessity; the destruction or wilful damage to historic monuments or to institutions dedicated to religion or art; and the plunder of public or private property. The sack of Troy could also be characterised as a widespread or systematic attack upon a civilian population. The fact that the city was defended did not divest it of its civilian character, and the underlying offences committed included murder; extermination; enslavement; deportation; imprisonment; rape; and persecutions on political, racial, and religious grounds.

The crimes committed at the legendary Troy would also have constituted genocide. Genocide is established when any of the following underlying offences are committed with intent to destroy, in whole or in part, a national, ethnical, racial, or religious group, as such: killing members of the group; causing serious bodily or mental harm to members of the group; deliberately inflicting on the group conditions of life calculated to bring about its physical destruction in whole or in part; imposing measures intended to prevent births within the group; or forcibly transferring children of the group to another group. Forcible displacement has been held by modern international criminal courts to come within this list of crimes; and, with the exception of preventing births within a group, each of these offences was committed at Troy with the required specific intent.

Further, regarding the intent of the perpetrators, personal motives are sufficient in order to fulfill the requisite criminal state of mind for the elements of these international crimes. For example, Agamemnon did not bear any specific ill-will towards Priam and his city, but rather wanted money and power and used his brother's betrayal as an opportunity to wage war against Troy. Menelaus either truly loved Helena and wanted to get her back or wanted to salvage his personal honour, which had been blemished by Paris' abduction of his wife—or both. Achilleus sailed to Troy for immortal glory. Odysseus did not want to go to Troy at all, but was forced to go. Whatever the reason, the Achaeans voluntarily decided to journey across the Aegean Sea and wage an aggressive war against the Trojans, which included the perpetration of crimes again innocent persons. And this assessment is not only made according to the standards of today, for the ancient texts record that the gods were displeased at the manner in which Troy was defeated and as a result punished the Achaeans on their journey home. Many never made it back, such as Locrian Aias who had raped a priestess of Athena and desecrated a sacred statute. Agamemnon received his due when he was killed by his wife Clytemnestra upon his return to Mycenae. Achilleus never witnessed the fall of Troy and died in battle. It took Odysseus ten years to return home, during which time he suffered countless tragedies while suitors despoiled his home back in Ithaca.

In respect of the forcible displacement of the women and children of Troy, it should be acknowledged that the Achaeans could have taken a number of different actions. Transporting the women and children all the way back to Greece could not have been a simple endeavour; and, they easily could have been killed instead, as was the case with Hector's son, Astyanax. They also could simply have been abandoned there in the ashes of Troy. But the Achaeans instead chose to displace them, so that they could be used as slaves. This type of displacement is what will be referred to later in this book as an "arrival-oriented displacement" because it is not so much the point of departure that motivates the transfer, as much as the destination and eventual treatment of the victims. In this case, the women and children, considered valuable human capital, were transferred to mainland Greece in order to serve as slaves.

The destruction of Troy is a cornerstone event in world literature, and one of its ultimate episodes centers around the displacement of a group of civilians. This displacement is interlinked with other crimes, such as murder, looting, and rape. They all form a piece of a pattern. This interconnectedness between different types of crimes is a phenomenon that appears in actual human conflicts: more often than not, displacements are perpetrated alongside other crimes, such as murder and rape: whether these other crimes are ends in and of themselves or means by which the displacements are accomplished depends upon the specific facts of the conflict. The notion of war crimes and crimes against humanity are by no means modern inventions, but rather have existed for thousands of years in both theory and practice.[8] What better evidence could there be that forcible displacement has been considered a crime for thousands of years other than the fact that one of our earliest recorded stories ends in the displacement of a group of civilians from their homes and the perpetrators suffering divine retribution for their acts?

2. The Babylonian Captivity: Displacement in the Ancient World

The Babylonian Captivity refers to three interrelated displacements of the Jews by the Babylonians in the 6th century BCE. There is a significant body of scholarship devoted to this period of Jewish history, as well as much debate over the details and dates of the displacements. The account below is principally taken from *The King James Bible*, which, for the purposes of this book, is considered to be primary source material.[9]

In the wake of the crumbling Assyrian Empire[10] the Jews were besieged by a hostile foreign power, the Babylonians, who had conquered Assyria and then "taken from the river of Egypt unto the river Euphrates all that pertained to the king of Egypt."[11] In the Second Book of Kings of the Bible, it is told that Jehoiachin, the King of Judah who reigned from the city of Jerusalem, defied the god of the

8 Georges Maridakis, *An Ancient Precedent to Nuremberg*, 4 Journal of International Criminal Justice 847 (2006) (arguing that the trial of the Athenian General Philocles in 405 BCE during the Peloponnesian War for "outrageous practices towards Greeks" was an ancient precursor of the Nuremberg trials following World War II).

9 The Bible, Authorized King James Version with Apocrypha (2008) (originally published in 1611). In addition to the references cited below, references to the Babylonian Captivity can also be found in Ezra; The Book of the Prophet Ezekiel; Tobit, chapter 14 (Apocrypha); and Judith, chapter 4 (Apocrypha).

10 John W. Betlyon, *Neo-Babylonian Military Operations Other Than War in Judah and Jerusalem*, *in* Judah and the Judeans in the Neo-Babylonian Period 263-64 (Joseph Blenkinsopp & Oded Lipschitz, eds., 2003).

11 2 Kings, chapter 24, verse 7.

Jews and greatly angered him. In 597,[12] King Nebuchadnezzar of Babylon took his forces to Jerusalem and besieged the city.[13] Jehoiachin, along with his royal family and court, surrendered to Nebuchadnezzar, who took them all into custody. In addition to plundering the royal treasures of Jerusalem, Nebuchadnezzar "carried away all Jerusalem, and all the princes, and all the mighty men of valour, even ten thousand captives, and all the craftsmen and smiths: none remained, save the poorest sort of people on the land."[14] Nebuchadnezzar made his uncle, Mattaniah (whose name was subsequently changed to Zedekiah), the new king of Jerusalem, where he reigned for eleven years, before then rebelling against Nebuchadnezzar himself.[15]

This first displacement is also described in the Second Book of Chronicles, where some further details are added. The Chaldeans, who were inhabitants of a country of which Babylon was the capital, sacked Jerusalem, killed the young men who had taken sanctuary in houses, "and had no compassion upon young man or maiden, old man, or him that stooped for age".[16] The fate of those who were carried off to Babylon was to be servants to Nebuchadnezzar and his sons "until the reign of the kingdom of Persia".[17]

The Book of Daniel relates additional tales of the first displacement as it concerned Daniel.[18] Among the people of King Jehoiachin's court whom Nebuchadnezzar had carried away to Babylon were Daniel, Hananiah, Mishael, and Azariah—"[c]hildren in whom was no blemish, but well favoured, and skilful in all wisdom, and cunning in knowledge, and understanding science, and such as had ability in them to stand in the king's palace, and whom they might teach the learning and the tongue of the Chaldeans."[19] After being nourished in Babylon for three years, they were brought before King Nebuchadnezzar, who spoke with them and found them "in all matters of wisdom and understanding … ten times better than all the magicians and astrologers that were in all his realm."[20] After Daniel was successful in interpreting a dream of Nebuchadnezzar, which the King's wise men had been unable to interpret, Nebuchadnezzar put Daniel, Hananiah, Mishael, and Azariah in charge of the entire province of Babylon and made Daniel chief of all the wise men.[21]

---

12 Ronald Herbert Sack, Images of Nebuchadnezzar: The Emergence of Legend x (2004).

13 2 Kings, chapter 24, verses 10-11.

14 *Id.* verses 12-16.

15 *Id.* chapter 24, verses 17-20.

16 2 Chronicles, chapter 36, verse 17.

17 *Id.* chapter 36, verse 20.

18 The Book of Daniel, chapters 1-6; *see also* The History of Susana (Apocrypha); The History of the Destruction of Bel and the Dragon (Apocrypha).

19 The Book of Daniel, chapter 1, verse 4.

20 *Id.* chapter 1, verses 18-20.

21 *Id.* chapters 2-4.

Ten years later, in 587 BCE,[22] Nebuchadnezzar besieged for a second time the city of Jerusalem, which was under the control of the rebellious Zedekiah. The Babylonian forces built forts around the city and settled in for a protracted siege, which lasted for one and a half years. When the food ran out in the city, Zedekiah and his military forces fled Jerusalem by night via the plains surrounding the city. However, the Chaldeans pursued Zedekiah and his forces, overtaking him on the plains of Jericho. Zedekiah's military forces were scattered by the Chaldeans, and Zedekiah himself was captured and taken before Nebuchadnezzar in Riblah. Judgement was passed upon Zedekiah, his sons were put to death before his very eyes, and then his own eyes were put out, after which he was shackled and brought to Babylon.[23] Nebuchadnezzar also executed all the nobles of Judah at Riblah.[24]

Nebuchadnezzar then sent his captain of the guard, Nebuzar-adan, along with the forces of the Chaldeans, to take the city of Jerusalem. They breached the walls of Jerusalem and burned all the houses and temples of the city. Nebuzar-adan brought some of the high priests before Nebuchadnezzar in Riblah in the land of Hamath, and they were executed. The people of the city were taken away to Babylon, along with the treasures of Jerusalem, but "the captain of the guard left the poor of the land to be vinedressers and husbandmen." Nebuchadnezzar made Gedaliah the ruler of those who were left.[25]

The third displacement of the Babylonian Captivity took place around 582 BCE.[26] Although Gedaliah assured his subjects that they would be unharmed as long as they submitted to the reign of Nebuchadnezzar, the Jews rebelled and killed Gedaliah.[27] The book of Jeremiah gives more details of the story: Baalis, the King of the Ammonites, sent Ishmael to kill Gedaliah, who was living on Mizpah. After dining together, Ishmael, together with ten men he had brought with him, smote and killed Gedaliah, along with other Chaldeans and Jews who were present at the banquet. Ishmael took all the dead bodies and cast them into a mass grave. He then took the Chaldeans captive, as well as the remainder of the people in Judah, and attempted to bring them by force back to the Ammonites. However, Johanan pursued them with a host of captains, catching up to them at the waters near the city of Gibeon. Johanan rescued the captives and returned

22 This date is disputed. Some scholars argue that Nebuchadnezzar laid siege to Jerusalem in 587 and that the city succumbed to the siege on 5 August 587, while others contend that Nebuchadnezzar entered the city in 586, and the city fell on 15 August 586. *See* Daniel L. Smith-Christopher, A Biblical Theology of Exile 59 (2002).

23 2 Kings, chapter 25, verses 1-7; Jeremiah, chapter 39, verses 1-7.

24 Jeremiah, chapter 39, verse 6.

25 2 Kings, chapter 24, verses 8-22; Jeremiah, chapter 39, verses 8-10.

26 Rainer Kessler, The Social History of Ancient Israel: An Introduction 119 (2008) (describing the third exile which took place in the wake of the assassination of Gedaliah).

27 2 Kings, chapter 24, verses 22-26.

them back to Mizpah. Ishmael managed to escape with eight other of his men and returned to the Ammonites.[28]

Following Ishmael's slaying of Gedaliah, the Jews feared Nebuchadnezzar's retribution and wanted to flee to Egypt.[29] The people petitioned the prophet Jeremiah to ask the god of the Jews what they should do. After ten days, the god of the Jews communicated with Jeremiah, commanding the Jews not to travel to Egypt: if they did, they would "die by the sword, by the famine, and by the pestilence". Nevertheless, led by Johanan and all his military forces, the remaining Jews in Judah fled to Egypt, and all the lands of Judah were emptied of their inhabitants.[30]

Babylon was conquered by the Persian Empire in 539 BCE.[31] It is recorded in the Second Book of Chronicles that, in his first year of his reign, Cyrus the Great ordered that the Temple of Jerusalem was to be rebuilt.[32] When Darius assumed power from Cyrus, he vowed to rebuild Jerusalem. When the time came, he made good on his word and also returned the Jews to their homes in Judah.[33]

As with the Sack of Troy, the Babylonian Captivity occupies an important place in human literature and history. The transfer of people from their homes was a common means of conquest in the ancient world, and the Babylonians used it for a variety of reasons: as punishment for insurrection,[34] as a means by which to remove the threat of continued resistance in the conquered lands, and in order to maintain a group of candidates to replace the rulers of other lands, in the event that they became unruly.[35] It is possible that the Babylonians hoped to plunder the material wealth of Jerusalem and to harness the valuable human capital of the Jewish learned class. In the 6th century BCE, the Babylonians were superior in military power to the Jews and easily overcame them on three separate occasions. But it is notable that the Jews were not always killed following their subjugation, but rather displaced and then enslaved. The resources involved in transporting and then incorporating over 50,000 people into Babylonian society must have been not insignificant, and the benefits of this servitude must have outweighed the costs, lest it would not have been attempted. Not only did Nebuchadnezzar

---

28 Jeremiah, chapters 40-41.

29 2 Kings, chapter 24, verses 22-26.

30 Jeremiah, chapters 42-44.

31 Amihai Mazar, Archaeology of the Land of the Bible: 10,000-586 B.C.E. 548 (1992).

32 2 Chronicles, chapter 36, verse 22-23; Ezra, chapter 1.

33 The following displaced persons were returned: 42,360 Jews, 7,347 servants, and 245 singing men and women. 1 Esdras (Apocrypha), chapters 1-6. *See also* Nehemiah, chapter 7, verses 66-67; Ezra, chapter 2, verses 64-65.

34 John W. Betlyon, *Neo-Babylonian Military Operations Other Than War in Judah and Jerusalem, in* Judah and the Judeans in the Neo-Babylonian Period 263-64 (Oded Lipschits & Joseph Blenkinsopp, eds., 2003).

35 Ephraim Stern, Archaeology of the Land of the Bible, Volume II: The Assyrian, Babylonian, and Persian Periods, 732-332 BCE 353 (2001).

place value upon the material wealth of Judah, plundering the many treasures that are described in great detail in the Bible, but he also recognised the worth of the human capital of the Jews. This is demonstrated in the remarkable story whereby Daniel and his compatriots are nourished for years in the King's court, after which Nebuchadnezzar replaces the incumbent Babylonian administrators with Daniel and his colleagues due to their superior skills. The account of the Babylonian Captivity in the Bible reveals a willingness to cross ethnic boundaries. Just as the captured Trojan women and children were transported back to Greece to become slaves, the Jews were sent to Babylon to be integrated into its society. This is a very different phenomenon than will be seen in later displacements where the crimes are premised upon ethnic, religious, or national differences between the displaced and the perpetrators.

There are, however, discrepancies in some of the treatment of the Jews by the Babylonians. It is not uncommon for the *intelligentsia* to be targeted in the course of a displacement of a population as a means of eroding opposition to the transfer. During the first displacement in 597, the Babylonians killed many young women and men and elderly people, but took back to Babylon the elite, leaving only "the poorest sort of people on the land". During the second displacement in 587, Nebuchadnezzar had all the high priests and nobles executed, and again left only "the poor of the land to be vinedressers and husbandmen" in Judah. Despite these mass killings, others were brought back to Babylon because of their worth as slaves. It thus can be seen that, at least in some instances, the Babylonians considered it conducive to the displacement of the Jews to Babylon to eliminate their leaders; and, in other instances, Jews thought to have great potential for independent thought were intentionally brought back to Babylon to play an integral and even leading role in Babylonian society.

Finally, with the first two displacements fresh in their minds, those who remained in Judah feared that Nebuchadnezzar would assault them a third time when his governor Gedaliah was dethroned by Ishmael. The third displacement was more indirect in a causal sense than the first two, and took on a decidedly different character. It also differed in that, instead of the Jews being displaced directly for the purpose of being brought to a foreign land as slaves, their displacement was motivated by a desire to remove themselves from harm's way in Judah. The example of the Babylonian Captivity is one of the earliest recorded displacements in human history, the aspects of which are far from simple to discern. From a very early time, humans' displacement of each other was a complex and erratic practice that significantly varied based upon the shifting facts pertaining to the particular transfer at hand.

The displacement of the Jews had a profound impact upon their culture and religion. Unlike many resettled groups of individuals, the Jewish people appear to have maintained a tightly-knit community, rarely venturing to mingle with outsiders during the 70 years of their captivity.[36] This may have contributed to

36 Mathew A. Berk, The History of the Jews from the Babylonian Captivity to the Present Time: Comprising Their Conquests, Dispersions,

the rather sudden transformation of Judaism, from a polytheistic to a monotheistic religion during the Babylonian captivity.[37] It was also immediately after the Babylonian captivity that worship in synagogues was instituted and that the Book of Kings was written (approximately 562 BCE).[38] The Babylonian Captivity therefore seems to have been an important causal factor in the transformation of certain elements of Jewish culture and religion.

3. The Muslim Conquest of North Africa: The Dispersement of the Berbers

History is replete with the rise and fall of empires, but often little attention is paid to the plight of the conquered. The Arab Conquests—also known as the Muslim or Islam Conquests—of the 7th and 8th centuries CE were among the most successful in history and continue to affect several populations. Our focus here is upon the Berbers, individuals who inhabited Northern Africa long before the Arabs or any of the other conquering empires. The Arab Conquests lasted a century, beginning just after the death of the prophet Muhammad in 632 CE, and resulted in an Islamic empire stretching from Spain to Pakistan and covering all of North Africa. By the time the Arab Conquests began, the Berbers already lived uneasily in the conquered land that formed part of the Byzantine Empire. The initial clashes between the Berbers and the conquering Arab armies resulted in the enslavement of many Berbers as well as the levying of taxes upon them.[39]

Although several of the Arab leaders immediately attempted to adopt a policy of assimilation of the Berbers and some Berber tribes were receptive to this, a great many fled their villages in the latter half of the 7th century CE.[40] Berber resistance arose upon the ascent to power of the Arab leader Uqba, who traveled across North Africa to fight the Berbers, whom he considered to be inferior to the Arabs. Some of the Berber tribes sided with Uqba, some mounted resistance against his army, and others renewed their ties with the Byzantines.[41]

Wanderings, Persecutions, Commercial Enterprises, Literature, Manners, Customs, and Forms of Worship, With an Account of the Various Efforts Made For Their Conversion 19-20 (1846).

37 For additional reading on this transformation, see Yehezkel Kaufman, The Babylonian Captivity and Deutero-Isaiah (1970).

38 *Id.* at 40-45 (1970) (describing the changes in Judaism that took place during and immediately after the Babylonian captivity).

39 *See* Michael Brett & Elizabeth Fentress, The Berbers 82-88 (1996) (describing the initial encounters between the Berbers and the Arabs).

40 *See* Abdulwād Dhanūn Tāha, The Muslim Conquest and Settlement of North Africa and Spain 64 (1989) (noting that many Berbers abandoned their homelands in the region of al-Qayrawān due to the Arab invasion and most Berbers moved to the area of the Aurās mountains).

41 For additional reading on the Arab conquests, see generally Jane Soames Nickerson, A Short History of North Africa (1968); Michael Brett and

Shortly after Uqba was killed in battle with the Berbers in 683 CE, a new leader, Hāssan, was appointed.[42] Hāssan conquered the remaining areas still held by the Byzantines, mostly along the coasts. After the last of the Byzantines left, Hāssan undertook to conquer the Berbers once and for all. His first attempt failed because many of the Berber tribes united under the Berber Queen al-Kāhinam and thus were able to successfully contend with Hāssan's army. In 696 CE, Queen al-Kāhinam issued an order to her troops, directing them to burn and destroy the crops and riches of the Berber villages so that there would be no wealth for the Arabs to plunder.[43] Her fateful order turned many Berbers against her, and the second time that Hāssan waged war against the Berbers, he prevailed. It was also at this time that Carthage fell for the last time, as a result of Hāssan's efforts.

But this was not the last of the resistance by the Berbers against the Arabs. Although Hāssan's successor attempted to quell Berber resistance to conversion to Islam with violent reprisals in the early 8th century CE, he was not completely successful.[44] While many Berbers allied themselves with the Arabs, a few remaining tribes refused to capitulate, while others grew resentful of their Arab conquerors, who had forced thousands of Berbers into slavery and denigrated the Berbers as second-class citizens.[45] This led to the last major episode of Berber insurrection against the Arab rulers, which took place from 739-743 CE. The Berbers ultimately lost the war, but they maintained strongholds across Northern Africa; and, as a result, Berber dynasties ruled much of Northwest Africa during the 11th and 13th centuries CE.

The effects of the Arab Conquests, which killed and enslaved thousands of Berbers and displaced numerous others, are visible even now, more than a thousand years later. The Berbers continue to live in the remote areas of North Africa whither they fled during the Arab Conquests, and these populations tend to have fewer resources and access to education than their Arab counterparts. Tensions can often run high between those who identify themselves as Arabs and those

---

Elizabeth Fentress, The Berbers (1996); and Walter E. Kaegi, Byzantium and the Early Islamic Conquests (1992).

42 *See* Trudy Ring, Robert M. Salkin, & Sharon La Boda, International Dictionary of Historic Places: Middle East and Africa 458 (1996) (describing Uqba's death).

43 *See* General History of Africa: Volume III: Africa from the Seventh to the Eleventh Century 125 (M. El Fasi, ed.) (2002) (examining Queen al-Kāhinam's "scorched earth" policy).

44 *See* Charles-André Julien, Histoire de l'Afrique du Nord: Des origines à 1830 359-360 (1994) (describing the conquests of Mousa ibn Noçaïr (in English generally spelled Mūsā ibn Nusyr) and his forceful policy of conversion of the Berbers).

45 *See* Jamil M. Abun-Nasr, A history of the Maghrib in the Islamic period 34 (1987) (explaining that the Arab ruling class demanded that Berbers pay tribute by giving their children into slavery and noting that 20,000 captured Berber slaves were purportedly given to one ruler during the time of Mūsā ibn Nusyr's rule).

who identify themselves as Berbers.[46] Although the vast majority of Berbers are Muslim, many Berber communities remain culturally and linguistically isolated from the predominantly Arab population. Berber languages are not recognised as official languages in Morocco, Algeria, or Tunisia, and discrimination on the basis of race is often present in Berber and Arab communities.[47]

4. The Incas: An Early Example of Mass Population Transfer for Territorial Gain

Several hundred years after the Arab Conquests, an equally aggressive campaign of invasion and displacement was being waged in the Americas. The Incas were a small ethnic group until their appearance in history in the 1200s CE; yet, by the late 1400s CE, they had established the largest empire in the Americas, with dominion over between six and 14 million people in South America at the height of their power.[48] Although the Inca Empire was built over the relatively short period of one hundred years, it was dispatched with great alacrity by the Spanish in the 1500s CE.

One of the mechanisms by which the Incas were able to consolidate their power so rapidly was through mass population transfer. Scholars vary in opinion as to the extent that mass population transfers took place under the Inca Empire, but most scholarship acknowledges that population transfer was indeed one of the methods the Incas used to successfully conquer communities.[49] The system employed by the Incas was referred to as "*mitima*", which means "resettlement".[50]

Today's understanding of the *mitima* system has been gleaned from a combination of the writings of the Spanish conquistadores and archeological findings. It is now thought that the Inca kings' custom was to coordinate mass population

---

46 *See* Nick Pelham, *Moroccan Berbers Demand Rights*, BBC News, 2 Jan. 2001, http://news.bbc.co.uk/2/hi/africa/1097087.stm (describing the backlash against continued "Arabisation" in Morocco and the growth of a Berber rights movement); *see also* Immigration and Refugee Board of Canada, Morocco: Brief history of the Berbers including their origins and geographic location, 16 Nov. 2000, http://www.unhcr.org/refworld/topic,463af2212,469f279a2,3df4be668,0.html (discussing the Berber rights movement in Morocco and providing a brief history of the Berbers).

47 *See* Assessment for Berbers in Algeria, Minorities at Risk Project, 31 Dec. 2003, http://www.unhcr.org/refworld/country,,MARP,,DZA,,469f3a531c,0.html.

48 Gordon F. McEwan, The Incas: New Perspectives 96 (2006) (describing the difficulty in estimating the number of persons conquered by the Incas but stating that "[m]ost modern Inca scholars seem to accept and work with figures ranging between 6 million and 14 million people").

49 *See* Barbara Somervill, Empire of the Inca 33 (2005) (describing the *mitima* practice); David P. Werlich, Peru: A Short History 34-34 (1978) ("The incas frequently moved newly conquered peoples from the fringes of the empire to more secure zones and replaced them with *mitmaes*, colonists from older dominions.").

50 Barbara Somervill, Empire of the Inca 33 (2005).

transfers immediately following new conquests.[51] At times, entire villages were moved thousands of miles.[52] In total, it is estimated that approximately six to seven thousand families were uprooted from their homes in conquered territories and transferred to other Inca territories. Thousands of other individuals were likewise transferred from Inca provinces to the newly conquered territory.[53] Each transfer was carefully orchestrated. Communities were transferred to provinces that resembled their own native provinces in order to increase the likelihood of successful adaptation;[54] thus, for example, communities native to warm climates were transferred to other warm climates.[55] The *mitimae* were then made to adopt the customs and language of Cuzco, the Inca capitol.[56]

Scholars have pointed to several purposes of the *mitima* system. First, the system allowed the Incas to thoroughly "mix" the populations of all Inca territory and to create a uniform civilization in terms of customs, law, and language.[57] Second, the Incas were able to confront opposition by requiring communities that resisted conquest to live with groups that were already successfully living under Inca dominion. One author describes the system as follows: "[a]n entire village or sections of that village were forcibly moved from their home to new, pro-Inca locations. *Mitima* broke up the rebels yet did not deprive the village of needed services, since loyal Inca workers moved in to replace the rebels and maintain normal levels of productivity."[58] A final purpose of the *mitima* system was to increase productivity by forcibly resettling communities to farm in areas that were thought to be promising agricultural lands.[59]

Had the Inca Empire not been destroyed by civil war[60] and the conquest of the Spanish in the 1500s CE, it is possible that the Incas would have extended their empire even further. At least in the short-term, the Incas' use of population transfer cemented their control over newly conquered territories and proved to be an effective method of controlling new territories. In the long-term, however,

---

51 Bernabe Cobo, History of the Inca Empire 189 (1979).

52 *See* Michael A. Malpass, Daily Life in the Inca Empire xxvi (1996) (describing reports of Ecuadorian individuals being moved all the way to Bolivia).

53 Bernabe Cobo, History of the Inca Empire 189 (1979).

54 *Id.* at 189-90.

55 *Id.*

56 *Id.* at 191.

57 *Id.*

58 Barbara Somervill, Empire of the Inca 33 (2005).

59 Michael Andrew Malpass, Daily Life in the Inca Empire 39 (1996) (describing the resettlement of populations to add to the labor force and thereby increase crop productivity); Barbara Somervill, Empire of the Inca 33 (2005) (noting that "[t]here are several cases where villages designated for resettlement were moved to places that the Inca wanted to rework and develop, such as the terraced maize fields in Cochabamba").

60 *See* Burr Cartwight Brundage, Empire of the Inca 305 (1963) (discussing the civil war, known as the "War of the Two Brothers").

the conquest and forcible displacement of other peoples may have engendered the Incas' own downfall. One theory is that communities conquered by the Incas never became integrated since the Incas conquered such a vast number of people in a relatively short period of time.[61] Given the precarious ties between communities within the Empire that had been uprooted, the Spanish were able to swiftly infiltrate the Empire and destroy it with relative ease. And so those who carried out displacement became the displaced, and the destructive cycle that the Incas had begun was thus perpetuated.

5. The Moors: Expulsion for Religious Purposes

In the 1600s CE, the practice of forcible displacement continued, this time under the ostensible auspices of religion. The Arab Conquests covered not only the territory of North Africa, but also resulted in the conquest of Spain and the movement of millions of people into Spain. The tables were turned in 1609 CE, when Spain decided to expel the Muslim Moors, an episode in Spain's history in which approximately 300,000 Moors, who had been compelled to convert to Catholicism, were forced out of Spain in the span of five years.

At the time of their expulsion, the Moors had lived in Spain for hundreds of years, since the Arab Conquests in the 7th and 8th centuries CE. Moorish culture had spread to much of Spain, influencing everything from architecture to farming techniques and land use.[62] Christians, who were present on the Iberian Peninsula since before the arrival of the Moors, had either fled, remained and retained their religion, or converted to Islam. However, the religious wars of the 15th and 16th centuries CE were to have a profound effect upon Spanish culture. With the capture of Granada, the last Muslim kingdom of Spain, and the expulsion of the Jewish population from Spain in 1492 CE, the Catholic kings of Spain firmly established Christian predominance in the region.

Although initially permitted to practice Islam, the Spanish monarchs declared in 1499 CE that all inhabitants of Grenada and the surrounding areas were required to convert to Catholicism. The converted Moors were termed "moriscos", but the extent to which the Catholic conversion was successful is a

---

61 Gordon F. McEwan. The Incas: New Perspectives 133 (2005) ("Despite the welfare cocoon provided by the Inca state and the fearful sanctions applied against those who rejected it, the Inca Empire was plagued with revolts. Having expanded so rapidly, the empire had had little time to consolidate its rule and to develop a real sense of integration of the people of the provinces. Their loyalty lay with their own *ayllus* and ethnic lords and not with the Inca state. Rebellions were frequent, bloody, and sometimes long-lived. This instability was the greatest weakness of the Inca Empire and probably accounts for the rapid success of the Spanish conquerors when the Europeans finally made contact.").

62 *See* Thomas G. Glick, From Muslim Fortress to Christian Castle: Social and Cultural Change in Medieval Spain (1995) (discussing the spread of Moorish culture in Spain with a focus on the use of Islamic land settlement and water management techniques).

topic debated by historians.[63] It is clear, however, that the Moriscos never fully assimilated into Spain's Catholic society. This led to the Spanish monarchy's century-long preoccupation with the threat that the Moriscos posed to Spain's Catholic hegemony. By the beginning of the 17th century CE, under Philip III's reign, the Moriscos had become a pressing problem for the monarchy, who were deeply distrustful of Moriscos and considered them heretics, despite the fact that all Moriscos had been baptised and were purported Catholics. The possibility of expulsion of the Moriscos was heatedly debated by the clergy and between King Phillip III and his advisors. One scholar suggests that "[b]ecause they were baptised Christians the Moriscos were a problem like no other minority group from the examples of history."[64] In spite of their conversion to Catholicism, the Moriscos were never able to overcome the Spanish perception that they were outsiders, and Phillip III ultimately decided to expel all Moriscos in April 1609 CE.[65] Several months later, the military undertook the campaign of expulsion.

The military's method was to expel the Moriscos one region at a time, starting with Valencia. In each region, the Moriscos were forced onto Spanish ships that simply deposited them onto the shores of Northern Africa. The exact method of the expulsion and the degree of violence accompanying the expulsion varied greatly. The local nobles carried out the King's order by accompanying the Moriscos to boats waiting to take them to North Africa; the belongings of the Moriscos were confiscated; bands of Christians stole from, raped, and even killed Moriscos in transit.[66] Young children were spared because they were seen as clean slates who could become true Catholics: they were thus separated from their parents. A number of Moriscos were also "exempted" from the expulsions, provided that they were able to convince someone close enough to an influential Spanish person to allow them to stay. By the end of 1614 CE, the Spanish government had expelled nearly 300,000 Moriscos, leaving entire villages empty. King Philip III declared an end to the expulsions in 1614 CE, proclaiming: "All Moriscos who have not left or have returned must leave under pain of slavery in the galleys and confiscation of goods. If it be woman or very old to be whipped with 200 lashes and branded."[67]

Religion played an important pretextual role in the expulsion of the Moors. On the one hand, Catholics were expelling Catholics, so religion did not operate as a deontological shield against the perpetration of crimes against a vulner-

63 *See* James B. Tueller, Good and Faithful Christians: Moriscos and Catholicism in Early Modern Spain 24 (2002) (noting that the Moriscos "lived complex religious lives with strands of their past weaving into their behavior").

64 *Id.* at 127.

65 *Id.* at 122.

66 *See* Antonio Dominguez Ortíz & Bernard Vincent, *La tragédie se répète: Le Bannissement des Morisques*, *in* Chrétiens, Musulmans et Juifs Dans L'Espagne Medieval 307 (Ron Barkaï, ed., 1994).

67 *See* James B. Tueller, Good and Faithful Christians: Moriscos and Catholicism in Early Modern Spain 199 (2002).

able group. On the other hand, Morisco children were spared because they could be "reprogrammed" and reintegrated into Spanish society, which could indicate either a willingness to show mercy where possible or a utilitarian goal of gaining more human capital for Spanish society, or both. With the expulsion of the Moriscos, Spain rid itself of a perceived threat to Catholicism. The decision to expel those who were not perceived as true Catholics had a lasting impact on Spain's religions constitution.[68]

6. The Highland Clearances: Displacement in the Name of Economic Progress

The examples of forcible displacement discussed thus far were motivated on some level by religion, as in the case of the Moors and the Arab Conquests, or by territorial gain and the search for political dominance, as in the case of the Incas. In contrast, the Highland Clearances represent an example of displacement that primarily was for economic reasons and that was in general accomplished with relatively less violence than the previous examples. Nevertheless, the Clearances had equally deleterious effects upon the displaced population; today, some even refer to the Clearances as genocide.[69]

The Highland Clearances, which occurred from 1780 to 1855 CE, constitute a relatively unknown period of British history, despite the fact that they involved the forcible displacement of thousands upon thousands of agrarian people living in the Scottish Highlands and islands in the north of Scotland and the concomitant near-destruction of the Gaelic culture, which was concentrated in the Highlands and made up of individuals that had emigrated to Scotland from Ireland. Described in simplest terms, the Clearances were a series of mass evictions carried out by wealthy Scottish landlords, who forced common tenants out in favor of using land for the then-lucrative industry of sheep farming. Viewed more closely, the Clearances involved a complex set of interacting dynamics, frequently with class undertones.[70]

The Highland Clearances took place in a time of great economic and cultural change. Through the 18th century CE, the Scottish Highlands followed a clan system, and the vast majority of the inhabitants were tenants living on land belonging to powerful landlords. The Highlands were quite remote from the rest of the British Isles and were considered to be "uncivilised" by most of the English: "the outer edge of civilization—remote, uncouth and dangerously

68 Central Intelligence Agency World Factbook 2011, Spain, https://www.cia.gov/library/publications/the-world-factbook/geos/sp.html.

69 Eric Richards, The Highland Clearances 312 (2000) (opining that "economic displacement" and "population control" are better labels but acknowledging that there is "widespread" use of the term "genocide" to describe the Clearances).

70 For a particularly thorough account of the Highland Clearances, see generally Eric Richards, A History of the Highland Clearances: Agrarian Transformation and the Evictions 1746-1886 (1982).

anarchic".[71] A wave of the economic movement known as capitalism, whose main proponent was Adam Smith, was sweeping across Europe, and the Scottish Highlands were considered to be much in need of its "progressive" influence. Thus, historians argue that landlords were already beginning to raise rents and buy into capitalist ideals before the commencement of the period now referred to as the Highland Clearances.

It was in this context that the first of the Clearances were carried out by individual landlords in the early 1780s CE, many of whom had thousands of tenants. Because they were carried out by individuals and not as part of an organised campaign, the Clearances varied in duration and severity. Early on, some of the landlords gave several years notice and free passage to Canada and the United States to tenants who were to be evicted.[72] As landlords became aware of the profits to be made in sheep farming, communities of tenants were increasingly forced from their land to make room for new sheep herds. A commentator writing in the 19th century CE aptly wrote, "[I]s it credible, that in the 19th century ... man shall be bartered for a fleece or a carcase of mutton—nay, held cheaper?"[73] Indeed, it seems that the promise of wealth outweighed the value of the human tenants that were pushed off the land.

While some of the landlords provided notice and/or alternative accommodations to tenants, there were also many mass evictions, sometimes involving the destruction of homes and buildings, giving the tenant no choice but to flee. The most notorious of the violent evictions is the Sutherland clearance of 1810 CE, which displaced approximately 15,000 people and converted nearly all of the emptied territory to sheep-grasing land.[74]

By the 1850s CE, tens of thousands of Highlanders had been forcibly displaced from their homes. The number of individuals who were forcibly removed is impossible to accurately estimate, however, because some of the departures have been classified as voluntary.[75]

Although the landlords did not specifically target individuals for ethnic or religious reasons, the effect of the Clearances was to destroy much of the Gaelic culture, which was dispersed along with the people that fled. According to Ross Noble, former Chairman of the Highland Folk Museum, "the Highland

71 *See* Eric Richards, Debating the Highland Clearances 8 (2007).

72 An example of this earlier and less drastic method of eviction is the Harris Clearances, instituted by Lord Dunmore, who gave tenants three years notice and free passage to Canada. The old and sick were sent to nearby lands. Eric Richards, Debating the Highland Clearances 47-48 (2007).

73 Alexander McKenzie, The History of the Highland Clearances 387 (1883) (quoting a work by George Ensor).

74 Eric Richards, Debating the Highland Clearances 53-54 (2007) (describing the Sutherland clearance).

75 Eric Richards, The Highland Clearances 322-23 (2000) (noting the difficulties inherent in providing a quantitative assessment of the number of displaced individuals).

Clearances transformed the cultural landscape of the Highlands of Scotland, probably forever."[76] First, the land that was inhabited for hundreds of years by the Highlanders was almost emptied of people. Today, the Highlands remain sparsely populated—even the sheep that once took the place of human beings are no longer there. The buildings too were demolished to make room for the sheep. The Gaelic language has also suffered due to the Clearances.[77] In large part, this is due to the dispersal of the Gaelic-speaking communities, many of whom were forced to speak English in the urban areas within Scotland to which they emigrated or in the countries of the New World.

7. Aborigines in Australia: A Story of Land Dispossession and Violence

The story of the aborigines, dispossessed of their lands and violently oppressed, may be assumed by some to mirror that of other experiences of indigenous persons whose lands were seized by foreign invaders. Yet the displacement of the aborigines was a unique episode of colonial domination due to the sheer scale of violence inflicted upon the aborigines by the British and the swiftness and ruthlessness with which the British carried out their colonial endeavor.

The British arrived in Australia in the late 1700s CE, more than 50,000 years after the arrival of the first aborigines.[78] Estimates of the numbers of aborigines in Australia when the British arrived range from a low of 300,000 to a high of 850,000.[79] Unlike in other colonial episodes in history, the British immediately encroached upon the aborigines' land without seeking their consent. This was a departure from normal British colonial practice, which included purported attempts to seek the consent of indigenous peoples by entering into treaties for land sharing.[80] There is a general consensus that this was because the aborigines lived in small semi-nomadic groups dispersed across the Australian continent:

---

76 Ross Noble, *The Cultural Impact of the Highland Clearances*, http://www.bbc.co.uk/history/british/civil_war_revolution/scotland_clearances_01.shtml#four.

77 *Id.*

78 Richard Broome, Aboriginal Australians: Black Responses to White Dominance 1788-1980 10 (1982) (noting that the exact date of the arrival of the aborigines is unknown, but the aborigines have lived in Australia for at least 50,000 years). *See also* John Rennie Short, Cartographic Encounters: Indigenous Peoples and the Exploration of the New World 119 (2009).

79 Malcolm Prentis, A Study in Black and White: The Aborigines in Australian History 26 (2009) (noting that the population of aborigines in Australia was thought to be 300,000, but recent research has shown that the number is more likely in the range of 500,000-850,000).

80 For example, the British entered into treaties with the Native Americans in what is now the United States and with the Maoris of what is now New Zealand. *See* Richard Broome, Aboriginal Australians: Black Responses to White Dominance 1788-1980 26 (1982).

because they had no permanent and established communities, the British perceived the land to be *terra nullius*, a term reflecting the European doctrine that native inhabitants of land only had sovereignty over it if they had established permanent towns and recognisable systems of governments, in which case European explorers generally sought "consent" before taking over the land.[81]

The beginning of British domination over the aborigines is considered to be 1770 CE, the year that Captain James Cook landed on Australia's east coast. The British motivations for colonising Australia appear to have changed over time: initially, Australia was seen as an outlet to construct penal colonies for the thousands of convicts that overcrowded English jails. During the mid-1800s CE, with the growth of capitalism and at the height of England's Industrial Revolution, Australia became increasingly appealing to England for its natural resources and land. The continent was swiftly overrun by sheep farmers, who sold wool to the booming textile industry, with the dispossession of aborigines' lands taking place over a period of roughly one hundred years. The colonists simply established settlements where they saw fit, including penal colonies, regardless of the land's use by the aborigines.

What started as land dispossession quickly escalated into violence, with the aborigines mounting a guerilla resistance against the British occupation. The resistance movement reached its culmination in the 1830s and 1840s CE, a time of rapid expansion of British settlements. It was at that time that immigration to Australia substantially increased, largely due to the decision of the British government to lower tariffs on Australian wool.[82] In "a fantastic land grab which was never again to be equaled," thousands of British immigrants settled in Australia, bringing over 20 million sheep and settling over 400 million hectares of aborigine land.[83] The violence between white settlers and aborigines continued far into the nineteenth century, but on a lesser scale. By conservative estimate, about 4,000 aborigines and 470 white settlers died in conflicts from 1861-1896.[84]

Many of the aborigines attempted to maintain their nomadic way of life, but to no avail. The British colonists had fundamentally changed the use of the land, which was overwhelmingly occupied by grasing sheep. The watering holes, hunting grounds, and sacred sites of aboriginal communities slowly but inevitably disappeared as the colonies expanded. Without the use of their land, it became increasingly difficult for the aborigines to provide for themselves, and they relied more and more upon food and jobs from British settlers. The British policies regarding land for the aborigines varied greatly from region to region, but there

81 *Id.* at 10.

82 For a detailed discussion of British immigration to Australia in the 19th century CE, see Richard Broome, Aboriginal Australians: Black Responses to White Dominance 1788-1980 36-51 (1982).

83 *Id.* at 37.

84 Luke Trainor, British Imperialism and Australian Nationalism: Manipulation, Conflict and Compromise in the Late Nineteenth Century 83 (1994).

were sporadic efforts to settle aborigines on "missions". The Christian missionaries, who undertook to convert the aborigines in the 19th century CE, also attempted to set up schools and settlements, but their success was only moderate.

The toll of British colonisation was heavy: 150 years subsequent to James Cook's landing in Australia, only 60,000 individuals considered themselves to be aborigines.[85] Those who had not died in clashes with the British or from disease were dispossessed of their land in the name of economic gain. The aborigines were not only displaced; they were also divested of the religious and cultural practices that were entwined with the use of their land. The case of displacement for the aborigines does not bear the immediacy of the Moriscos in Spain, but the result of displacing the aborigines from their land is the same result that we see repeated time and again.

8. Crimean Tatars in the former USSR: Ethnically Motivated Displacement in the Name of Politics

The former Union of Soviet Socialist Republics (USSR) has been called the regime "that most consistently and insistently implemented" a policy of forcible migration.[86] The Soviet Union accomplished the forced displacement of over six million people within its own borders and the forced displacement of millions more outside its borders in the 20th century CE.[87] Mass expulsions of those thought to be "anti-Soviet" took place well before World War II: they were increasingly common throughout World War I and in the interregnum period.[88] It was during World War II, however, that Joseph Stalin, head of the Communist Party and leader of the USSR, adopted a more systematic approach to removing groups of people who were either thought to be cooperating with the Germans or who were undesirable for other reasons. To this end, at least a million Muslims were expelled from the Caucasus region, alone, and an even

85 Richard Broome, Aboriginal Australians: Black Responses to White Dominance 1788-1980 10 (1982) (explaining that the population of aborigines remaining in Australia may have been greater than 60,000, given that many individuals who were part-aborigine were reluctant to self-identify as aborigine given the pervasive race issues).

86 *See* Pavel Polian, Against Their Will: The History and Geography of Forced Migrations in the USSR 3 (2004).

87 The exact number of persons that were forcibly displaced across international borders is unknown, but it is estimated to be greater than the number of internally displaced persons. *See id.* at 4.

88 For additional reading on the Soviet Union's history of displacement, see Benjamin Lieberman, Terrible Fate: Ethnic Cleansing in the Making of Modern Europe (2006). For an insightful chapter on one of Stalin's pre-World War II campaigns of deportation and mass killing, see Nicolas Werth, *The Mechanism of Mass Crime: The Great Terror in the Soviet Union, 1937-1938*, *in* The Specter of Genocide: Mass Murder in Historical Perspective (Robert Gellately & Ben Kiernan, eds., 2003).

greater number of Russians of German origin were forced to leave their homes.[89] However, detailing the sheer scale of the displacement perpetrated by the Soviet Union would require many volumes; therefore, the focus of this section is upon one of the many groups that were expelled: the Crimean Tatars.

The reasons for focusing upon the forcible displacement of the Crimean Tatars are twofold: first, the displacement of the Tatars is an example of the speed with which a single mass displacement can be carried out; second, the motivation for the displacement mirrored many displacements perpetrated today, in that it was purportedly political, but in reality was likely due to the cultural threat posed by the Crimean Tatars, who resisted assimilation into Soviet culture much more so than other populations of Soviet-annexed lands. The Soviet distrust of the Crimean Tatars was such that all Tartar place names were changed to Russian ones, and the eventual return of some of the Crimean Tatars took place decades after the return of many of the other ethnic groups that had been expelled.[90]

The origins of the Crimean Tatars date from the 13th and 14th centuries CE, when they began to dominate the Crimean Peninsula.[91] The Crimean state, however, was not established until the mid-15th century CE, when the Crimean Tatars established the Crimean Khanate. Since Russia's annexation of the Crimean Khanate in 1783 CE, the Crimeans had fought to maintain their cultural identity; and, for a brief period of time in the aftermath of the Tsar's fall from power, they succeeded in reclaiming their own state. After the Soviet Union claimed the Crimean state as its own, the Soviet Union sought to rid the Crimean Tatars of their leadership, either by killing them or by banishing them to workcamps. The motivation was to stamp out the nationalist beliefs of the Crimean Tatars and to force them to assimilate into Soviet culture. However, it was not until 1944 CE, in the midst of World War II, that the USSR attempted to completely eliminate the Crimean Tatar culture through the forcible displacement of thousands.

The reasons for the deportation were purportedly political. The Soviet leadership claimed at the time that the Crimean Tatars had collaborated with the Germans, which was in fact the case for a portion of the Tatar population.[92]

89 The Muslim groups that were deported included the Kalmyks, the Karachai, the Chechens, and the Ingushes. *See* Benjamin Lieberman, Terrible Fate: Ethnic Cleansing in the Making of Modern Europe 204-05 (2006).

90 Note that the Soviets also changed Greek and German names. Many of the other ethnic Muslim groups returned in the 1950s. *Id.* at 207-08.

91 *See generally* Alan Fisher, The Crimean Tatars (1978) (providing a thorough history of the Crimean Tatars).

92 German accounts describe the extent of Crimean Tatar collaboration as limited to the recruitment of approximately 15,000-20,000 Tatars to form self-defense battalions in support of the German occupation of the Crimea and the creation of Germans-supported "Muslim Committees", constituted of Crimean Tatars that were tasked to manage the religious and cultural activities of the Crimean Tatar-

There were other versions of the story, however. Historian Alan Fisher has described two other versions of the conduct leading up to the deportation: he argues that the Germans themselves considered the Tatars to be of little significance and largely ignored them; therefore, any collaboration between the Tatars and the Germans had little if any significance or impact.[93] The third version of the extent of Tatar collaboration with Nazi Germany originates from the Tatars themselves, who claim that the vast majority of Tatars did not support the Germans and that many of the Crimean Tatars experienced oppression from both the Germans and the Soviets.

Regardless of the extent of Crimean Tatar participation in World War II, the swift deportation and elimination of vast numbers of Crimean Tatars took place in the course of a single night—on 18 May 1944 CE. The deportation was sudden and entirely unexpected, and the Tatars were given little if any time to collect their belongings. One account of the deportation describes it in the following manner:

> It was a journey of lingering death in cattle cars, crammed with people, like mobile gas chambers. The journey lasted three to four weeks, and took them across the scorching summer steppes of Kazakhstan .... [T]hey crammed [the Tatars'] women and children into the trucks .... On the long stages, the corpses decomposed in the huddle of the trucks, and at the short halts, where water and food were handed out, the people were not allowed to bury their dead and had to leave them beside the railway track.[94]

The reasons for this sudden and mass forcible displacement of the Crimean Tatars from the Soviet Union are not completely understood to this day. Crimean Tatar support of the German forces was far less significant than support of other ethnic minorities in the USSR who were not subsequently deported as the Crimean Tatars were, and there were thousands of Crimean Tatars who in fact fought in the Red Army.[95] What is clear, however, is that the central government in the former Soviet Union distrusted the Crimean Tatars, who, unlike some of the other ethnicities within the USSR, never fully assimilated into Soviet society and attempted to maintain some semblance of their own culture. The expulsion of the Crimean Tatars is not unlike the expulsion of the Moriscos from Spain, a

dominated areas. *See* ALAN FISHER, BETWEEN RUSSIANS, OTTOMANS AND TURKS: CRIMEA AND CRIMEAN TATARS 190 (1998).

93 *Id.* at 151 (1978) (explaining that the Germans "dismisse[d] the Tatars as Orientals and as a prime example of *Untermenschen*, who were not important subjects for German consideration during the war").

94 *Id.* at 166 (quoting an "Open Letter from the Russian Friends of the Crimean Tatars").

95 It has been suggested that the Crimean Tatars were deported in order to facilitate greater Russian control of the Soviet-Turkish border, although this is merely one of several theories. *See id.* at 192.

group that was also deeply distrusted, in that case by the Catholic Kings. In both cases, there was a fear of the "other" and a deep-seated suspicion that led to tragic episodes of mass displacement.

9. The Bangladesh War of Independence: Conflict and Displacement

The next example that will be examined in this chapter is the forcible displacement that took place during the Bangladesh War of Independence of 1971. The genocide and mass displacement of millions of Bengalis during the Bangladesh liberation war has recently gained attention due to renewed efforts to prosecute those responsible for these atrocities.

The origins of the conflict can be traced to the colonial history of present-day Bangladesh. The region that now constitutes India, Pakistan, and Bangladesh was once under British colonial rule for nearly a century. After the British relinquished control of the region in 1947 CE, Pakistan, formerly part of India, came into being.[96] The newly formed national boundaries of Pakistan now enclosed a host of different groups of people that had no cultural or linguistic commonalities. From the beginning, East Bengal, one of the provinces of Pakistan, agitated for independence. Compared to much of the rest of Pakistan, the population in East Bengal was relatively homogenous and shared the same language—Bengali. In 1949 CE, the Muslim League leaders of East Bengal formed the Awami Muslim League Party, later known as the Awami League, to lead the struggle for East Bengal's autonomy. The relationship between the Awami League and the Muslim League of Pakistan was turbulent for the next decade, as the East Bengalis continued to assert a right to autonomy.

In 1958 CE, Iskander Mirza, who was the President of Pakistan, and the Commander-in-Chief of its army, General Ayub Khan, carried out a military coup and declared martial law to be in effect. General Ayub soon expelled Mirza from the government and took control for himself, eventually becoming the party leader of the Muslim League. The East Bengalis, in the hopes of gaining more political control over East Bengal, attempted to participate in Ayub's government but were largely frustrated. General Ayub transferred leadership to General Yahya Khan in 1969 CE, who attempted to tackle the East Bengali problem by holding legislative elections in 1970 CE. To the surprise of many, the Awami League won a majority of seats in the government under the leadership of the head of the Awami League, Sheikh Mujib. West Pakistan, led by Zulfikar Ali Bhutto, refused to recognise the leadership of the Awami League, including Sheikh Mujib's leadership, and General Yahya consequently postponed the

96 The following section on the Bangladesh War of Independence draws from three sources: Mizanur Rahman Shelley, Emergency of a New Nation in a Multi-Polar World: Bangladesh (2000); Ali Riaz, Unfolding State: the Transformation of Bangladesh (2005); Richard Sisson & Leo E. Rose, War and Secession: Pakistan, India and the Creation of Bangladesh (1991).

National Assembly's first session. Sensing that their efforts were once again being frustrated, the East Bengalis launched a Civil Disobedience Movement beginning on 1 March 1971 CE.

The response of the West Pakistan-led army was brutal. On 25 March 1971 CE, General Yahya led a full-scale attack in Dhaka, the centrally-located city that would become the capital city of Bangladesh. The most heavily targeted areas were the Hindu parts of Dhaka, as well as the University of Dhaka, home to many students who supported the movement for East Bengali independence.[97] In Dhaka alone, thousands were murdered and countless homes and buildings were destroyed.

The Dhaka massacre only served to further encourage nationalist East Bengalis, some of whom unsuccessfully attempted to wage a resistance using guerilla tactics. Over the next few months, the Pakistan army continued to raze the countryside and cities of East Bengal, assisted by East Bengali collaborators, referred to as *razakars*. Hundreds of thousands of East Bengalis fled their homes to escape the violence, many of them crossing into India at a steady rate: the mass exodus reached approximately 50,000 people per day during the months following the Dhaka Massacre. A contemporary news report described that the column of displaced persons moving "into India never ends, day or night. It has been four months since civil war broke out between East and West Pakistan, and the refugees still pour in."[98] Rape and sexual violence against women, as well as killing and torture, were widespread. It was not until December 1971 CE that the conflict abated, when India invaded what is now Bangladesh and the Pakistani army surrendered.

During the 1971 war, approximately 40 million East Bengalis were displaced from their homes—ten million of whom fled to India.[99] Another three million people were killed.[100] Countless women were raped, and the perpetrators have never been completely identified. The full extent of the crimes committed in East Bengal has begun to attract attention, with the recent establishment of a special war crimes tribunal in Dhaka. To date, charges have been filed against four individuals accused of committing war crimes, including the killing of 345 people during the conflict.[101] Unlike the other examples considered in this chap-

97 S. Mahmud Ali, Understanding Bangladesh 56 (2010).

98 *Pakistan: The Ravaging of Golden Bengal*, Time (2 Aug. 1971).

99 Samuel Totten & William S. Parsons, Century of Genocide: Critical Essays and Eyewitness Accounts 249 (2008).

100 Liberation War Museum, Genocide and Atrocities, http://www.liberationwarmuseum.org/liberation-war/51-genocide-and-atrocities. The museum houses the skeletal remains of individuals killed in the war, found in several of the fields that have been excavated in recent years.

101 The individuals charged, Motiur Rahman Nizami, Ali Ahsan Mohammad Mujahid, Muhammad Kamaruzzaman, and Abdul Quader Mollah, are all prominent members of the Jamaat-e-Islami party, the largest Islamic political party in Bangladesh. *See* Bangladesh accuses Islamic leaders of war crimes, Reuters (25 July 2010), http://

ter, there may be repercussions for those who carried out the displacement. The same is to be said of the perpetrators of atrocities in the conflicts in Cambodia, Rwanda, and the former Yugoslavia. The recent efforts to hold perpetrators of forcible displacement responsible for their crimes may signal a significant shift from what appears to be customary impunity for the centuries-old practice of forcible displacement.

10. The Three Gorges Dam: Justifying Displacement in the Name of Progress

The final example of displacement in this chapter concerns displacement caused by development. While development-induced displacement may seem quite different at first glance than some of the other forms of displacement examined thus far, it shares the same objective as other forms of displacement: to forcibly remove individuals from their lands, which often results in the impoverishment of the displaced and damage to their cultures.

In the past few decades, the world has witnessed unprecedented growth of large-scale energy-producing structures. Dams account for a large portion of these development projects; and, since the late 1970s CE,[102] resort to the hydroelectric generation of power has become more and more prevalent. In many developing countries, dams provide a relatively straightforward means of generating the energy that is needed to sustain rapidly expanding economies. Much as they may assist economic development, however, dams can have detrimental effects not only upon the environment, but also upon the populations that are often displaced by their construction. Estimates of the number of persons in the world displaced by dam construction alone range from 40 to 80 million people.[103] China's Three Gorges Dam, the greatest undertaking in dam construction ever attempted, is an example of such displacement on a massive scale.

The Three Gorges Dam was built upon China's Yangtze River, in Southwestern China. The idea of building the Three Gorges Dam was first set forth in the early 20th century CE, although it was not until the 1990s CE that the Chinese government seriously began to move forward with the project.[104] In

---

in.reuters.com/article/idINSGE66O01L20100725. Further details regarding the charges are not available as of the time of this writing.

102 MEGAPROJECT: A CASE STUDY OF CHINA'S THREE GORGES PROJECT 3 (Shiu-hung Luk & Joseph Witney, eds., 1993).

103 World Commission on Dams, *Dams and Development: A New Framework for Decision-Making*, Chapter 4, People and Large Dams – Social Performance, p. 8. The World Commission on Dams was sponsored by the World Bank and by the World Conservation Union. The final report of the Commission focused on providing a comprehensive overview of the environmental, economic, and social impacts of dam construction.

104 MEGAPROJECT: A CASE STUDY OF CHINA'S THREE GORGES PROJECT 3 (Shiu-hung Luk & Joseph Witney, eds., 1993).

the face of a great deal of academic controversy, China completed the first phase of the dam's construction in 2006 CE, with high hopes that the dam would boost the economy, prevent downstream flooding, and ameliorate river transport.[105] The dam itself is one of the largest engineering projects ever undertaken. It is approximately two kilometers wide, and has created a reservoir that is just greater than 632 square kilometers in size—the length of Lake Superior in North America.[106]

It is this reservoir that has caused the vast majority of the displacement. According to one source, the reservoir inundated 13 cities, 140 towns, and 1,352 villages.[107] This translates into the displacement of over 1.4 million people, a number that does not take into account other negative effects upon communities in the area, such as loss of livelihood and environmental degradation.[108] The initial plan of the Chinese government was for the displaced to be moved to land above the reservoir. When the government began evacuating citizens in 1997 CE, it promised that living standards would not change and that the displaced would be compensated. However, many of those resettled are far worse off now that they have been resettled; many of the lands to which they were resettled were either non-arable or could not sustain additional farming, and the compensation provided was not enough to build new homes.[109] In fact, there are reports that much of the money set aside to be used as compensation for the displaced was embezzled by corrupt government officials.[110] The displaced have also lost

105 Dai Qing, The River Dragon Has Come! The Three Gorges Dam and the Fate of China's Yangtze River and Its People xviii (1998) (noting that the Chinese government expected a national increase of electricity of 10% resulting from the Three Gorges Dam).

106 *Id.* (noting that the Dam is two kilometers wide and that the reservoir it creates is the length of Lake Superior); *see also* Sarah C. Aird, *China's Three Gorges: The Impact of Dam Construction on Emerging Human Rights,* 8 No. 2 Hum. Rts. Brief 24 (2001) (arguing that the displacement caused by the Three Gorges Dam violates various international human rights treaties as well as the Guiding Principles on Internal Displacement).

107 Sarah C. Aird, *China's Three Gorges: The Impact of Dam Construction on Emerging Human Rights,* 8 No. 2 Hum. Rts. Brief 24 (2001).

108 World Commission on Dams, *Dams and Development: A New Framework for Decision-Making*, Chapter 4, People and Large Dams – Social Performance, p. 8.

109 *See* Jim Yardley, *Chinese Dam Projects Criticized for Their Human Costs*, The New York Times (19 Nov. 2007), at http://www.nytimes.com/2007/11/19/world/asia/19dam.html?pagewanted=1&_r=1&ref=three_gorges_dam (discussing the poor living conditions of resettled individuals).

110 *See Three Gorges Dam Money Missing*, BBC News (26 January 2007), http://news.bbc.co.uk/2/hi/asia-pacific/6301075.stm (citing reports that over 30 million United States dollars were embezzled from funds for the displaced); Jill McGivering, *Three Gorges Dam Social Impact*, BBC News (20 May 2006), http://news.bbc.co.uk/2/hi/asia-pacific/5000198.stm (noting that "[o]fficial accounts seem to support [the] complaints [of the displaced] that millions of dollars have been embezzled").

something less tangible than money; entire communities have been dispersed and forever separated from ancestral homes, some of which were built over more than a thousand years ago.

Unlike most of the previous examples explored, the displacement caused by the Three Gorges Dam project is not a result of conflict, nor is it ethnically or politically motivated, as is often the case in situations of mass displacement. Yet, one may draw a parallel between the displacement caused by the Three Gorges Dam and that carried out in the Scottish Highlands: both were in the name of economic progress. In the Highlands, landowners sought to further capitalism and their own corresponding wealth by replacing farmers and other tenants with sheep farms. In the case of the Three Gorges Dam, China too seeks to gain economic advantage. The question to be asked is whether development-induced displacement—displacement for economic gain—is somehow more justifiable than other forms of displacement. It may be that one must look to the result of the displacement in assessing whether it is more or less justified. The issue may be phrased in terms of whether the displacement of 1.4 million people and the concomitant damage to their ways of life are less reprehensible because they are committed in the name of economic progress, rather than in the name of ethnic hatred.

* * *

There are countless other examples of displacement that have not been included herein, such as the Native American experience in the 18th and 19th centuries CE, the genocide in Cambodia in the 1970s CE, and the more recent situations in Sudan, East Timor, and the Democratic Republic of the Congo. Other examples of displacement will be considered later in this book, such as those during the conflicts in the former Yugoslavia and Rwanda. It is apparent that displacement is not a thing of the past, but a problem still facing humanity today; and, the manner in which displacements have been perpetrated has not changed that much over the millennia. Many displacements that have purportedly been motivated by religion, politics, or ethnic hatred have been—in reality—mere "land-grabs", with the ideological reason simply an expedient excuse and/or a means of setting the perpetrators into motion in order to effect the displacement. In other words, the contest for resources has often constituted the root objective for displacements. Despite the motivations of the perpetrators, a displacement—from the victims' perspective—is just as damaging.

The remainder of this book is dedicated to examining what we as an international community have done to deal with this problem, from adopting international treaties to deal with some of the effects of forcible displacement to recently creating international tribunals to prosecute those who still insist on displacing their fellow humans. But these efforts have not stopped displacement from occurring, and it is for this reason that new strategies must be risked if we are to discipline ourselves not to uproot each other from our homes.

Chapter Three

Law of Forcible Displacement

The greatest problem for the human species is that of attaining a civil society which can administer universal justice.[1]

1. Definitions

A number of terms are employed to refer to the forcible displacement of people, including deportation, expulsion, forced migration, and forcible transfer. Some terms, such as expulsion, refer to requiring individuals to move across international borders involuntarily. Other terms, such as internal displacement or forced relocation, refer to the involuntary transfer of individuals within their countries of origin.[2] Throughout this book, the term "forcible displacement" is used. The word "displacement" means to move something or someone away or apart. It is a term that is preferable to the word "transfer", which means to carry something or someone across, because whether someone is moved across a boundary, he or she is still the victim of a crime if moved away from his or her home. The term "migration" can be used in a non-criminal context as part of the natural movement of populations, and so can obscure the discussion at times. The word "forcible" is added to "displacement" in order to indicate that the objects of the movement are not doing so voluntarily. As will be explored later during the discussion of the jurisprudence of the ICTY in chapter four below, terminology can sometimes be of great importance in defining the law of forcible displacement; but, if not chosen carefully, it has the potential to distort the proper application of the law to the facts of a case.

At the heart of forcible displacement lies the notion that communities are in some way connected to specific territories, which allow them to survive, persevere, and ultimately thrive. Special Rapporteur Al-Khasawneh, author of an

---

1 Immanuel Kant, quoted in *Idea for a Universal History with a Cosmopolitan Purpose*, *in* KANT: POLITICAL WRITINGS 45, translated by H.B. Nisbet, second edition (Hans Reiss, ed., 1991).

2 JEAN-MARIE HENCKAERTS, MASS EXPULSION IN MODERN INTERNATIONAL LAW AND PRACTICE 2 (1995) (defining internal displacement as "uprooting caused by civil war, internal strife, ethnic tensions and other situations where serious human rights violations occur" and forced relocation as "forcible resettlement pursuant to governmental policies, such as the implementation of development projects").

influential report by the Commission on Human Rights on population transfer,[3] has made this very point, stating:

> The basic ideas would seem to be that belonging to a community is important and that a stable community is normally related to a particular territorial zone. In the normal case, territory, both socially and legally, connotes population, and to regard a population in the normal case, as related to particular areas of territory is to recognize a political reality which underlies modern territorial settlements.[4]

Most often then, the goal of forcible displacement is to change the demographic composition of a given region by either requiring people to relocate involuntarily to a given location or by expelling people from a given location, thereby endangering the population's very existence, both at an individual level and at a communal level. This is a pattern that has been repeated time and again throughout history. Such was the case when, in the 1990s, Iraq attempted to change the demographic composition of Kuwait by expelling Kuwaitis out of Kuwait and resettling Iraqis there in their place.[5] In the same decade, hundreds of thousands of individuals were displaced in the massive ethnic cleansing campaigns carried out in the former Yugoslavia and in Rwanda.[6] These are only a few examples of forcible displacement carried out in our own time.

In spite of the international community's recognition that forcible displacement constitutes a pervasive problem, the challenge of defining the dimensions of the problem and its root causes—let alone its eradication—has thus far proved difficult. In attempting to characterise the phenomenon of forcible displacement, the Special Rapporteur on Population Transfer for the Commission of Human Rights has identified seven scenarios where forcible displacement violates international law. These seven categories consist of the following:

---

3 Commission on Human Rights, Sub-Commission on Prevention of Discrimination and Protection of Minorities, *Final Report: Freedom of Movement, Human Rights and Population Transfer*, U.N. Doc. E/CN.4/Sub.2/1997/23 (27 June 1997) (*prepared by* Special Rapporteur Al-Khasawneh) [hereinafter *Final Report on Freedom of Movement*].

4 *Id.* ¶ 20.

5 *See* JEAN-MARIE HENCKAERTS, MASS EXPULSION IN MODERN INTERNATIONAL LAW AND PRACTICE 158 (1995).

6 At the end of 2001, there were more than 400,000 refugees in the former Yugoslavia and 277,000 internally displaced persons. *See* United States Committee for Refugees and Immigrants, *U.S. Committee for Refugees World Refugee Survey 2002 – Yugoslavia (including Kosovo)* (10 June 2002), http://www.unhcr.org/refworld/docid/3d04c1561c.html. At the end of 2000, there were approximately 55,000 Rwandan refugees and asylum seekers and 150,000 internally displaced persons. United States Committee for Refugees and Immigrants, *U.S. Committee for Refugees World Refugee Survey 2001 – Rwanda* (20 June 2001), http://www.unhcr.org/refworld/docid/3b31e16810.html.

1. Transfers that are collective in nature, affecting a group of persons. Population transfers can involve large numbers of people in a single event or they can be gradual, incremental, or phased.
2. Transfers that are carried out by force or threat of force.
3. Transfers that are involuntary, without the full informed consent of the affected populations.
4. Transfers that are deliberate on the part of the government or other party conducting the transfer, with or without whose knowledge the violations occur.
5. Transfers that are systematic, forming a pattern of policy or practice.
6. Transfers that are discriminatory, affecting a distinct population or distinct populations.
7. Transfers that take place without due process.[7]

Such a broad interpretation of forcible displacement is consistent with the international consensus that the involuntary dislocation of individuals from their homes is a violation of human dignity and a practice that must be eliminated. While the different legal instruments explored in this book vary in their conceptualisation of forcible displacement and apply to forcible displacement in different contexts, they all share the core value that forcibly moving individuals away from their homes is a crime that should not be tolerated: this is the agreed, starting premise.

There is a prodigious body of law set forth in a variety of instruments, both "hard law" and "soft law", which recognises that the forcible displacement of persons from their lawful places of residence is impermissible under international law. Humanitarian instruments prohibiting forcible displacement include the Geneva Conventions and the Optional Protocols to the Conventions. Human Rights instruments include the International Covenant on Civil and Political Rights, the International Convention on the Elimination of All Forms of Racial Discrimination, the Universal Declaration of Human Rights, the Convention on the Prevention and Punishment of the Crime of Genocide, and the 1951 Convention Relating to the Status of Refugees. The relevant "soft law" instruments are the draft Code of Crimes Against the Peace and Security of Mankind, the International Law Association's Declaration of Principles of International Law on Mass Expulsion, and the International Law Association's Declaration of International Law Principles on Internally Displaced Persons. The Security Council has also adopted numerous resolutions, several of them binding under Chapter VII of the UN Charter, denouncing forcible displacement.

A further set of legal instruments becomes applicable to those persons who have been forcibly displaced from their historical territory and become stateless persons, refugees, or internally displaced persons. Apart from a brief discussion of the Refugee Convention, this chapter does not attempt to delve into this body of law, but rather focuses upon the law that prohibits the act of forcible displace-

7 *Final Report on Freedom of Movement*, ¶ 10.

ment and the law that affirms an individual's right to freedom of movement and the right not to be forcibly displaced.

The first section of this chapter considers the Nuremberg Trials, which constituted one of the first significant advancements in prohibiting forcible displacement. The second section addresses the prohibition of forcible displacement in humanitarian law. The third section considers applicable human rights instruments. The fourth section examines soft law applicable to forcible displacement, including several relevant Security Council Resolutions. The fifth section reviews the ICJ's approach to the crime of forcible displacement.

2. The Nuremberg Trials: Early Attempts to Legally Define Forcible Displacement

Prior to World War II, there existed at least one national legal instrument prohibiting forcible displacement, referred to as the Lieber Code, a code for military conduct for the Union Army in the United States Civil War that was written by Francis Lieber and approved by the members of the army in 1863. It provided that "private citizens are no longer ... carried off to distant parts."[8]

More than half a century later, in 1919, reference was also made to deportation of civilians as a war crime in a report by a Commission created by the delegates present at the Preliminary Peace Conference, convened just after World War I.[9] The Commission was tasked with conducting an inquiry into the extent of state responsibility for World War I and the crimes committed by responsible states.[10] In its enumerated list of crimes to be investigated, the Commission listed both deportation of civilians and forced labour of civilians.[11]

However, it was not until 1942, before the close of World War II, that the first international legal document explicitly categorising forcible displacement as a war crime was created. The First Inter-Allied Declaration on war crimes was signed in London by nine signatories: Belgium, Czechoslovakia, France, Greece, Luxembourg, The Netherlands, Norway, Poland, and Yugoslavia.[12] The docu-

---

8 *See* U.S. War Department, General Orders No. 100, 24 April 1863.

9 *See generally* Commission on the Responsibility of the Authors of the War and on Enforcement of Penalties, Report Presented to the Preliminary Peace Conference, 29 March 1919, 14 American Journal of Int'l Law 95 (1920) (reporting the Commission's work to the delegates of the Preliminary Peace Conference).

10 *Id.* at 96.

11 *Id.* at 114.

12 The Human Rights Dimensions of Population Transfer, Including the Implantation of Settlers, Preliminary report prepared by A.S. Al-Khasawneh and R. Hatano, Commission on Human Rights, Sub-Commission on Prevention of Discrimination and Protection of Minorities, Forty-fifth session, ¶ 144 (E/CN.4/Sub.2/1993/172 (6 Jul. 1993); Nina Jørgensen, The Responsibility of States for International Crimes 15 (2003) (providing the exact date upon which the document was signed and the signatories).

ment listed "mass expulsion" as an example of the atrocities committed by the Nazis, in reference to their widespread deportation programmes. This brief mention was a precursor to the International Military Tribunal (IMT), also called the Nuremberg Trials, which played a key role in criminalising forcible displacement.

At the close of World War II, there were some thirty million individuals who had been dislocated from their homes,[13] many of whom were forcibly displaced at the hands of the Nazi regime. Ironically, after the war, the German people were themselves the subject of massive forcible displacements.[14]

The creation of the IMT was a watershed event in modern human history and in many ways was the first criminal tribunal of its kind.[15] It was established in 1945 by the United States, France, Russia, and the United Kingdom in order to prosecute atrocities committed by individuals during World War II, and it explicitly recognised the crime of forcible displacement. Article 6(b) of the London Charter of the IMT (also referred to as the "London Charter" or the "Nuremberg Charter") defined war crimes as including, but not limited to

> murder, ill-treatment or deportation to slave labor or for any other purpose of civilian population of or in occupied territory, murder or ill-treatment of prisoners of war or persons on the seas, killing of hostages, plunder of public or private property, wanton destruction of cities, towns or villages, or devastation not justified by military necessity.[16]

Article 6(c), which defined crimes against humanity, also included deportation.[17]

There were three counts in the Nuremberg indictment that addressed the crime of deportation.[18] In describing the Nazis' methodical policy of deportation and slave labor, the Tribunal explained that by mid-April 1940 the Government General had ordered compulsory deportation of hundreds of thousands of labor-

13 Francois Bugnion, *Refugees and the Right of Return*, 28 FORDHAM INT'L L.J. 1397, 1398 (2008).

14 *See generally* ALFRED-MAURICE DE ZAYAS, NEMESIS OF POTSDAM (1979) (describing the Allied displacement of Germans living in Central and Eastern Europe during and after World War II).

15 *See generally* WHITNEY R. HARRIS, TYRANNY ON TRIAL, THE TRIAL OF THE MAJOR GERMAN WAR CRIMINALS AT THE END OF WORLD WAR II AT NUREMBERG, GERMANY, 1945-1946 (1999); TELFORD TAYLOR, THE ANATOMY OF THE NUREMBERG TRIALS (1992).

16 London Charter of the International Military Tribunal, Annexed to the London Agreement for the Establishment of an International Military Tribunal, art. 6(b), 9 *Int. Leg.* 632, 637 (1945).

17 *Id.*

18 JEAN-MARIE HENCKAERTS, MASS EXPULSION IN MODERN INTERNATIONAL LAW AND PRACTICE 155 (1995).

ers living in occupied territories to Germany.[19] However, the forcible displacement described by the judgement was not limited to displacement across national borders, and the IMT did not overly concern itself with defining the legal status of the occupied territories within which, and from which, victims were displaced. As Judge Wolfgang Schomburg of the ICTY has noted, the crime of forcible displacement as considered by the IMT was conceptualised as a crime of transferring people from their homes, without regard to the ultimate destination of the displaced.[20] The IMT concluded that the war crimes set forth in 6(b) of the London Charter, including deportation, were already considered to be war crimes under customary international law.[21] The individual considered to be the driving force behind the implementation of the deportation policy, Fritz Sauckel, was sentenced to death.[22]

In the years immediately following World War II, with the horrors of the war still fresh, the international community debated the best way to prevent such atrocities from recurring. One of the first steps taken was the endorsement by the United Nations' General Assembly of the Nuremberg Principles, which codified the principles of international law identified in the London Charter and the Judgement of the Nuremberg Tribunal.[23] Principle VI included deportation as both a war crime and a crime against humanity. The adoption of the Nuremberg Principles was a crucial step toward a more comprehensive discourse on the crime of forcible displacement. This was also the era in which the humanitarian law framework was further developed, in large part as a response to World War II. The following section explores the role of humanitarian law in prohibiting forcible displacement.

3. Humanitarian Law

a. The Hague Conventions as Progenitors of the Geneva Conventions

The purpose of humanitarian law is to regulate armed conflict in order to curb its unnecessary excesses and to minimise harm to civilians and other protected

---

19 IMT Judgement, *War Crimes and Crimes Against Humanity*, http://avalon.law.yale.edu/imt/judwarcr.asp.

20 *See Prosecutor v. Naletilić and Martinović*, Case No. IT-98-34-A, Judgement, 3 May 2006, Separate and Partially Dissenting Opinion of Judge Schomburg, ¶¶ 11-12.

21 IMT Judgement, *The Law Relating to War Crimes and Crimes Against Humanity*, http://avalon.law.yale.edu/imt/judlawre.asp.

22 Jean-Marie Henckaerts, Mass Expulsion in Modern International Law and Practice 155 (1995).

23 Through Resolution 177 (II), the General Assembly gave the work of formulating the Nuremberg Principles to the International Law Commission. *See* International Law Commission (2nd session), *Principles of International Law Recognized in the Charter of the Nuremberg Tribunal and in the Judgment of the Tribunal*, U.N. Doc. A/1316 (6 June-29 July 1950).

persons or property. Humanitarian law is applicable to forcible displacement in many, but not all, instances, because forcible displacement often takes place in times of armed conflict. For example, customary international law requires that a grave breach of the Geneva Conventions or a violation of the laws or customs of war (otherwise known as a "war crime") be committed during an armed conflict, the former during an international armed conflict and the latter during either an international or internal armed conflict. However, there is no such requirement in customary international law for a crime against humanity; therefore, a forcible displacement as a crime against humanity could be committed by a government against a group of people within its territory when there is no armed conflict ongoing at the time. But the same would not be the case for a forcible displacement charged as a war crime.

Several of the principal sources of humanitarian law relied upon today are the Hague Conventions, the Geneva Conventions of 1949, the 1977 Additional Protocols to the Geneva Conventions, and customary international law. The predominant view is that many of the rules contained in humanitarian law instruments have passed into customary law.[24] Accordingly, those countries that have not ratified instruments such as the Additional Protocols to the Geneva Conventions may still be bound by the norms contained within them as a matter of a customary international law.

There are two sets of Hague Conventions, one signed in 1899 and the other in 1907.[25] According to Judge Theodor Meron of the ICTY, the 1899 Convention was "the first general, multilateral codification of the laws of land war", while the second was essentially "a revamped version" of the 1899 Convention.[26] The Hague Conventions address the rights and duties of combatants in war, while the Geneva Conventions of 1949 each address a specific category of affected persons in time of war.[27] The Additional Protocols to the Geneva Conventions clarify and expand upon several of the provisions found in the Geneva Conventions them-

---

24 *See* The Human Rights Dimensions of Population Transfer, Including the Implantation of Settlers, Preliminary report prepared by A.S. Al-Khasawneh and R. Hatano, Commission on Human Rights, Sub-Commission on Prevention of Discrimination and Protection of Minorities, Forty-fifth session, ¶ 153 (E/CN.4/Sub.2/1993/172 (6 Jul. 1993) ("According to most opinions today, the provisions of the Hague and the Geneva Conventions constitute customary international law.").

25 *See* Convention with Respect to the Laws and Customs of War on Land, 29 July 1899, 32 Stat. 1803, 1 Bevans 247; Convention Respecting the Laws and Customs of War on Land, 19 Oct. 1907, 36 Stat. 2277, 1 Bevans 631.

26 *See* Theodor Meron, *Reflections on the Prosecution of War Crimes by International Tribunals*, 100 A.J.I.L. 551, 554 (2006).

27 The four Geneva Conventions of 1949 are the Geneva Convention for the Amelioration of the Condition of Wounded and Sick in Armed Forces in the Field, 12 Aug. 1949, 6 U.S.T. 3114, 75 U.N.T.S. 31; the Geneva Convention for the Amelioration of the Condition of Wounded, Sick and Shipwrecked Members of Armed Forces at Sea, 12 Aug. 1949, 6 U.S.T. 3217, 75 U.N.T.S. 85; the Geneva Convention Relative to the Treatment of Prisoners of War, 12 Aug. 1949, 6 U.S.T. 3316, 75 U.N.T.S. 135; and the

selves. Prior to the adoption of the Geneva Conventions and their Protocols, the primary source of humanitarian law was the Hague Conventions.[28] While the Hague Conventions provided a comprehensive guide to legal warfare, neither Convention contained any mention of forcible displacement or deportation. Recognising this omission, the drafters of the Geneva Conventions and their Protocols set out to create a set of legal instruments that would prohibit forcible displacement and that would better fit the paradigms of modern warfare.

b. The Geneva Conventions

Support for a provision in the Geneva Conventions prohibiting forcible displacement was widespread, given the then-recent revelation of the painful details of the deportation and forced labor system employed by the Nazis during World War II.[29] In fact, the authors of Geneva Convention IV agreed unanimously on the need for an explicit prohibition of forcible displacement.[30] This prohibition is found in Article 49, which provides:

> Individual or mass forcible transfers, as well as deportations of protected persons from occupied territory to the territory of the Occupying Power or to that of any other country, occupied or not, are prohibited, regardless of their motive.
>
> Nevertheless, the Occupying Power may undertake total or partial evacuation of a given area if the security of the population or imperative military reasons so demand. Such evacuations may not involve the displacement of protected persons outside the bounds of the occupied territory except when for material reasons it is impossible to avoid such displacement. Persons thus evacuated shall be transferred back to their homes as soon as hostilities in the area in question have ceased.
>
> The Occupying Power undertaking such transfers or evacuations shall ensure, to the greatest practicable extent, that proper accommodation is provided to receive the protected persons, that the removals are effected in satisfactory conditions of hygiene, health, safety and nutrition, and that members of the same family are not separated.

Geneva Convention Relative to the Protection of Civilian Persons in Time of War, 12 Aug. 1949, 6 U.S.T. 3516, 75 U.N.T.S. 287 [hereinafter Geneva Convention IV].

28 *See* Theodor Meron, *Reflections on the Prosecution of War Crimes by International Tribunals*, 100 A.J.I.L. 551, 554 (noting that "it was not until the turn of the twentieth century, at the 1899 and 1907 Hague Peace Conferences, that the modern law of war and war crimes began to take shape").

29 This was noted by the International Committee of the Red Cross, in its Commentaries on the Geneva Conventions (ICRC Commentaries). ICRC Commentaries, *Commentary on Article 49*, http://www.icrc.org/ihl.nsf/COM/380-600056?OpenDocument.

30 ICRC Commentaries, *Commentary on Article 49*, http://www.icrc.org/ihl.nsf/COM/380-600056?OpenDocument.

> The Protecting Power shall be informed of any transfers and evacuations as soon as they have taken place.
>
> The Occupying Power shall not detain protected persons in an area particularly exposed to the dangers of war unless the security of the population or imperative military reasons so demand.
>
> The Occupying Power shall not deport or transfer parts of its own civilian population into the territory it occupies.[31]

The language of Article 49 has several important implications, according to Jean-Marie Henckaerts. First, it prohibits relocation within occupied territory *and* relocation outside of occupied territory. Second, it is applicable to both individual and mass deportations. Third, any kind of deportation is prohibited, regardless of the destination. Fourth, it forbids transfer of a state's own civilian population into occupied territory.[32] This last point has become increasingly relevant as states such as Iraq have moved to populate occupied territories with their own citizens. These observations are also relevant to the United Nations International Criminal Tribunal for the former Yugoslavia's observations on the cross-border requirement, to be discussed later in chapter four.

As the text of Article 49 clearly indicates, the prohibition of displacement is not absolute because the article contemplates the possibility that a population could be evacuated temporarily where either "the security of the population" is at risk or where "imperative military reasons so demand."[33] The overarching purpose behind the first exception relating to the security of the population is to protect civilians from being unnecessarily exposed to warfare. In fact, states have a corresponding duty to remove civilians from "the vicinity of military objectives", although this duty is "without prejudice to Article 49."[34] The second "imperative military reasons" exception allows for the evacuation of civilians where their "presence ... in an area hampers military operations."[35] The ICRC Commentary provides little guidance as to what exactly constitutes "imperative military reasons", merely stating that "[e]vacuation is only permitted ... when overriding military considerations make it imperative; if it is not imperative, evacuation ceases to be legitimate."[36] The ICTY has provided some insight into when a pop-

31 Geneva Convention IV, art. 49.

32 *See* Bonaventure Rutinwa, *Refugee Claims Based on Violation of International Humanitarian Law: The "Victim's" Perspective*, 15 Geo. Immigr. L.J. 497, 500 (citing Jean-Marie Henckaerts, Mass Expulsion in Modern International Law and Practice 144 (1992)).

33 Geneva Convention IV, art. 49.

34 Protocol Additional to the Geneva Conventions of 12 August 1949, and Relating to the Protection of Victims of International Armed Conflicts, 8 June 1977, 16 I.L.M. 1391 [hereinafter Additional Protocol I], art. 58.

35 ICRC Commentaries, *Commentary on Article 49*, http://www.icrc.org/ihl.nsf/COM/380-600056?OpenDocument.

36 *Id.*

ulation may be lawfully displaced, as will be discussed below in the discussion of the *Stakić* case in chapter four.[37] As will be seen, the general language of international instruments can often be understood best when applied in the context of a concrete set of facts, such as the armed conflicts of the former Yugoslavia of the 1990s. Although both exceptions to Article 49 employ general language that could be open to a variety of interpretations, they also set baseline standards for which actions are permitted during armed conflict. Evacuated persons may not be transferred to areas outside of the occupied territory unless it is impossible to avoid such transfer, and in the case that transfer to occupied territory is imperative, individuals transferred must be returned to their homes upon the cessation of hostilities in the area. The occupying power is further charged with providing appropriate accommodation, nutrition, safety, and hygienic conditions to individuals who are transferred.[38]

In addition to Article 49, several other provisions in Geneva Convention IV are applicable to forcible displacement. Article 27(1), for example, provides for the general protection of civilians and stipulates that protected persons are entitled "in all circumstances" to respect for their family rights, religious practices, manners and customs, and humane treatment.[39] While it can be inferred that maintaining these rights involves allowing a community to remain within its home territory, Article 27 does not contain any explicit mention of forcible displacement. Nevertheless, the article has been invoked by some scholars as a potential prohibition against forcible displacement.[40]

The drafters of the Geneva Conventions specifically categorised some forms of forcible displacement as war crimes. Article 147 provides a list of crimes that are considered as grave breaches of the Convention and war crimes and includes "unlawful deportation or transfer" in this list.[41] According to the ICRC Commentary, the purpose behind Article 147 was to "draw up as a warning to possible offenders a clear list of crimes whose authors would be sought for in all countries." The drafters included both unlawful deportation and transfer in the list of enumerated war crimes, in the wake of the atrocities committed during World War II.[42]

The only provision of the Geneva Conventions that applies to internal armed conflict is Common Article III, in which there is no express mention of forci-

---

37 *Prosecutor v. Stakić*, Case No. IT-97-24-A, Judgement, 22 March 2006, ¶¶ 286-87.

38 Geneva Convention IV, art. 49.

39 Geneva Convention IV, art. 27(1).

40 *See, e.g.*, Bonaventure Rutinwa, *Refugee Claims Based on Violation of International Humanitarian Law: The "Victim's" Perspective*, 15 Geo. Immigr. L.J. 497, 499 ("[Article 27(1)] does not expressly prohibit population displacement. However, some of the elements of this provision may have bearing on the legality of forcible population displacement.").

41 Geneva Convention IV, art. 147.

42 ICRC Commentaries, *Commentary on Article 17*, http://www.icrc.org/ihl.nsf/COM/380-600169?OpenDocument.

ble displacement; however, it can be inferred that the prohibitions contained in Common Article III of "violence to life and person" and "outrages upon personal dignity, in particular humiliating and degrading treatment" would also act as a blanket prohibition of forcible displacement.[43] The significance of Common Article III is thus not that it specifically prohibits forcible displacement, but rather that it provides what the ICJ has termed the "minimum yardstick" of protection available to individuals in internal conflict, and thus extends to individuals not otherwise within the protective scope of the other instruments discussed in this section.[44] However, with the adoption of the Additional Protocols to the Geneva Conventions in 1977, many of the protections within the Conventions were extended to a broader set of circumstances in relation to the conduct of hostilities, including situations of internal armed conflict.

Prior to the adoption of the Additional Protocols to the Geneva Conventions, there was a gap in humanitarian law regarding forcible displacement because the Geneva Conventions, with the exception of Common Article III, applied only to situations of international armed conflict.[45] The drafters of the Additional Protocols were keenly aware of this problem, and the ICRC noted in its Commentary that "the problem [of forcible displacement] is particularly acute in situations of non-international armed conflict in which there have been cases, for example, of the forced movement of ethnic groups and national groups opposed to the central government."[46]

The Additional Protocols, which supplemented and updated the Geneva Conventions, are an attempt to compensate for this gap. Additional Protocol II extended the scope of many of the protections contained in the Geneva Conventions to conflicts of an internal character.[47] This was a much-needed change, given that 80% of victims of war were victims of internal conflicts in the time that had elapsed since the end of World War II and the Additional Protocols.[48] Additional Protocol I also increased the scope of the Geneva

43 The Human Rights Dimensions of Population Transfer, Including the Implantation of Settlers, Preliminary report prepared by A.S. Al-Khasawneh and R. Hatano, Commission on Human Rights, Sub-Commission on Prevention of Discrimination and Protection of Minorities, Forty-fifth session, ¶ 186 (E/CN.4/Sub.2/1993/172 (6 Jul. 1993).

44 Military and Paramilitary Activities in and Against Nicaragua (Nicar. v. U.S.), Merits, 1986 ICJ REP. 14, 114, ¶ 218 (27 June).

45 Additional Protocol I; Protocol Additional to the Geneva Conventions of 12 August 1949, and Relating to the Protection of Victims of Non-International Armed Conflicts, 8 June 1977, 16 I.L.M. 1442 [hereinafter Additional Protocol II].

46 ICRC Commentaries, *Commentary on Article 17*, http://www.icrc.org/ihl.nsf/COM/475-760023?OpenDocument.

47 Article 3, common to all four of the Geneva Conventions (Common Article III), is the only article in the four Geneva Conventions applicable to non-international conflicts.

48 Additional Protocol II, Introduction.

Conventions by making them applicable to situations of armed conflict "in which people are fighting against colonial domination and alien occupation and against racist régimes in the exercise of the right to self-determination."[49]

In addition to expanding the legal reach of the Geneva Conventions, the Additional Protocols also provided substantive additions to the prohibitions and rules set forth by the Geneva Conventions. One such addition was Article 17 of Additional Protocol II, prohibiting the forced movement of civilians. The first section of Article 17 reads much like Article 49 of Geneva Convention IV, prohibiting the displacement of civilians unless "the security of the civilians involved or imperative military reasons so demand."[50] The second section of Article 17, however, is an entirely new addition, providing that "[c]ivilians shall not be compelled to leave their own territory for reasons connected with the conflict."[51] The ICRC Commentary to Article 17 explains that the concept of the term "territory" encompasses not only the national territory of a country, but also *parts* of a country's territory.[52] This distinction substantially broadens the scope of protection by explicitly prohibiting forcible displacement of communities *within* national boundaries. This is quite different from Article 49: while Article 49 arguably prohibited involuntary movement of communities within national boundaries in the context of international conflict, it was not drafted in such a way that a natural reading led to this conclusion; rather, it was through scholarly interpretation that this conclusion became accepted. The drafting of Article 17 cemented the prohibition on intra-state transfers by more explicitly clarifying that such transfers were unlawful.

But even when no armed conflict exists, people are still protected under international law from being forced from their homes, and this protection largely takes the form of international human rights law. The relationship between international humanitarian law and human rights law is discussed below.

4. Human Rights Law

International human rights law (IHRL) and international humanitarian law (IHL) have a specific relationship to each other in international law. They both co-exist during armed conflict, with some matters being exclusively within the ambit of IHRL and others within IHL. Where both govern a situation in the context of armed conflict, the IHL norm will usually be considered the *lex specialis*, and the IHRL norm the *lex generalis*; but, when human rights law sets a standard that is higher than the coordinate humanitarian law standard, the

49 Additional Protocol I, art. 1(4).

50 Additional Protocol II, art. 17(1).

51 Additional Protocol II, art. 17(2).

52 ICRC Commentaries, *Commentary on Article 17*, http://www.icrc.org/ihl.nsf/COM/475-760023?OpenDocument.

human rights norm applies.[53] So IHL, by its own terms, does not always trump IHRL in times of armed conflict.

The interplay between IHL and IHRL has been discussed by the International Court of Justice. In its 1996 Advisory Opinion on the Legality of the Threat or Use of Nuclear Weapons, the Court noted that application of the International Covenant of Civil and Political Rights does not cease to operate in times of war.[54] Several years later, the court again considered that "the protection offered by human rights conventions does not cease in case of armed conflict, save through the effect of provisions for derogation of the kind to be found in Article 4 of the International Covenant on Civil and Political Rights."[55] Additionally, humanitarian law often contains human rights norms, and portions of both have become customary international law.[56] Due to the fact that international humanitarian law generally requires that, where human rights law sets a higher minimum threshold of rights, the higher threshold is the controlling standard,[57] in situations of non-international armed conflict, human rights law can regulate the authority of a state in relation to its actions towards civilians and those not taking an active part in hostilities.[58]

a. The Right to Freedom of Movement and Residence

Apart from the 1948 Convention on the Prevention and Punishment of the Crime of Genocide and the 1951 Convention Relating to the Status of Refugees, both of which are relevant to a discussion of forcible displacement, there are numerous human rights instruments that include provisions that can be broadly interpreted as prohibitions of forcible displacement. Among the pertinent human rights instruments are the Universal Declaration of Human Rights (UDHR), the International Covenant on Civil and Political Rights (ICCPR),

---

53 *See* Douglas Cassel, *Symposium: Redefining International Criminal Law: New Interpretations and New Solutions: Criminal Law: Pretrial and Preventive Detention of Suspected Terrorists: Options and Constraints under International Law*, 98 J. Crim. L. & Criminology 811, 819 (2008); *see also* Monica Hakimi, *International Standards for Detaining Terrorism Suspects: Moving Beyond the Armed Conflict-Criminal Divide*, 33 Yale J. Int'l L. 369, 370 (2008).

54 International Court of Justice, Advisory Opinion on the Legality of the Threat or Use of Nuclear Weapons, Advisory Opinion, 1996, ICJ Reports, ¶ 25 (8 July 1996).

55 *Id.* at ¶ 106.

56 Douglass Cassel, *Criminal Law: Pretrial and Preventive Detention of Suspected Terrorists: Options and Constraints Under International Law*, 98 J. Crim. L. & Criminology 811, 819-20 (2008).

57 *Id.* at 819-20.

58 ICCPR, art. 4; *see also* Douglas Cassel, *Symposium: Redefining International Criminal Law: New Interpretations and New Solutions: Criminal Law: Pretrial and Preventive Detention of Suspected Terrorists: Options and Constraints under International Law*, 98 J. Crim. L. & Criminology 811, 821 (2008).

and the International Convention on the Elimination of All Forms of Racial Discrimination (CERD). These instruments are of significance given that they apply at all times, unlike humanitarian law instruments, which are limited to times of war. These instruments each include a general right to choose one's residence. The UDHR provides that "everyone has the right to freedom of movement and residence within the borders of each State …. Everyone has the right to leave any country, including his own, and to return to his country." [59] The ICCPR provides that "everyone lawfully within the territory of a State shall, within that territory, have the right to liberty of movement and freedom to choose his residence."[60] In his Final Report on Freedom of Movement, Special Rapporteur Al-Khasawneh noted that "forced removal of populations by expulsion or eviction from their ordinary places of residence to uncertain modes of livelihood and adverse conditions of life prima facie violates" state obligations under the ICCPR.[61] The language contained in CERD is nearly identical to that of the UDHR, requiring state signatories to undertake to prohibit and to eliminate racial discrimination in the enjoyment of the right to freedom of movement and residence within the borders of the state, the right to nationality, and the right to own property alone as well as in association with others.[62]

These human rights instruments are of importance to the prohibition against the forcible displacement of people for a number of reasons. When one speaks of the prohibition of forcible displacement, it is frequently a concept cast in negative terms: thou shalt not displace one's neighbor. But there is also a positive right—the fundamental international human rights norm—to live in peace in one's own home. Before a right can be protected, it must first be identified, and it is in the UDHR, the ICCPR, and the CERD that the basic right is codified. Another reason for the importance of these instruments is the large number of states that have signed, ratified, or acceded to them. The widespread acceptance of the principles within these international human rights treaties indicates that it is a matter of common agreement that liberty of movement and freedom to choose one's own residence are rights afforded to individuals that must not be abrogated.

---

59 Universal Declaration of Human Rights, art. 13, 10 Dec. 1948, G.A. Res. 217A, U.N. GAOR 3rd Sess., U.N. Doc. A/810 [hereinafter UDHR].

60 International Covenant on Civil and Political Rights, art. 12(1), *entered into force* 23 March 1976, 999 U.N.T.S. 171 [hereinafter ICCPR].

61 Commission on Human Rights, Sub-Commission on Prevention of Discrimination and Protection of Minorities, *Final Report: Freedom of Movement, Human Rights and Population Transfer*, U.N. Doc. E/CN.4/Sub.2/1997/23 (27 June 1997) (*prepared by* Special Rapporteur Al-Khasawneh), ¶ 53.

62 International Convention on the Elimination of All Forms of Racial Discrimination, art. 5(d)(i), (iii), (v), 21 Dec. 1965, 660 U.N.T.S. 195.

b. The Genocide Convention

The crime of genocide is defined in Article 2 of the Genocide Convention as "any of the following acts committed with intent to destroy, in whole or in part, a national, ethnic, racial or religious group, as such: (a) Killing members of the group; (b) Causing serious bodily or mental harm to members of the group; (c) Deliberately inflicting on the group conditions of life calculated to bring about its physical destruction in whole or in part; (d) Imposing measures intended to prevent births within the group; (e) Forcibly transferring children of the group to another group."[63]

The Genocide Convention therefore provides that the forcible transfer of children can constitute genocide. It has also been argued that it can be inferred from the list of acts of genocide contained within the Genocide Convention that the crime of genocide can take the form of forcible displacement, outside the context of forcibly transferring children of one group to another group. As explained by one legal scholar, "[b]ecause of the human rights violations involved in forcing individuals from their homes and across international borders into refugee camps where mortality and morbidity rates are exceptionally high and completely foreseeable, military action with these objectives is arguably committed with the intent to destroy a national, ethnic, racial or religious group in whole or in part."[64] Such an interpretation of the Genocide Convention is also borne out by the jurisprudence of the ICTY, as is discussed in chapter four. In this regard, the provision in the Genocide Convention concerning the infliction of conditions of life calculated to bring about physical destruction of a group is the most relevant to forcible displacement because it can logically encompass a prohibition of the displacement of any part of a population, given that such acts often result in the severe disruption of the lives of the displaced group. In spite of this argument, the crime of forcible displacement may evade the perimeters of the Genocide Convention, given that the Convention specifically requires the *intent* to destroy the group or part of the group. For example, the application of the Genocide Convention to forcible displacement would not necessarily be a straightforward matter if the perpetrators claim that the transfer is for security or economic reasons or that the transfer is temporary. On the other hand, the context in which the crime of genocide may occur may be broader than that in which war crimes may occur. Article 1 of the Genocide Convention provides that genocide may occur in times of peace and in times of war. Thus, on the one hand, the level of intent required for a genocide is quite specific—intent to destroy, in whole or in part, a national, ethnic, racial or religious group, as such—while, on the other hand, the jurisdictional context in which genocide can be committed is broader than for some other international crimes.

---

63 Convention on the Prevention and Punishment of the Crime of Genocide of 1948, art. 2, 9 Dec. 1948, 78 U.N.T.S. 277 [hereinafter Genocide Convention].

64 *See* Kathleen Sarah Galbraith, *Moving People: Forced Migration and International Law*, 13 Geo. Immig. L.J. 597, 606 (1999).

The ICJ has held that the principles contained in the Genocide Convention represent customary international law and that the substance of the Convention is therefore binding upon states parties to the Convention and non-states parties alike.[65] As a result, many states that are not bound by other human rights instruments or humanitarian law instruments may be bound by the Genocide Convention. This has the potential to fill a legal gap applicable to the specific factual scenario where a rogue state that has not ratified certain key human rights instruments is taken to task for actions that may constitute genocide through the displacement of people. But it remains to be seen whether states will attempt to use the Genocide Convention as an instrument to prohibit forcible displacement. The ICJ has briefly considered the possibility in a recent case, the Case Concerning Application of the Convention on the Prevention and Punishment of the Crime of Genocide, Bosnia and Herzegovina v. Yugoslavia (Serbia and Montenegro), which will be further examined later in this chapter; however, the ICJ's treatment of this issue was not exhaustive in the circumstances of that case.

c. *The Refugee Convention*

The Refugee Convention and its 1967 Protocol form the cornerstone for the protection of certain persons, known as refugees, displaced across an international boundary. The Refugee Convention was established with the express purpose of addressing the plight of millions of persons who became refugees during the Holocaust and World War II and who often had no place to turn after fleeing their homes.[66]

A refugee is defined by the Convention as an individual unable or unwilling to return to his or her country of origin or, in the case of stateless individuals, country of habitual residence, due to "a well-founded fear of being persecuted for reasons of race, religion, nationality, membership of a particular social group

65 *See* Reservations to the Convention on the Prevention and Punishment of the Crime of Genocide, 1951 I.C.J. 15, 23 (stating that "the principles underlying the Convention are principles which are recognized by civilized nations as binding on States, even without any convention obligation").

66 Naomi S. Stern, *Evian's Legacy: The Holocaust, the United Nations Refugee Convention, and Post-War Refugee Legislation in the United States*, 19 GEO. IMMIG. L.J. 313, 315 (2004-2005) (noting that "the U.N. Convention was a direct response to the Jewish refugee crisis created by the Holocaust and other refugee crises that emerged in the wake of World War II, including the escape of political refugees from newly-emerged Communist regimes in Eastern Europe").

or political opinion."[67] Although UNHCR's guidelines[68] provide that a "well-founded fear of persecution" need not necessarily be based on one's own personal experience, to fall under the Refugee Convention definition, one must still demonstrate a well-founded fear of persecution based upon one of the five grounds set out in the Convention. Therefore, while the Refugee Convention definition can be applied broadly, it does not cover, and was not intended to cover, individuals that flee their countries on account of generalised violence or grounds outside of the five enumerated by the Refugee Convention.

The cornerstone of the Refugee Convention is the principle of *nonrefoulement*, provided for in Article 33 of the Convention. At the heart of the principle of *nonrefoulement* is a state's obligation not to return an individual to his or her country if his or her life or freedom would be threatened upon return.[69] Thus, the Refugee Convention is concerned with protecting individuals who have fled their countries and who object to being forced to return based upon persecution or the threat of persecution on account of the grounds enumerated in the Convention.[70]

The Refugee Convention provides much-needed protection to many individuals who have involuntarily left their country of origin or, in the case of stateless persons, their country of habitual residence. While the Convention is certainly relevant to a discussion of forcible displacement, it does not, and was not intended to, place any positive obligation on governments to *refrain* from displacing individuals within their borders or to apprehend those who commit forcible displacement within their borders. Instead, it plays the integral role of triggering a receiving state's obligations once an individual meeting the Convention definition of a refugee crosses into its territory.

5. Regional Human Rights Treaties

There are several regional instruments that address the protection of displaced individuals. The 1969 Organisation of African Unity (OAU) Convention

67 Convention Relating to the Status of Refugees, 28 July 1951, 189 U.N.T.S. 137 [hereinafter Refugee Convention]. The Refugee Convention was supplemented by the Protocol Relating to the Status of Refugees, 31 Jan. 1967, 19 U.S.T. 6223, 606 U.N.T.S. 267 [hereinafter 1967 Protocol]. The 1967 Protocol incorporates articles 2 through 34 of the Refugee Convention, thereby binding signatories to the 1967 Protocol to the provisions of the Refugee Convention.

68 UNHCR, *Handbook on Procedures and Criteria for Determining Refugee Status*, 1979, Geneva, re-edited 1992, ¶ 43.

69 *See* Jean-Marie Henckaerts, Mass Expulsion in Modern International Law and Practice 101 (1995).

70 For a general discussion on the protections offered by the Refugee Convention, see Guy Goodwin-Gill, *Introduction to the 1951 Convention Relating to the Status of Refugees and the Protocol Relating to the Status of Refugees*, http://untreaty.un.org/cod/avl/ha/prsr/prsr.html.

Governing the Specific Aspects of Refugee Problems in Africa, for example, obliges parties to provide significant protections to refugees in Africa.[71] Similarly, the 1984 Cartagena Declaration on Refugees (Cartagena Declaration), while not a binding legal instrument, recommends that its signatories observe the protections to refugees mandated by the Refugee Convention and expands the Refugee Convention definition of refugee to include "persons who have fled their country because their lives, safety or freedom have been threatened by generalized violence, foreign aggression, internal conflicts, massive violation of human rights or other circumstances which have seriously disturbed public order."[72] The Cartagena Declaration also addresses internally displaced persons, "call[ing] on national authorities and the competent international organizations to offer protection and assistance to those persons and to help relieve the hardship which many [persons displaced within their territory] face."[73] Beginning in 1999, the Council of the European Union has adopted several directives comprising the EU asylum *acquis*. These directives require that member states adopt legislation for, *inter alia*, temporary protection in the event of a mass influx of displaced persons, minimum standards for receiving asylum-seekers, and minimum requirements for granting and withdrawing refugee status.[74]

In October 2009, a landmark regional human rights treaty was adopted by the African Union, which is the first binding legal instrument to comprehensively address the *positive obligation* of states to prevent forcible displacement. The Convention, called the Convention for the Protection and Assistance of Internally Displaced Persons in Africa (Kampala Convention), aims to address the rights of the more than ten million forcibly displaced persons in sub-Saharan Africa, 6.3 million of whom are internally displaced.[75] Notably, the Kampala Convention is based on the Guiding Principles.[76]

Although the Kampala Convention is limited to situations of internal displacement, it encompasses a broad array of individual rights and state responsibilities and could provide a model for an international convention prohibiting all types of forcible displacement. Among the state responsibilities engaged by the Kampala Convention are the responsibilities to prevent and prohibit arbi-

71 Convention Governing the Specific Aspects of Refugee Problems in Africa, 1001 U.N.T.S. 45, *entered into force* 20 June 1974.

72 Cartagena Declaration on Refugees, Conclusion 3, Annual Report of the Inter-American Commission on Human Rights, OAS Doc. OEA/Ser.L/V/II.66/doc.10, rev. 1, at 190-93 (1984-1985).

73 *Id.* Conclusion 9.

74 Such directives are published in the Official Journal of the European Union and are also available on UNHCR's website at http://www.unhcr-centraleurope.org/en/resources/legal-documents/european-union-asylum-acquis.html.

75 *See* Press Release N: /2010, *African Union Addressing the Challenges of Forced Displacement in Africa*, 1 Jan. 2010, http://www.africa-union.org/root/au/index/index.htm.

76 Andrew Solomon, *Introductory Note to African Union Convention for the Protection and Assistance of Internally Displace Persons in Africa*, 49 I.L.M. 83, 83-84 (2010).

trary relocation, Article 3(1)(a); to hold individuals accountable for committing crimes of arbitrary displacement, Article 3(1)(g); and to provide protection and assistance to displaced persons, Article 5. The Kampala Convention also prohibits internal displacement in situations of armed conflict, which includes holding individuals engaged in the conflict accountable for committing arbitrary displacement in the context of armed conflict.

6. Soft Law Instruments

There are several "soft law" instruments that specifically address forcible displacement. "Soft law" is a term that refers to documents that are endorsed in some way by states or international organisations, but that do not have the status of a binding treaty.[77] One example would be a United Nations declaration, such as the Universal Declaration of Human Rights (UDHR). Soft law documents usually focus upon fundamental norms in a variety of areas and, although not legally binding, can provide guidance and concrete goals for future state action. The particular norms of a soft law instrument, such as the UDHR, may also *become* binding as customary international law, which "consists of rules of law derived from the consistent conduct of States acting out of the belief that the law required them to act that way."[78]

There are a number of soft law instruments containing direct prohibitions of forcible displacement. A notable soft law instrument is the Proposed Draft Code of Crimes Against the Peace and Security of Mankind (Draft Code), the most recent version of which is from 1996.[79] The Draft Code includes "arbitrary deportation of forcible transfer of population" as a crime against humanity.[80] Although more than ten years have elapsed since the International Law Commission presented its last Draft Code, the instrument nevertheless continues to be considered a significant step forward in prohibiting forcible displacement.[81] The International Law Association has also taken significant action

77 Richard B. Lillich et al., International Human Rights Problems of Law, Policy, and Practice (4th ed. 2006).

78 Shabtai Rosenne, Practice and Methods of International Law 55 (1984).

79 The first version of the Draft Code of Crimes Against the Peace and Security of Mankind was presented by the International Law Commission in 1954, but was never passed due to disagreement among the states over what constituted "an act of aggression" by a state. *See* William N. Gianaris, *The New World Order and the Need for an International Criminal Court*, 16 Fordham Int'l L.J. 88, 95 (1992).

80 Draft Code of Crimes Against the Peace and Security of Mankind, art. 18(g), U.N. GAOR, 51st Sess., Report of the International Law Commission on the Work of its Forty-eighth session Supp. No. 10, U.N. Doc. A/51(10) (6 May-22 July 1996) [hereinafter Draft Code].

81 *See, e.g.*, Marco Simmons, *The Emergence of a Norm Against Arbitrary Forced Relocation*, 34 Colum. Human Rights L. Rev. 95, 130 (2002) (citing the 1996 Draft Code as an important development in the emergence of a prohibition on forced relocation).

regarding forcible displacement, adopting in 1986 the Declaration of Principles of International Law on Mass Expulsion (Declaration on Mass Expulsion) and the Declaration of International Law Principles on Internally Displaced Persons (Declaration on Internally Displaced Persons) in 2000. The Declaration on Mass Expulsion defines mass expulsion as "an act, or a failure to act, by a State with the intended effect of forcing the departure of persons against their will from its territory for reasons of race, nationality, membership in a particular social group or political opinion."[82] Principle 3 notes that mass expulsion may fall under the purview of the Genocide Convention if committed with the requisite intent, while Principle 4 deems mass expulsion to be an international crime.[83] The Declaration on Internally Displaced Persons addresses the rights of internally displaced persons within a state and that state's obligations towards them. In particular, the Declaration espouses the right to freedom from arbitrary displacement[84] and the right to freedom from genocide and ethnic cleansing.[85] The Declaration on Internally Displaced Persons complements a number of soft law instruments addressing internal displacement.[86]

One of the most important soft law instruments that exists for the protection of internally displaced persons is the Guiding Principles on Internal Displacement (Guiding Principles), first presented to the Commission on Human Rights in 1998 by Francis Deng, who was at the time the Representative to the United Nations Secretary-General on internally displaced persons. The Guiding Principles identify the rights of internally displaced persons and the guarantees that governments should afford to them within their borders. "Internally displaced persons" are defined broadly as

> persons or groups of persons who have been forced or obliged to flee or to leave their homes or places of habitual residence, in particular as a result of or in

82 Declaration of Principles of International Law on Mass Expulsion, Preamble, 62nd Conference of the International Law Association (24-30 Aug. 1986) [hereinafter Declaration on Mass Expulsion].

83 Principle 4 states that, "in view of the violation of all human rights of citizens who are expelled en masse, the act of mass expulsion partakes of the attributes of 'international crime,' with all the consequences that go with it." Declaration on Mass Expulsion.

84 Declaration of International Law Principles on Internally Displaced Persons, art. 4(1), 69 ILA, Conference Report (2000).

85 Declaration of International Law Principles on Internally Displaced Persons, art. 4(3), 69 ILA, Conference Report (2000).

86 There is a prodigious body of scholarship on the subject of internal displacement, much of which is beyond the scope of this book, which therefore does not include a discussion of all of the soft law addressing internal displacement, although many of these instruments provide similar protections to internally displaced persons as those provided in the Declaration on Internally Displaced Persons. *See, e.g.*, Guiding Principles on Internal Displacement, E/CN.4/1998/53/Add.2 (11 Feb. 1998) (*prepared by* Francis M. Deng).

> order to avoid the effects of armed conflict, situations of generalized violence, violations of human rights or natural or human-made disasters, and who have not crossed an internationally recognized State border.[87]

While the Guiding Principles do not constitute binding obligations upon governments, they have been widely disseminated and promoted by the United Nations and have been recognised by the General Assembly as "an important international framework for the protection of internally displaced persons."[88]

In addition to the documents cited above, several agencies and commissions of the United Nations have mandates that extend to the protection of refugees and displaced persons and have adopted reports and resolutions that contribute to the corpus of soft law that is relevant to incidents of forcible displacement. The newly-created Human Rights Council is one such UN organ. The Council replaced the Human Rights Commission in 2006 and is one of the principle bodies within the UN charged with the protection and promotion of human rights. The Human Rights Council has been at the forefront of advocating for the rights of displaced persons, electing a Special Rapporteur to study the human rights dimensions of population transfer and adopting several resolutions to promote the Special Rapporteur's work. The Special Rapporteur's final report culminated in a significant resolution on population transfer by the UN Sub-Commission on the Promotion and Protection of Human Rights, which catalogued much of the existing international law pertaining to unlawful forcible displacement.[89]

Another relevant entity within the UN is the Special Rapporteur on the Human Rights of Internally Displaced Persons, who is tasked specifically with promoting the rights of internally displaced persons and who issued the Guiding Principles on Internal Displacement, discussed above.[90] When it was first established by the Secretary-General in 1992, the title of this position was the "Representative on internally displaced persons." The Commission on Human Rights (now the Human Rights Council) subsequently indicated to the Secretary-General that additional attention to the human rights of internally displaced persons was warranted, and the Secretary-General thereafter appointed Walter Kälin as the Representative on the human rights of internally displaced persons.

---

87 Guiding Principles on Internal Displacement, Introduction.

88 2005 World Summit Outcome, G.A. Res. 60/L.1, ¶ 132, U.N. Doc. A/60/L.1 (2005).

89 *See* Commission on Human Rights, Sub-Commission on Prevention of Discrimination and Protection of Minorities, *Final Report: Freedom of Movement, Human Rights and Population Transfer*, U.N. Doc. E/CN.4/Sub.2/1997/23 (27 June 1997) (*prepared by* Special Rapporteur Al-Khasawneh). *See* UN Sub-Commission on the Promotion and Protection of Human Rights, *Resolution 1997/29 on Freedom of Movement and Population Transfer*, E/CN.4/Sub.2/RES/1997/29 (28 Aug. 1997).

90 *See* Introduction to the Mandate of the Special Rapporteur of Internally Displaced Persons, Dr. Chaloka Beyani, http://www2.ohchr.org/english/issues/idp/mandate.htm.

The Representative had a relatively broad mandate and was charged with promoting the protection of internally displaced persons by working with national governments and non-governmental organisations, which included the task of distributing and promoting the Guiding Principles on Internal Displacement. One of the most significant duties of the Representative was to create an integrated approach within the UN itself to the protection of internally displaced persons, a function that mirrors the streamlining of human rights within the UN system by the United Nations High Commissioner for Human Rights.[91] In an organisation as complex as the United Nations, such coordination is an essential ingredient for effectively ameliorating the situation of internally displaced persons.

In 2010, Dr. Chaloka Beyani was appointed by the Human Rights Council as the "Special Rapporteur on the Human Rights of Internally Displaced Persons." Although the title of the mandate holder changed, as did the appointing authority, the mandate remains largely the same, and the Special Rapporteur continues to be responsible for disseminating the Guiding Principles and focusing national, regional, and international attention on the challenges faced by IDPs and the necessary protection that must be afforded to them.[92]

7. Security Council Resolutions

The Security Council has also added its voice to the efforts to prohibit forcible displacement. Under Chapter VII of the United Nations Charter, the Security Council may require states parties to take appropriate action when it deems that there is a threat to the peace, a breach of the peace, or acts of aggression by one or more states and when action is required "to maintain or restore international peace and security." A number of Security Council resolutions have condemned specific incidents of forcible displacement, and the Council has, on more than one occasion, taken measures under Chapter VII of the UN Charter to force states engaging in the practice to cease doing so, in compliance with international obligations. The increasing attention that the Security Council has paid to the issue of forcible displacement is an indication that the international community is becoming more attuned to the problem. Some examples of Security Council involvement are explored below.

The Security Council has issued several resolutions regarding deportations of Palestinians by Israel. In a 1990 resolution, the Security Council stated that it "[d]eplore[d] the decision by the Government of Israel, the occupying Power, to resume the deportation of Palestinian civilians in the occupied territories."[93] Two years later, the Security Council issued another resolution, in which it deplored the decision by Israel, the "occupying Power", to resume the deporta-

91 *See id.*

92 *See id.*

93 S.C. Res. 673, S/RES/673 (24 Oct. 1990).

tion of Palestinian civilians in the occupied territories; reaffirmed the application of Geneva Convention IV to the situation there; and requested Israel to refrain from deporting any Palestinian civilian and to ensure the safe and immediate return to the occupied territories of all those deported.[94]

Also in 1990, as a result of widespread reports that Iraq was deporting Kuwaitis to Iraq and settling Iraqi groups in Kuwait, the Security Council issued a number of Chapter VII resolutions regarding these forcible displacements. Resolution 670 condemned "the treatment of Iraqi forces of Kuwaiti nationals, including measures to force them to leave their own country" and reaffirmed Iraq's duty to comply with its international treaty obligations, including its obligations to civilians under Geneva Convention IV.[95] In the same year, the Security Council issued two more resolutions reiterating Iraq's international obligations to refrain from forcibly displacing groups of people out of and into Kuwait.[96] The Security Council also considered the prosecution of individuals who were carrying out these deportations and relocation policies, but ultimately did not press forward with this plan.[97] It was only three years later that the Security Council decided to create the ICTY, and so it may indeed be the case that the Council's experience with the Iraq-Kuwait situation may have made the historic creation of the ICTY more politically feasible when the right time and set of circumstances presented themselves.

In the 1990s, the Security Council issued repeated resolutions in response to the ethnic cleansing campaigns in the former Yugoslavia. In 1992 alone, the Security Council issued four different resolutions calling upon countries in the former Yugoslavia to cease campaigns of forcible displacement.[98] The Security Council's creation of the International Criminal Tribunal for the former Yugoslavia represented, at the time, a novel measure to address the issue of forcible displacement in a specific region afflicted by armed conflict. The Tribunal was established in 1993 pursuant to a Security Council resolution issued under Chapter VII of the UN Charter. The purpose of the Tribunal was to prose-

94 S.C. Res. 726, S/RES/726, (6 Jan. 1992); *see also* S.C. Res. 799, S/RES/799 (18 Dec. 1992) ("Strongly condemn[ing] the action taken by Israel, the occupying Power, to deport hundreds of Palestinian civilians, and express[ing] its firm opposition to any such deportation by Israel").

95 S.C. Res. 670, S/RES/670 (25 Sept. 1990).

96 *See* S.C. Res. 674, S/RES/674 (29 Oct. 1990); S.C. Res. 677, S/RES/677 (28 Nov. 1990).

97 Jean-Marie Henckaerts, Mass Expulsion in Modern International Law and Practice 159 (1995).

98 *See* S.C. Res. 752, S/RES/752 (15 May 1992) (calling upon all parties to the conflict "to ensure that forcible expulsions of persons … cease"); S.C. Res. 757, S/RES/757 (30 May 1992) (calling for "immediate cessation of forcible expulsion"); S.C. Res. 771, S/RES/771 (13 Aug. 1992) (expressing "grave alarm" at the mass forcible expulsions and deportation); S.C. Res. 779, S/RES/779 (6 Oct. 1992) (expressing grave alarm due to ethnic cleansing and forcible expulsion).

cute "persons responsible for serious violations of international humanitarian law committed in the territory of the former Yugoslavia."[99] The jurisprudence of the ICTY has contributed substantially to the body of law regarding forcible displacement and is the subject of the next chapter. Although it is always difficult to empirically measure the deterrent effect of measures taken to curb crimes, it is beyond dispute that the ICTY has tried high-level political and military leaders for the crime of forcible displacement who otherwise never would have faced prosecution for their actions or inactions. But this is still an area of much political controversy.

The actions of the Security Council, a political body, can be a valid way to assess whether a situation involves forcible displacement. Although the Council is not a law-making body and the member states of the Council do not legislate norms that can necessarily be applied in other settings, when the Council acts, especially under Chapter VII of the UN Charter, it is not uncommon for it to cite relevant international law as a basis for its intervention in a particular situation. In such cases, the Council can be considered to be applying various sources of international law, such as the Geneva Conventions and their Protocols, treaty law between the warring states, or international instruments such as the ICCPR. Moreover, when the Security Council decides to take action in relation to a situation, it is often the product of compromise and eventual consensus between the different members states, and thus the very declaration that forcible displacement is occurring has a certain amount of authority behind it due to the deliberative process by which that determination has been made.

8. The International Court of Justice

The ICJ, as the principle judicial organ of the United Nations, has issued several opinions discussing state obligations to refrain from forcible displacement. Because the ICJ deals with the specific cases that are brought before it and because the prohibitions of forcible displacement are spread out among various legal instruments, the ICJ's cases dealing with forcible displacement tend to be fact-specific.[100]

In the Case Concerning Application of the Convention on the Prevention and Punishment of the Crime of Genocide, Bosnia and Herzegovina v. Yugoslavia (Serbia and Montenegro) (Case Concerning Application of the Genocide Convention), the ICJ considered whether forcible displacement constituted genocide within the scope of the Genocide Convention. The ICJ concluded that, where the intent behind deportation and displacement of a group in the context of ethnic cleansing is *only* to *remove* the group from a region rather than to *destroy* the group, the acts of displacement do not necessarily constitute geno-

99 S.C. Res. 827, S/RES/827 (15 May 1993).

100 The European Court of Human Rights generally has addressed expulsion of the individual in an immigration context, but not in the context of forcible displacement. Its case law is therefore not dealt with herein.

cide under the Convention.[101] The Court did, however, leave open the possibility that ethnic cleansing could fall within the scope of the Genocide Convention if the perpetrators exhibited the requisite intent to destroy a group and specifically used forcible displacement as a method of destruction.[102] This holding is consistent with what Chambers of the ICTY had previously held in the *Blagojević and Jokić* and *Brđanin* cases, which are examined in the next chapter.

In its Advisory Opinion on Legal Consequences of the Construction of a Wall in the Occupied Palestinian Territory in 2003, the ICJ relied upon Article 49 of Geneva Convention IV. It determined that the Israeli practice of establishing Israeli settlements in occupied Palestinian territory was in breach of Article 49, holding that Article 49 "prohibits not only deportations or forced transfers of population such as those carried out during the Second World War, but also any measures taken by an occupying Power in order to organize or encourage transfers of parts of its own population into the occupied territory."[103]

In 2008, Georgia commenced a case before the ICJ, claiming that Russia was violating certain provisions of CERD by practicing and supporting racial discrimination through violence and mass expulsion of ethnic Georgians and other ethnic groups, which resulted in "significant changes in the ethnic composition of South Ossetia and Abkhazia."[104] According to Georgia, Russia's continued violence and expulsion of ethnic Georgians could result in irreparable violation of Georgia's rights under CERD, and thus provisional measures were sought to prevent this.[105] The ICJ issued provisional measures pursuant to CERD, ordering a halt to the mass expulsion and violence against residents of two regions of Georgia, South Ossetia, and Abkhazia. In particular, the Court found that the rights under Article 5(b) of the CERD, regarding security of the person against violence or bodily harm, and Article 5(d)(i), regarding freedom of movement and residence within the state, required immediate action in order to be preserved.[106] Among other measures, the ICJ ordered both Georgia and Russia to do all in

101 Case Concerning Application of the Convention on the Prevention and Punishment of the Crime of Genocide, Bosnia and Herzegovina v. Yugoslavia (Serbia and Montenegro), Judgement, 2007 I.C.J. ¶ 190 (27 Feb.).

102 *Id.*

103 Legal Consequences of the Construction of a Wall in the Occupied Palestinian Territory, 2004 I.C.J. 20, ¶ 120 (9 July).

104 Application of the International Convention on the Elimination of All Forms of Racial Discrimination (Geor. v. Russ.) (Application Instituting Proceedings) (12 Aug. 2008).

105 Application of the International Convention on the Elimination of All Forms of Racial Discrimination (Geor. v. Russ.) (Request for the Indication of Provisional Measures of Protection Submitted by the Government of the Republic of Georgia) (14 Aug. 2008).

106 Case Concerning the Application of the International Convention on the Elimination of All Forms of Racial Discrimination (Geor. v. Russ) (Request for the Indication of Provisional Measures) (Order of 15 Oct. 2008), ¶ 142.

their power to ensure, without distinction as to national or ethnic origin, the security of persons, the right of persons to freedom of movement and residence within the borders of the state, and the protection of the property of displaced persons and refugees.[107]

As can be seen from the three cases discussed above, the ICJ has squarely confronted the crime of forcible displacement on a number of occasions. Of course, the enforcement of the ICJ's opinions is always a thorny area, and often an ICJ ruling will be made but then not enforced by the relevant state party. The Court's power as a preventive mechanism is therefore limited by its institutional competence.

* * *

The Genocide Convention has had a profound effect upon the manner in which states, NGOs, and the international community view the crime of genocide. The Convention clearly and unequivocally sets forth the legal definition of the crime, along with its mental and physical elements. Debates and discussion of the legal contours of the crime of genocide are far less common than debates over the scope of other crimes, such as forcible displacement, and this is why the invocation of the crime of genocide is such a powerful, and feared, political tool in international affairs. When a powerful state or the Security Council decides to use the word "genocide" to describe a situation, it is a significant event because there is widespread agreement that genocide is to be prevented and punished. It is therefore in the *application* of the legal term "genocide" to a situation where the analysis and political decisions take place, rather than in efforts to ascertain what the definition of genocide is in the first place. Forcible displacement, on the other hand, is still a crime in search of a definition upon which everyone agrees.

The patchwork quilt of legal norms discussed in this chapter is an essential and important source for the prohibition of forcible displacement. But because the law in this area is derived from many different sources, it tends to be of a more diffuse nature than, for example, the law of genocide. Unlike genocide, there is no one authoritative definition of forcible displacement, and the elements of the crime may differ depending upon the forum in which one finds oneself. This may have the unfortunate consequence of weakening the prohibition because what may be considered forcible displacement in one forum may not necessarily be considered forcible displacement in another: such a state of affairs calls into question the veracity of the crime because, without a single, agreed-upon definition, efforts to enforce the prohibition may seem arbitrary and/or politically motivated. It is for this reason that, although the law in this area has been developing—most significantly since the end of World War II,—it would be beneficial to have a single, authoritative source to point to when attempting to convince individuals and governments that they should be taking actions to prevent the displacement of people from their homes and to punish perpetrators

107 *Id.* ¶ 149.

of displacement when it has occurred. With such an international instrument in place, the general, agreed-upon definition of forcible displacement could then be domesticated into the national law of states for even greater preventive effect.

Chapter Four

The Modern Tribunals

Forcible displacement is a consequence, and sometimes even an intended outcome, of most armed conflicts.[1]

1. The International Criminal Tribunal for the former Yugoslavia: The Great Experiment

The visionary events of the post-World War II era in respect of international criminal justice encompassed the Nuremberg and Tokyo Tribunals, the domestic trials conducted in Germany under Control Council Law No. 10 by the United States Nuremberg Military Tribunals, and the many military trials conducted under United States law in Asia and the Pacific of hundreds of political and military leaders of the defeated Axis Powers who had committed violations of international law during the war. What followed this bold new age of individual criminal responsibility for atrocity crimes during wartime was a period of relative quiet, as the World powers squared off for almost 50 years of the Cold War. Following the collapse of the Union of Soviet Socialist Republics, Slovenia, Croatia, and Bosnia and Herzegovina, in relatively quick succession, declared their independence from the Socialist Federated Republic of Yugoslavia. In 1991, Slovenia managed an extremely brief war, and Croatia began its own. In 1992, Bosnia and Herzegovina declared its independence, Sarajevo was soon under siege, people were being killed and displaced, and detention camps began to crop up in April of that year. Images of emaciated IDPs behind barbed wire fences galvanised the public and the international community into action.[2]

The United Nations' creation of an *ad hoc* tribunal was the international community's direct response to the armed conflicts following the dissolution of Yugoslavia, which included the forcible displacement of civilians on a massive

1 Catherine Phuong, Forcible Displacement in Peace Agreements, The International Council on Human Rights Policy, Review Meeting, Peace Agreements: The Role of Human Rights in Negotiations, Belfast, 7-8 March 2005. In this paper, Ms. Phuong argues that, in many peace processes, the return of refugees and other persons displaced by an armed conflict is considered to be essential to a lasting peace.

2 Laura Silber & Allan Little, The Death of Yugoslavia 37-41, 70-264 (1996); Tim Judah, Kosovo, War and Revenge 65 (2002) ("On 16 July 1990 the Serbian League of Communists officially transformed itself into the Socialist Party of Serbia (SPS) and elected Milošević as its head.").

scale.[3] In 1992, the United Nations Security Council determined under Chapter VII of the United Nations Charter that the situation in Yugoslavia constituted a threat to international peace and security and passed Resolution 771, declaring that individuals who had committed or ordered the commission of grave breaches of the Geneva Conventions were individually and criminally responsible for such breaches and calling upon the international community to cooperate in the collection of evidence of those crimes. The Security Council asked the United Nations Secretary-General to assemble and task a group of experts to examine this evidence; and, after this report was received, the Security Council asked the Secretary-General to make a proposal for the establishment of an international criminal tribunal. On 25 May 1993, after having received this proposal, the Security Council, again acting under Chapter VII, passed Resolution 827, by which ICTY was created.[4] But the creation of ICTY had seemingly little deterrent effect upon the warring parties. In July 1995, the United Nations safe haven at Srebrenica was taken by Bosnian Serb forces, and thousands of Bosnian Muslims were executed or displaced. The following month, the North Atlantic Treaty Organisation (NATO) began to bomb Serb positions, and Croatian forces drove the Serb population from the Krajina. In November, the Dayton Peace Accords were signed by the warring factions, ending the active hostilities.[5]

---

3 *See generally* LAURA SILBER & ALLAN LITTLE, THE DEATH OF YUGOSLAVIA (1996) (first published in 1995). This source is a compelling and contemporaneously-written book on the conflicts during the dissolution of the former Yugoslavia.

4 *See generally* Report of the Secretary-General Pursuant to Paragraph 2 of Security Council Resolution 808 (1993), Presented 3 May 1993 (S/25704). On 19 April 1993, the Secretary-General addressed a letter to the President of the UN Security Council informing him that the report would be made available to the UN Security Council no later than 6 May 1993. The ICTY was considered an *ad hoc* tribunal due to the manner in which it was created and its specific temporal and territorial jurisdiction. It is commonly considered the first truly international criminal court to try individuals for the alleged commission of international crimes, as opposed to the post-World War II tribunals, whose membership was restricted to the allied powers that had emerged victorious from that conflict. The personal jurisdiction of the ICTY is limited to individuals, as opposed to states. *See* ICTY Statute, articles 1, 6. The temporal jurisdiction is over crimes alleged to have been committed from 1 January 1991 (ICTY Statute, articles 1, 8), and the geographic jurisdiction is over crimes alleged to have been committed on the territory of the former Yugoslavia (ICTY Statute, articles 1, 8). Finally, the ICTY has both concurrent and primary jurisdiction over national courts (ICTY Statute, article 9), unlike the later-established International Criminal Court, which operates jurisdictionally upon the principle of complementarity.

5 LAURA SILBER & ALLAN LITTLE, THE DEATH OF YUGOSLAVIA 265-387 (1996); TIM JUDAH, KOSOVO, WAR AND REVENGE 109-126 (2002); CHRIS STEPHEN, JUDGEMENT DAY, THE TRIAL OF SLOBODAN MILOŠEVIĆ 52-76 (2004); Human Rights Watch, *Weighing the Evidence, Lessons from the Slobodan Milosevic Trial*, Volume 18, No. 10(D), at 7-9 (Dec. 2006).

Although it is impossible to generalise an entire armed conflict, there are certain features or patterns that, either contemporaneously or in hindsight, can be discerned and perhaps even be used to understand the events that occurred. The events in Rwanda in the summer of 1994 and in Cambodia from 1975 to 1979 were complex sets of fact patterns involving numerous actors, but they can also be considered clear instances of genocide. The civil war in Sierra Leone from 1991 to 1999 was remarkable for its use of child soldiers. The attacks in Lebanon between 2004 and 2005, specifically the assassination of Lebanese Prime Minister Rafik Hariri by car-bomb explosion in Beirut on 14 February 2005, have been aptly termed terrorism. All these conflicts have their own individual characters. The dissolution of the former Yugoslavia in the 1990s—although it involved genocide, murder, extermination, rape, torture, and many other crimes—can arguably be termed, at its core, a conflict where forcible displacement was the goal of the warring parties. Given the extremely multi-ethnic population spread out over the entire territory, military actions were violent "land grabs" and efforts to consolidate territory populated by a single ethnicity.

What follows is an analysis of the United Nations Security Council's great experiment in the implementation of international humanitarian and human rights law. No other international tribunal has dealt with the crime of forcible displacement to such an extent as the ICTY has in its almost two decades of existence. It was in the courtrooms of the ICTY that the parties and the judges wrestled with a burgeoning area of modern international law in an attempt to assess the responsibility of individuals accused of forcibly displacing their fellow human beings during the conflicts in the Balkans. The experiences of the International Criminal Tribunal for Rwanda, the Special Court for Sierra Leone, and the International Criminal Court are also considered below, but to a more limited extent than that of ICTY due to the latter's more extensive treatment of the subject.

a. *Forcible Displacement as Crimes under the ICTY Statute*

Forcible displacement is criminalised via the ICTY Statute under several provisions. Article 5(d) identifies deportation as a crime against humanity. The Appeals Chamber has held that deportation and forcible transfer are acts constituting persecution, a crime against humanity, under Article 5(h).[6] Article 5(i), which prohibits "other inhumane acts" as crimes against humanity, has also been interpreted as proscribing forcible transfer.[7] Article 2(g) of the Statute makes the

6 *See Prosecutor v. Krnojelac*, Case No. IT-97-25-A, Judgement, 17 September 2003 (*Krnojelac* Appeal Judgement), ¶ 222.

7 *See Prosecutor v. Blagojević and Jokić*, Case No. IT-02-60-T, Judgement, 17 January 2005 (*Blagojević* Trial Judgement), ¶¶ 623-32; *Prosecutor v. Brđanin*, Case No. IT-99-36-T, Judgement, 1 September 2004 (*Brđanin* Trial Judgement), ¶ 539; *Prosecutor v. Krstić*, Case No. IT-98-33-T, Judgement, 2 August 2001 (*Krstić* Trial Judgement), ¶ 519.

unlawful deportation or transfer of a civilian punishable as a grave breach of the Geneva Conventions. Chambers have also considered that forcible transfer and deportation can constitute genocidal acts under Article 4 of the ICTY Statute.[8]

Articles 2, 4, and 5 have certain general legal requirements that must be satisfied in order for the Prosecution to prove that a crime has been committed; however, the elements—the *actus reus* and the *mens rea*—of an underlying offence do not change according to the particular Article under which it is charged. For the purposes of this book, we are generally only concerned with the *actus reus* and *mens rea* of forcible displacement, rather than the general requirements for the various articles pursuant to which the displacement is charged.

b. Development of ICTY Jurisprudence Ante *the* Stakić *Appeal Judgement*

As in many common law jurisdictions, the elements of the underlying offence of forcible displacement developed over time in cases before the Tribunal. Whereas it can take hundreds of years in a domestic jurisdiction for agreed and settled definitions of the elements of a crime to develop, the process took a comparatively short amount of time at the Tribunal. One of the main reasons for this is most likely the fact that the Tribunal is meant to be applying the law that is already in existence at the time that the offences are committed, rather than "creating" the law *ex post facto*. Despite this fact, it can be difficult to discern differences between efforts to uncover the state of pre-existing law, especially when one is dealing with customary international law, and a Chamber's efforts to define elements of an international crime, when the elements have never been defined before. Put another way, if a Chamber is supposed to be merely applying the law that already existed at the time of the offence, but yet has to articulate elements of that offence for the very first time, issues in connection with the doctrine of *nullum crimen sine lege* can arise. In order to deal with this problem, the Secretary-General in his report to the Security Council stated that the competence of the ICTY in respect to its *ratione materiae* is derived from the Geneva Conventions, the Hague Conventions, the Genocide Convention, and the Nuremberg Charter.[9] It is no coincidence that all of these sources of law are discussed in the preceding chapter, because they indeed are the legal basis for the criminalisation of forcible displacement and the other crimes in the ICTY Statute.

---

8 *See Prosecutor v. Stakić*, Case No. IT-97-24-T, Judgement, 31 July 2003 (*Stakić* Trial Judgement), ¶¶ 516-19. The Trial Chamber's findings were undisturbed by the Appeals Chamber. *See Prosecutor v. Stakić*, Case No. IT-97-24-A, Judgement, 22 March 2006 (*Stakić* Appeal Judgement), ¶¶ 37-57. *See also Brđanin* Trial Judgement, ¶ 906. The Trial Chamber's findings were undisturbed by the Appeals Chamber. *See Prosecutor v. Brđanin*, Case No. IT-99-36-A, Judgement, 3 April 2007 (*Brđanin* Appeal Judgement).

9 Report of the Secretary-General Pursuant to Paragraph 2 of Security Council Resolution 808 (1993), S/25704, 3 May 1993, ¶ 35.

The task of delineating the elements of a crime that already existed in its basic form in other legal documents was therefore a challenging one that did not take place overnight. Although it would not be fair to call the ICTY's efforts to define the legal elements of forcible displacement as heuristic, the jurisprudence on forcible displacement was honed over the course of several years. A review of the cases leading up to the *Stakić* case, in which the Tribunal gave its most developed treatment of forcible displacement, provides a window into the conceptual challenge of delineating a crime that continually evades the confines of legal construction.

In the case of *Prosecutor v. Blaškić* (March 2000), the Trial Chamber considered that the offence of "deportation or forcible transfer of civilians" was a form of persecution and defined it as the "forced displacement of the persons concerned by expulsion or other coercive acts from the area in which they are lawfully present, without grounds permitted under international law".[10] The Trial Chamber did not set forth a requisite *mens rea* for forcible transfer, but rather focused upon the *mens rea* required for the underlying offence of persecution, which it defined as "the specific intent to cause injury to a human being because he belongs to a particular community or group".[11] The Trial Chamber heard testimony from witnesses during the trial that, once the soldiers of the Croatian Defence Council had taken control of the village of Gačice, they took the residents (247 Muslim civilians) on a forced march towards Vitez and forced them to sit opposite the Hotel Vitez as human shields for approximately three hours. Afterwards, the residents were taken back to the village and made to live in the seven houses that remained standing. They were then loaded onto trucks and driven by force out of the village by the soldiers of the Croatian Defence Council.[12] Based upon this evidence, the Trial Chamber concluded that these events amounted to devastation without any military necessity and forcible transfer of civilians.[13]

The Trial Chamber in the case of *Prosecutor v. Krstić* (August 2001) explained that "both deportation and forcible transfer relate to the involuntary and unlawful

---

10 *Prosecutor v. Blaškić*, Case No. IT-95-14-T, Judgement, 3 March 2000, ¶ 234 (*Blaškić* Trial Judgement) (citing Article 7(2)(d) of the Statute of the International Criminal Court; 1996 International Law Commission Report, pp. 100-01).

11 *Id.* ¶ 235.

12 *Id.* ¶ 549.

13 *Id.* ¶ 550. Blaškić's conviction under count 1, which included the crime of persecution, was reversed on appeal in light of the Appeals Chamber's determination that the Trial Chamber applied an incorrect legal standard in relation to the *mens rea* in finding him to have ordered the attacks that gave rise to crimes against civilians and civilian property. The Appeals Chamber stated that a person who orders an act or omission with the awareness of the substantial likelihood that a crime will be committed in the execution of that order had the requisite *mens rea* for establishing responsibility under Article 7(1). *Prosecutor v. Blaškić*, Case No. IT-95-14-A, Judgement, 29 July 2004, ¶ 481.

evacuation of individuals from the territory in which they reside. Yet, the two are not synonymous in customary international law. Deportation presumes transfer beyond State borders, whereas forcible transfer relates to displacements within a State".[14] The Trial Chamber also stated that "any forced displacement is by definition a traumatic experience which involves abandoning one's home, losing property and being displaced under duress to another location".[15] The Trial Chamber concluded that, on 12 and 13 July 1995, despite a United Nations Security Council resolution declaring that the United Nations-protected Srebrenica enclave was to be "free from armed attack or any other hostile act", units of the Bosnian Serb Army (VRS) launched an assault upon the enclave and captured the town of Srebrenica. About 25,000 Bosnian Muslim civilians (Bosnian Muslim women, children, and elderly persons), "in an atmosphere of terror", were then forcibly bused out of the enclave (from Potočari) to territory under the control of Bosnia and Herzegovina at Kladanj. The Trial Chamber found that Krstić, who was the Commander of the VRS Drina Corps, was guilty of forcible transfer as an inhumane act constituting a crime against humanity.[16]

In *Prosecutor v. Naletilić and Martinović* (March 2003), the Trial Chamber noted that the jurisprudence of the Tribunal held that deportation required transfer beyond state borders, while forcible transfer may take place within national borders.[17] With regard to the *mens rea* element of the crime, the Trial Chamber stated that the Prosecution must prove that a perpetrator had the intent to have persons removed, which implies the aim that the person will not return.[18] In arriving at this conclusion, the Trial Chamber looked to the Commentary of Geneva Convention IV, which states that, "unlike deportation and forcible transfer, evacuation is a provisional measure": the Chamber regarded this as indicative of the fact that deportation and forcible transfer were not by their nature provisional.[19]

Because the indictment did not contain any averments of displacement across a state border and no evidence had been admitted to that effect, the Trial Chamber concluded that there was no basis to find that persecution was con-

---

14 *Krstić* Trial Judgement, ¶¶ 521-22 (noting that Article 2(g) of the ICTY Statute, Articles 49 and 147 of the Geneva Convention Concerning the Protection of Civilian Persons in Time of War (Geneva Convention IV), Article 85(4)(a) of Additional Protocol I, Article 18 of the ILC Draft Code, and Article 7(1)(d) of the Statute of the International Criminal Court all condemn deportation or forcible transfer of protected persons and that Article 17 of Protocol II likewise condemns the "displacement" of civilians).

15 *Id.* ¶ 523. While the Trial Chamber defined the *actus reus* of deportation and forcible transfer as described above, it did not state the requisite *mens rea* element.

16 *Id.* ¶¶ 1, 519, 532, 727. These findings were upheld on appeal. *Prosecutor v. Krstić*, Case No. IT-98-33-A, Judgement, 19 April 2004, ¶ 151.

17 *Prosecutor v. Naletilić and Martinović*, Case No. IT-98-34-T, Judgement, 31 March 2003, ¶ 670 (*Naletilić and Martinović* Trial Judgement).

18 *Id.* ¶ 520.

19 *Id.* ¶ 520, note 1362.

ducted by means of deportation. The Trial Chamber did, however, find that forcible transfers had taken place. In assessing the individual criminal responsibility of the specific accused for these transfers, the Trial Chamber noted that Naletilić had lived most of his life in Germany and returned to Široki Brijeg in Bosnia and Herzegovina to set up a military group called the Convicts' Battalion, which under his leadership battled the Serb forces in Mostar during the spring of 1992.[20] Martinović, a civilan before the war, joined the Croatian Defence Forces and became a commander.[21] The Trial Chamber found these two men to be criminally responsible for the forcible transfer of Muslim civilians, explaining that "the forcible transfers were carried out on discriminatory grounds as [Bosnian] Muslims were selected and forced out of their homes while their [Bosnian] Croat neighbours were allowed to stay".[22] Moreover, the Chamber found that "[t]he forcible transfers were part of a well-organised campaign aimed at removing the [Bosnian] Muslim civilian population from the West bank of Mostar" and that "[b]oth accused were aware of and participated in this campaign".[23]

In *Prosecutor v. Stakić* (July 2003), in determining the *actus reus* for deportation, the Trial Chamber looked to the definition of the term "deportation". The Trial Chamber observed that the English version of the Statute uses the term "deportation", which according to Black's Law Dictionary was "the act or an instance of removing a person to another country", especially the expulsion or transfer of an alien from a country[24] The Trial Chamber also noted that Black's Law Dictionary referred to the Roman law term "*deportatio*" as an act "of carrying away" a person from the area where he was living under previously safe conditions and as

> [p]erpetual banishment of a person condemned for a crime. It was the severest form of banishment since it included additional penalties, such as seizure of the whole property, loss of Roman citizenship, confinement to a definite place .... Places of *deportatio* were islands (*in insulam*) near the Italian shore ....[25]

The Trial Chamber considered that, because under Roman law the term *deportatio* referred to "instances where persons were dislocated from one area to another area also under the control of the Roman Empire", there was no cross-border requirement originally envisaged by the term. In other words, whether an inter-

20 *Id.* ¶ 2.

21 *Id.* ¶ 3.

22 *Id.* ¶ 672.

23 *Id.* ¶¶ 670-72. Both Naletilić and Martinović's convictions were upheld on appeal and the findings were not disturbed. *Prosecutor v. Naletilić and Martinović*, Case No. IT-98-34-A, Judgement, 3 May 2006, ¶¶ 154, 570-71 (*Naletilić and Martinović* Appeal Judgement).

24 *Prosecutor v. Stakić*, Case No. IT-97-24-T, Judgement, 31 July 2003, ¶ 674 (*Stakić* Trial Judgement).

25 *Id.*

national boundary was crossed or not, the removal of the person was still called "deportation". The Trial Chamber also considered that the concept of deportation meant the removal of someone from an area over which the perpetrator exercises authority or the removal of someone from an area where he or she hitherto enjoyed the "protection" of that authority.[26] The "core aspect of deportation" was therefore "to take someone out of the place where he or she was lawfully staying, *and* ... to remove that person from the protection of the authority concerned".[27]

The Chamber then examined the French version of the Statute and the Secretary-General's report to the Security Council accompanying the ICTY Statute, which is considered the legislative history of the legal instrument that created the Tribunal.[28] The Chamber considered that the fundamental right underlying the prohibition of deportation—what it termed "the protected interests"—was "the right and expectation of individuals to be able to remain in their homes and communities without interference by an aggressor, whether from the same or another state".[29] The Trial Chamber was therefore of the view that "it is the *actus reus* of forcibly removing individuals from the territory and the environment in which they have been lawfully present, in many cases for decades and generations, which is the rationale for imposing criminal responsibility and not the destination resulting from such a removal."[30] In articulating the *actus reus* of the offence as such, the Trial Chamber was alert to the concern that a definite destination requirement would often make it difficult to determine whether and when the crime occurred due to the fact that the deportation of persons may have been accomplished in several stages and through several territories, as well as "across borders that may have changed every day."[31] For these reasons, the Trial Chamber found that Article 5(d) of the Statute had to be read "to encompass forced population displacements both across internationally recognised borders and *de facto* boundaries, such as constantly changing frontlines, which are not internationally recognised" and defined deportation "as the forced displacement of persons by expulsion or other coercive acts for reasons not permitted under international law from an area in which they are lawfully present to an area under the control of another party".[32]

Having articulated the legal elements of deportation as such, the Trial Chamber determined that the evidence adduced in the case illustrated that the persons leaving the municipality of Prijedor, in Bosnia and Herzegovina, during the time relevant to the indictment, could not be considered as having voluntarily decided to give up their homes in light of the coercive nature of the atmos-

26 *Id.*

27 *Id.* ¶ 674 (footnotes omitted).

28 *Id.* ¶¶ 675-76.

29 *Id.* ¶ 677.

30 *Id.*

31 *Id.*

32 *Id.* ¶ 679.

phere in the municipality. The Trial Chamber therefore concluded that Stakić, the President of the Municipality of Prijedor Crisis Staff, located in present day Republika Srpska in Bosnia and Herzegovina,[33] had intended to deport the non-Serb population from the Prijedor municipality and that, based upon this intent, he committed, planned, and ordered the crime of deportation. Stakić was accordingly found guilty of the crime of deportation.[34]

The Appeals Chamber, in *Prosecutor v. Krnojelac* (September 2003), held that acts of forcible displacement underlying the crime of persecution were not limited to displacements across a national border. It further stated that "the prohibition against forcible displacements aims at safeguarding the right and aspiration of individuals to live in their communities and homes without outside interference." Similar to the Trial Chamber in *Stakić*, the *Krnojelac* Appeals Chamber was of the view that it is "[t]he forced character of displacement and the forced uprooting of the inhabitants of a territory" that entail "the criminal responsibility of the perpetrator, not the destination to which these inhabitants are sent."[35]

At trial, it had been found that living conditions in the Foča Kazneno-Popravni Dom (KP Dom)—a detention facility—subjected the non-Serb detainees to a coercive prison regime such that they were not in a position to exercise genuine choice with regard to a prisoner exchange. Evidence of the conditions under which the victims were detained included testimony of beatings of detainees by prison guards, as well as the disappearances of detainees.[36] The Appeals Chamber concluded that the 35 detainees were under duress and that the Trial Chamber erred in finding that they had freely chosen to be exchanged.[37] The Appeals Chamber explained that, even though the evidence showed that "the prisoners were happy about the exchanges … it is impossible to infer genuine choice from the fact that consent was expressed, given that the circumstances may deprive the consent of any value".[38] In respect of the *mens rea* of Krnojelac, the commander of the KP Dom, the Appeals Chamber found that he had shared the intent of the principal perpetrators in a joint criminal enterprise aimed at

33 *Prosecutor v. Stakić*, Case No. IT-97-24-A, Judgement, 22 March 2006 (*Stakić* Appeal Judgement), ¶¶ 2-3.

34 *Stakić* Trial Judgement, ¶¶ 707, 712. The factual finding regarding the coercive nature of the atmosphere in the municipality remained undisturbed on appeal. *Stakić* Appeal Judgement, ¶ 310. The Appeals Chamber, however, found that the Trial Chamber was correct in its finding with respect to deportation in relation to the Trnopolje-Karlovac transfer, but should have entered a conviction for other inhumane acts resulting from the forcible transfer of persons across frontlines between the parties to the conflict, as well as between locations under Serb control. *Stakić* Appeal Judgement, ¶¶ 320-21.

35 *Prosecutor v. Krnojelac*, Case No. IT-97-25-A, Judgement, 17 September 2003, ¶ 218 (*Krnojelac* Appeal Judgement).

36 *Id.* note 2, ¶ 231-32.

37 *Id.* ¶ 233.

38 *Id.* ¶ 229.

removing the non-Serb detainees from the KP Dom facility and found him responsible, as a co-perpetrator, of persecution by way of forcible displacement.[39]

In *Prosecutor v. Blagoje Simić et al.* (October 2003), the Trial Chamber stated that the following common elements must be ascertained in order to establish that an act of deportation or forcible transfer has occurred: the unlawful character of the displacement, the area where the displaced person lawfully resided and the destination to which the person was displaced, and the intent of the perpetrator to deport or forcibly transfer the victim.[40] With respect to the *mens rea* requirement, the Trial Chamber concluded that a finding of forced displacement, either as deportation or forcible transfer, required an element of permanency in relation to the intention of the accused.[41] The Trial Chamber found that sixteen non-Serb civilians were unlawfully deported through exchanges from Bosanski Šamac, in Bosnia and Herzegovina, to Croatia and that one non-Serb civilian was forcibly transferred from Bosanski Šamac to Dubica, within the territory of Bosnia and Herzegovina.[42] The Trial Chamber found that the fact that some non-Serb civilians were asked whether they wanted to cross over to the other side did "not necessarily indicate that these persons voluntarily agreed to be exchanged, as they could have been left without a genuine choice as to whether to leave or to remain in the area when they made their statement."[43] The Trial Chamber considered the atmosphere of fear and terror in which the non-Serbs were taken from their homes, as well as evidence that some of the non-Serb civilians who were exchanged were not asked whether they wanted to be exchanged.[44] The Trial Chamber concluded that this evidence was "a strong indicator that these civilians were not voluntarily exchanged."[45] In its reasoning, the Trial Chamber noted that the detention and living conditions of these victims constituted a coercive environment that left them without a real choice as to whether or not they wanted to be exchanged.[46] It was thus found that the only reasonable inference from the extensive and continuing mistreatment of non-Serb civilians and their subsequent displacement was that the perpetrators intended that the victims should not return.[47]

---

39 This ground of appeal was accordingly upheld. *Id.* ¶¶ 246-48.

40 *Prosecutor v. Blagoje Simić et al.*, Case No. IT-95-9-T, Judgement, 17 October 2003, ¶ 124 (*Simić et al.* Trial Judgement).

41 *Id.* ¶ 134 (emphasis added).

42 *Id.* ¶¶ 968, 972, 1036-38.

43 *Id.* ¶ 967.

44 *Id.*

45 *Id.*

46 *Id.* ¶ 968.

47 *Id.* ¶¶ 967-68, 972, 1038 (internal citations omitted). The Trial Chamber's findings were upheld on appeal. *Prosecutor v. Blagoje Simić et al.*, Case No. IT-95-9-A, Judgement, 28 November 2006, ¶ 188.

Turning to the case of *Prosecutor v. Slobodan Milošević*,[48] it first should be noted that the trial encompassed three armed conflicts, those that unfolded in Croatia, Bosnia and Herzegovina, and finally Kosovo.[49] The last of these involved the participation of NATO in its first armed conflict, and set at odds the United States and the newly-emerging Russian Federation. At the half-way point in the trial, after the close of the Prosecution's case-in-chief, the *amicus curiae* lawyers assigned to assist Milošević made a motion to dismiss many of the charges against him. A number of these charges included forcible displacement. In its written decision upon the motion, the Trial Chamber stated that the elements of deportation and forcible transfer were the following: cross-border transfer, the involuntary nature of the movement, and the intent of the perpetrator.[50] The Trial Chamber further explained that offences of both deportation and forcible transfer required evidence of the perpetrator's intent to transfer the victim from his or her home or community and evidence that the perpetrator either directly intended that the victim would leave or that it was reasonably foreseeable that this would occur as a consequence of his action. Additionally, if the removal of the victim resulted in the crossing of a national border, the crime committed was deportation, while, if there was no such crossing, the crime committed was forcible transfer.[51]

Based upon evidence adduced by the Prosecution at the half-way point in the trial, the Trial Chamber concluded that there was sufficient evidence to find Milošević guilty of deportation in Kosovo and Bosnia and Herzegovina and therefore rejected Milošević's motion for the charges against him to be dismissed before he even lodged a defence to answer them.[52] The *Milošević* Trial Chamber relied heavily upon statistical demographic evidence in reaching its conclusions. At the beginning of each section dealing with a municipality where crimes were alleged to have taken place, the Trial Chamber gave a brief break-down of the statistical data that had been admitted into evidence though a demographic expert

48 Milošević was the first former head of state to be brought before and tried by an international criminal tribunal. As Human Rights Watch has stated, "the trial of Milosevic marked an end of the era when being a head of state meant immunity from prosecution. Since then other former heads of state, including Saddam Hussein and Charles Taylor, have been brought to justice." Human Rights Watch, *Weighing the Evidence, Lessons from the Slobodan Milosevic Trial*, Volume 18, No. 10(D), at 1 (Dec. 2006).

49 *See generally* Gideon Boas, The Milošević Trial, Lessons for the Conduct of Complex International Criminal Proceedings (2007) (an insider's assessment of the proceedings); Chris Stephen, Judgement Day, The Trial of Slobodan Milošević (2004) (providing a contextual summary of the proceedings up to the half-way point).

50 *Prosecutor v. Slobodan Milošević*, Case No. IT-02-54-T, Decision on Motion for Judgement of Acquittal, 16 June 2004, ¶ 46 (*Milošević* Rule 98 *bis* Decision).

51 *Milošević* Rule 98 *bis* Decision, ¶ 78.

52 *Id.* ¶¶ 82 (Table), 309 (d) (Schedule D).

witness. For example, the Trial Chamber noted that, in 1991, the population of Srebrenica was 29,198 people, 21,361 of whom were of Muslim ethnicity (73.2 percent). However, in 1997, the population of Srebrenica was 7,442, only seven of whom were of Muslim ethnicity (0.1 percent). This evidence was used to conclude that the Prosecution had adduced sufficient evidence that a genocide had been committed at Srebrenica, one of the means of which was the forcible transfer of the Bosnian Muslim population out of the UN-protected safe haven.[53] Although the trial of Milošević never reached a conclusion due to his death near the end of the trial,[54] the question of the forcible displacement of the Kosovo Albanians in the summer of 1999 was taken up in *Prosecutor v. Milutinović et al.*—otherwise known as the "Milošević Generals Trial"—which took place from 2006 to 2009 and which is dealt with later in this chapter.

In *Prosecutor v. Brđanin* (September 2004), the Trial Chamber stated that the *actus reus* of deportation consisted of the forcible displacement of individuals across a state border from an area in which they were lawfully present, without grounds permitted under international law, whereas displacement within the boundaries of a state constituted forcible transfer. Both deportation and forcible transfer required that the displacement took place under coercion, and the essential element in establishing coercion was that the displacement was involuntary in nature: in other words, the persons concerned had no real choice.[55] The Trial Chamber further stated that the requisite *mens rea* for both deportation and forcible transfer was the intent that the removal of the victims be permanent.[56]

Based upon the evidence presented at trial, the Trial Chamber concluded that "in forcibly displacing the Bosnian Muslims and Bosnian Croats within and from [the Autonomous Region of Krajina], the Bosnian Serb authorities had no other intention but to ensure that the departure of these populations would be on a permanent basis."[57] Specifically, the Trial Chamber noted that this intention was illustrated by the fact that Bosnian Muslims and Bosnian Croats' homes, business premises, and religious buildings were destroyed and their property was confiscated by or relinquished without compensation to the Assembly of the Serbian People in Bosnia and Herzegovina.[58] The Trial Chamber also articulated the test for whether the conditions imposed *during the course of the deportation or forcible transfer* constituted genocidal destruction as:

---

53 *Id.* ¶ 202.

54 *Prosecutor v. Slobodan Milošević*, Case No. IT-02-54-T, Order Terminating the Proceedings, 14 March 2006; Report to the President, Death of Slobodan Milošević, 30 May 2006, http://www.icty.org/case/slobodan_milosevic/4#presord.

55 *Prosecutor v. Brđanin*, Case No. IT-99-36-T, Judgement, 1 September 2004, ¶¶ 543-44 (*Brđanin* Trial Judgement).

56 *Id.* ¶ 545.

57 *Id.* ¶ 555 (internal citations omitted).

58 *Id.* ¶ 555.

> the objective probability of these conditions leading to the physical destruction of the group in part. In evaluating this objective probability, the Trial Chamber has focused on the actual nature of the "conditions of life" and on the length of time that members of the group were subjected to them. It has also been guided, when available, by factors such as the characteristics of the members of the group upon which they were inflicted.[59]

This holding was significant in that it purported to take into account conditions that were related to the displacement of the victims, and not just their strict movement *per se*. In making its findings in this case, the Trial Chamber relied upon evidence that the prisoners of the various camps had been held in small spaces and had to sleep on the floor, that the hygienic circumstances had been poor, that they had received insufficient food and water, and that they had been forced to perform strenuous physical work.[60] The Trial Chamber ultimately concluded that Brđanin, a prominent politician in the Autonomous Region of Krajina,[61] had aided and abetted the crimes of forcible transfer and deportation.[62]

In *Prosecutor v. Blagojević and Jokić* (January 2005), the Trial Chamber defined forcible transfer as the "forced character of displacement and the forced uprooting of the inhabitants of a territory" that gives rise to criminal responsibility.[63] The Trial Chamber further explained that the requirement of "forcible" describes a situation where individuals do not have a free or genuine choice to remain in the territory where they were present; includes threats or the use of force, fear of violence, and illegal detention; and requires that the displacement take place under coercion.[64] With respect to the *mens rea* requirement, the Trial Chamber stated that the perpetrator must have had the intention to remove the victims and that this intention implied that the victims should not return.[65] After evaluating the evidence, the Trial Chamber held that thousands of Bosnian Muslims were forcibly transferred from Srebrenica.[66] The Trial Chamber specifically relied upon evidence illustrating that women, children, and the eld-

59 *Id.* ¶ 906. The Trial Chamber's findings were undisturbed by the Appeals Chamber. *See Prosecutor v. Brđanin*, Case No. IT-99-36-A, Judgement, 3 April 2007 (*Brđanin* Appeal Judgement).

60 *Brđanin* Trial Judgement, ¶¶ 904-62.

61 *Id.* ¶ 9.

62 *Id.* ¶¶ 577, 583. The Trial Chamber's findings were not disturbed on appeal. *Brđanin* Appeal Judgement, ¶ 320.

63 *Prosecutor v. Blagojević and Jokić*, Case No. IT-02-60-T, Judgement, 17 January 2005 (*Blagojević and Jokić* Trial Judgement), ¶ 596 (citing *Krnojelac* Appeal Judgement, ¶ 218).

64 *Blagojević and Jokić* Trial Judgement, ¶ 596 (internal citations omitted).

65 *Id.* ¶ 601 (citing *Naletilić and Martinović* Trial Judgement, ¶ 520, note 1362).

66 *Blagojević and Jokić* Trial Judgement, ¶¶ 616-18. The Trial Chamber's findings were upheld on appeal. *Prosecutor v. Blagojević and Jokić*, Case No. IT-02-60-A, Judgement, 9 May 2007, ¶¶ 108-09.

erly were transported from Potočari in the Srebrenica enclave to Kladanj, while the men were initially taken to Bratunac town. From this evidence, the Trial Chamber concluded that the people transferred from Potočari did not have a genuine choice to remain in the Srebrenica enclave.[67] It is also interesting to note that, in establishing that the forcible transfer of women, children, and the elderly from Srebrenica caused them serious mental harm as an underlying act of genocide under Article 4(2)(b), the Trial Chamber relied upon the fact that they had been brutally separated from the men, had feared for the security of their male relatives and of themselves, had been forced to leave their homes and possessions, and had known that they would never be able to return. In addition, their changed economic and emotional situation was taken into account.[68] Regarding the *mens rea* requirement, the Trial Chamber found that the evidence demonstrated that the perpetrators did not intend for the displaced people to return once the situation had normalised.[69]

In the recently decided case of *Prosecutor v. Popović et al.* (June 2010), the Trial Chamber defined forced displacement in a manner consistent with both the *Krstić* and *Blagojević* Judgements, stating that both forcible transfer and deportation consist of "(i) the forced displacement of persons by expulsion or other forms of coercion (ii) from an area in which they are lawfully present (iii) without grounds permitted under international law".[70] The Trial Chamber noted that the *actus reus* for the crime of deportation consists of an additional element, namely that the acts of the accused caused displaced persons to be transferred across a border, which the *actus reus* for the crime of forcible transfer does not include.[71] The Trial Chamber further noted that both forcible transfer and deportation must be carried out by expulsion or other forms of coercion.[72] The Trial Chamber also held that the *mens rea* for forcible transfer required only proof of the intent to forcibly displace persons, without regard to their ultimate destination, while the *mens rea* for the crime of deportation required the Prosecution to prove the intent of the accused to displace persons across a *de jure* or *de facto* border.[73] In neither case, according to the Trial Chamber, did the Prosecution need to prove that the accused intended to permanently displace victims.[74]

---

67 *Blagojević and Jokić* Trial Judgement, ¶¶ 616-17.

68 *Id.* ¶¶ 650-54, 646; *Krstić* Trial Judgement, ¶ 513; *Prosecutor v. Karadžić and Mladić*, Case Nos. IT-95-5-R61 & IT-95-18-R61, Review of the Indictments Pursuant to Rule 61 of the Rules of Procedure and Evidence, 11 July 1996, ¶ 93.

69 *Blagojević and Jokić* Trial Judgement, ¶ 618.

70 *Prosecutor v. Popović et al.*, Case No. IT-05-88-T, Trial Judgement, 10 June 2010, ¶ 891 (*Popović et al.* Trial Judgement).

71 *Id.* ¶ 892.

72 *Id.* ¶ 896.

73 *Id.* ¶ 904.

74 *Id.* ¶ 905.

In addition to these pronouncements of the law, which were consistent with previous jurisprudence, the Trial Chamber had occasion to develop the element of "lawful presence", which Chambers hitherto had not discussed. One of the defendants claimed that, in order to be lawfully *present* in an area, victims had to meet legal requirements for *residency* in the area whence they were displaced.[75] The Trial Chamber roundly rejected this argument, finding that the requirement of lawful presence is intended to protect "those who have, for whatever reason, come to 'live' in the community—whether long term or temporarily" and that "the requirement for lawful presence is intended to exclude only those situations where the individuals are occupying houses or premises unlawfully or illegally and not to impose a requirement for 'residency' to be demonstrated as a legal standard."[76]

Applying each of these elements to the evidence adduced at trial, the Trial Chamber held that forcible transfer occurred when Bosnian Muslim women, children, and elderly persons were forcibly bused from their temporary safety in the enclave at Potočari to territory controlled by the Army of Bosnia and Herzegovina.[77] The Trial Chamber found that the requisite intent to displace the individuals in question was present, because the busing formed part of a greater scheme of the Bosnian Serb Forces to remove all Bosnian Muslims from Srebrenica and the surrounding areas.[78] The Trial Chamber also found that the women, children, and elderly persons were made to leave under coercive circumstances. In determining the coercive nature of the departure of these individuals, the Trial Chamber considered both the force and intimidation used to load the victims onto the buses at Potočari.[79] The Trial Chamber also took into account the circumstances leading up to the presence of the individuals at Potočari and found that the individuals in question had fled Srebrenica to seek shelter in Potočari due to fear of the ongoing violence in Srebrenica and the violence and threat of violence directed specifically at the civilian population.[80] The Trial Chamber concluded that the violence that caused the departure of the population of Srebrenica to Potocari and the fear-inducing atmosphere at Potočari both demonstrated the involuntary nature of the departure from Potočari.[81] The Trial Chamber therefore was satisfied that the departure of the Bosnian Muslim women, children, and elderly persons from Srebrenica to Potočari was involuntary and that their removal constituted forcible transfer as part of the greater plan of the Bosnian Serb Forces to remove Bosnian Muslims from the region.[82]

75 *Id.* ¶ 899.

76 *Id.* ¶ 900.

77 *Id.* ¶ 925.

78 *Id.* ¶¶ 915-17.

79 *Id.* ¶ 917.

80 *Id.*

81 *Id.* ¶¶ 917-18.

82 *Id.* ¶ 917.

c. *The* Stakić *Appeal Judgement and the Categorisation of Deportation and Forcible Transfer*

During the appeal of *Prosecutor v. Milomir Stakić*, the Appeals Chamber squarely confronted two issues that had been dealt with in the Trial Chambers, namely the cross-border transfer requirement and the requisite *mens rea* in relation to the permanency of the transfer. The Appeals Chamber first defined the *actus reus* of deportation as "the forced displacement of persons by expulsion or other forms of coercion from the area in which they are lawfully present, across a *de jure* state border or, in certain circumstances, a *de facto* border, without grounds permitted under international law".[83] One would have expected the Appeals Chamber to then set out the *mens rea* of deportation, but instead it stated this element in the negative: "the *mens rea* of the offence does not require that the perpetrator intend to displace the individual across the border on a permanent basis".[84] Similarly, the Appeals Chamber held that the *mens rea* for forcible transfer does not require the intent to transfer permanently.[85]

The Appeals Chamber then went on to discuss three issues: the forced character of the displacement, cross-border transfer, and the intended permanency of the displacement.

i. Forced Character of the Displacement

Stakić argued on appeal that the Trial Chamber erred when it found that departures organised by international humanitarian organisations were not permitted under international law and that he was criminally responsible for participating in such activities. According to Stakić, displacement, even if involuntary, did not constitute the crime of deportation when it was conducted as part of humanitarian efforts to evacuate civilians from a conflict zone.[86] The Appeals Chamber rejected this contention and held that "the participation of an NGO in facilitating displacements does not in and of itself render an otherwise unlawful transfer lawful."[87] The Appeals Chamber did not categorically preclude the possibility that displacement for humanitarian reasons may be justifiable in certain situations, but stated that this could not be the case "where the humanitarian crisis that caused the displacement is itself the result of the accused's own unlawful activity."[88] This ground of appeal by Stakić was therefore not successful because

83 *Stakić* Appeal Judgement, ¶¶ 278, 308.
84 *Id.* ¶ 278 (emphasis added).
85 *Id.* ¶ 317.
86 *Id.* ¶ 267.
87 *Id.* ¶ 286.
88 *Id.* ¶ 287.

the displacement of the Bosnian Muslims from Prijedor was caused by Stakić and his co-perpetrators.[89]

ii. Cross-Border Transfer

The Appeals Chamber then turned to the issue of cross-border transfer, noting that the Trial Chamber had held as follows:

> Article 5(d) of the Statute must be read to encompass forced population displacements both across internationally recognised borders and *de facto* boundaries, such as constantly changing frontlines, which are not internationally recognised. The crime of deportation in this context is therefore to be defined as the forced displacement of persons by expulsion or other coercive acts for reasons not permitted under international law from an area in which they are lawfully present to an area under the control of another party.[90]

The Appeals Chamber observed that the Trial Chamber therefore had endorsed the view that the value of a cross-border requirement for the crime of deportation was negligible because "what has in the jurisprudence been considered two separate crimes deportation and forcible transfer is in reality one and the same crime."[91]

After surveying various international law sources, the Appeals Chamber pronounced its opinion on this issue:

> The default principle under customary international law with respect to the nature of the border is that there must be expulsion across a *de jure* border to another country, as illustrated in Article 49 of Geneva Convention IV and the other references set out above.... In general, the question whether a particular *de facto* border is sufficient for the purposes of the crime of deportation should be examined on a case by case basis in light of customary international law.[92]

As a result, the Appeals Chamber held that the Trial Chamber, by convicting Stakić of the crime of deportation for displacements across constantly changing front lines, had expanded criminal responsibility by giving greater scope to the crime of deportation than existed under customary international law and thus violated the principle of *nullum crimen sine lege*.[93]

Judge Shahabuddeen lodged a *Blitzkrieg* dissenting opinion.

---

89 *Id.*

90 *Stakić* Trial Judgement, ¶ 679.

91 *Stakić* Appeal Judgement, ¶ 288 (citing *Stakić* Trial Judgement, ¶ 680).

92 *Id.* ¶ 300.

93 *Id.* ¶¶ 302-03.

First, Judge Shahabuddeen argued that customary international law did not confine "deportation" to the crossing of a border; rather, the crossing of a front line was enough, whether or not it was a border. He first pointed out that the European Commission on Human Rights had used the term "deportation" in the context the forcible displacement of Greek Cypriots from the territory controlled by Turkish Cypriots across the demarcation line separating Cyprus.[94] He then examined the sources of law surveyed by the majority, *e.g.*, Article 49 of Geneva Convention IV and Article 17 of Additional Protocol II, and showed that they do not speak to the issue at hand: "to say that 'deportation' has been used in several cases in relation to the crossing of a border is not the same as saying that it can *only* be so used."[95] Judge Shahabuddeen also warned that, when attempting to ascertain the state of customary law, "[h]ints and allusions must be separated from categorical proposition".[96]

Second, Judge Shahabuddeen argued that, even if customary international law always used the term "deportation" in relation to the crossing of a border, the term was reasonably capable of applying to a front line. In discussing the Tribunal's power to ascertain the state of customary international law, he made the following insight: "[i]n appreciating the 'essence' of a clarification, the question to be attended to is not whether a particular set of circumstances was ever concretely recognized by the existing law, but whether those circumstances reasonably fall within the scope of the existing law."[97] He then went on to critique the majority for reversing the Trial Chamber's application of the crime of deportation to the crossing of a front line. Judge Shahabuddeen reasoned that the term "deportation" should be used to refer to the crossing of "a coercive demarcation line represented by the border" because "[a] front line also represents a coercive demarcation line".[98] In his view, this was the case because "the law applicable to deportation across a border was always reasonably capable of applying to such displacement".[99]

Third, Judge Shahabuddeen looked to the plain language of Article 5 of the Statute. He observed that the Security Council, in adopting the language of Article 5, placed the enumerated offence of "deportation" under the chapeau paragraph that makes a crime against humanity applicable to both international and non-international armed conflict.[100] This evinced a clear intention to criminalise "deportation" both across a national boundary and within one, as well.

Fourth, Judge Shahabuddeen argued that there could be a deportation even across a constantly changing front line. He asserted that the interpretation of

94 *Id.* Dissenting Opinion of Judge Shahabuddeen, ¶ 23.

95 *Id.* ¶¶ 22-32.

96 *Id.* ¶ 32.

97 *Id.* ¶ 39.

98 *Id.* ¶ 33.

99 *Id.*

100 *Id.* ¶¶ 48-49.

Article 5(d) as applying to both the crossing of a national border and the crossing of a front line within a national border was more consistent with the Security Council's purpose for creating the ICTY in the first place, *i.e.*, the cessation of ethnic cleansing in the former Yugoslavia, which included transfers across constantly disputed and changing borders.[101]

Fifth, in a five-part argument, Judge Shahabuddeen pointed out that the majority's interpretation of Article 5(d) and Article 5(i) created an imbalance in the statutory regime erected by the Security Council to prosecute individuals for essentially the same factual conduct. He pointed out that, by relegating intra-state transfers to "other inhumane acts" under Article 5(i)—rather than characterising them as "deportation" proper under Article 5(d)—the majority required the Prosecution to prove additional elements for intra-state transfer *that it did not need to prove* for transfers across an international boundary. This is because other inhumane acts require elements, such as the fact that the act or omission caused serious mental or physical suffering or that it constituted a serious attack on human dignity, that deportation does not.[102] In other words, the effect of the holding of the majority of the Appeals Chamber was that it was now more difficult to prove an intra-state transfer than it was to prove a transfer across an international boundary. In the words of Judge Shahabuddeen,

> [t]here being an observable disequilibrium in available remedies for what in substance is the same thing, namely, forcible displacement of civilians in pursuit of ethnic cleansing, the consequence [of the majority's holding] is a partial nullification of the presumed intention of the Security Council to provide an equal remedial regime for an act which was of obvious concern to the Council in whichever way it was done.[103]

---

101 *Id.* ¶¶ 50-53.

102 *Id.* ¶¶ 54-62. For a person's act or omission to constitute an inhumane act as a crime against humanity under Article 5(i), the Prosecution must prove the following: the conduct must cause serious mental or physical suffering to the victim or constitute a serious attack upon human dignity; the conduct must be of equal gravity to the conduct enumerated in Article 5; and the physical perpetrator must have performed the act or omission deliberately and with the intent to inflict serious physical or mental harm upon the victim or commit a serious attack upon human dignity or with the knowledge that his act or omission would probably cause serious physical or mental harm to the victim or constitute a serious attack upon human dignity. *Prosecutor v. Kordić and Čerkez*, Case No. IT-95-14/2-A, Judgement, 17 December 2004, ¶ 117; *Prosecutor v. Milutinović et al.*, Case No. IT-05-87-T, Judgement, 26 February 2009, vol. 1, ¶ 170; *Prosecutor v. Tadić*, Case No. IT-94-1-T, Opinion and Judgement, 7 May 1997, ¶ 729.

103 *Stakić* Appeal Judgement, Dissenting Opinion of Judge Shahabuddeen, ¶ 60. Judge Shahabuddeen also remarks upon the fact that displacement across "constantly changing front lines" was a justifiable term for the Trial Chamber to use in reference to displacement across a "*de facto* border" because of the obvious criminality under

In short, there is no reason why the Security Council would make it more difficult to prosecute intra-state transfers than extra-state ones.

Sixth, Judge Shahabuddeen took issue with the majority's view that the Trial Chamber expanded Stakić's criminal responsibility by giving greater scope to the crime of deportation than existed under customary international law at the time of the crimes and thus violated the principle of *nullum crimen sine lege*. In Judge Shahabuddeen's view, "the crime always existed", and "all that the Security Council was doing in the Statute was to vest the Tribunal with jurisdiction over the crime." Whether the Security Council decided to prosecute the crime under a particular name or another therefore made no difference, and it was nothing more than a matter of nomenclature.[104]

Seventh, Judge Shahabuddeen, in his final point, emphasised that international law was concerned with substance, not labels.[105] Along these lines, he sought to draw attention back to the heart of the matter, and his eloquent reasoning warrants quotation in full:

> When one speaks of deportation across a border, what is involved is a "forced displacement" of civilians; but that also happens in the case of a "forced displacement" of civilians across a front line separating an area of a state under the control of one party from an area of the same state under the control of an opposing party. To the victim, the consequences of either act are not distinguishable. To him, the legally recognized lines on a map mean no more than a front line enforced at the point of a gun. This corresponds also to the attitude of the perpetrators; these, when they expel civilians across a front line, mean to jettison those civilians, to end the exercise by them of rights of citizenship in the territory from which they come, and in general to terminate public responsibility for them in that territory. Such a forcible displacement cannot reasonably be described as a "transfer". A power that expels civilians across a front line into an area controlled by another power is not just transferring the victims from one place to another: it is getting rid of them. The distinction strongly suggests that forcible displacement across a front line falls into the category of "deportation" rather than "transfer".
>
> It bears noting that the mission of the Tribunal is different from that of an international civil judicial body. The Trial Chamber was not called upon to determine what in law was the boundary between states for the purpose of settling a dispute between those states as to the course of the boundary; it was concerned with ascertaining facts on the ground at a particular point of time and with giving effect to them for the purpose of determining the criminal responsibility of an individual. This purpose is essential to the role of a criminal tribunal, which is better equipped to determine whether a given act on a given

customary international law of the forcible displacement of the civilian population across any boundary as it exists at the time of the displacement. *Id.* ¶¶ 63-65.

104 *Id.* ¶¶ 66-68.

105 *Id.* ¶ 69.

> day had the effect of moving people across front lines that existed on that day rather than to determine whether the crossing related to any boundary which existed over time. The legal implications of the latter exercise are not involved in the former.[106]

iii. Intended Permanency of the Displacement

Yet another issue of contention between the judges of the ICTY Appeals Chamber related to the *mens rea* of the perpetrator of forcible displacement. In the *Stakić* Appeal Judgement, the Chamber noted that there was a lack of consistency in the jurisprudence of the Tribunal with respect to the *mens rea* for the offence of deportation, noting that the *Blagojević and Jokić*, *Brđanin*, *Simić et al.*, and *Naletilić and Martinović* Trial Chambers all had required the perpetrators to act with the intent to permanently remove the victims.[107] The Appeals Chamber observed that the holdings of those Trial Chambers relied upon a distinction in the ICRC commentary to Article 49 of Geneva Convention IV between a lawful evacuation and unlawful displacement, but that the text of Article 49 did not contain any suggestion that deportation required an intent that deportees should not return.[108] The Appeals Chamber stated that it "chose" to follow the text of Article 49, therefore concluding that deportation did not require an intent that deportees should not return.[109] The Appeals Chamber ultimately found, however, that the Trial Chamber's error was harmless and did not require a reversal because Stakić had intended to permanently displace the deportees.[110]

The effect of the ruling of the Appeals Chamber is that a perpetrator can intend to only remove victims on a temporary basis and still commit deportation. It is difficult to envision a factual scenario where a perpetrator would do such a thing: it would require a perpetrator actively seeking to displace a population with either the intention of then transferring them back or the knowledge that they would otherwise successfully return. Nevertheless, there is a formalistic validity in such a position, for if a person—for some reason—actively decided to displace a group of people across a border but did not intend for the displacement to be permanent, the damage done to the victims could still be significant and the perpetrator could still be prosecuted.

d. *The* Naletilić and Martinović *Appeal Judgement*

About two months after the *Stakić* Appeal Judgement was rendered, the appeal in *Naletilić and Martinović* was decided. Due to the fact that the parties in *Naletilić*

106 *Id.* ¶¶ 70-71.

107 *Stakić* Appeal Judgement, ¶ 304.

108 *Id.* ¶¶ 305-06.

109 *Id.* ¶ 307.

110 *Id.* ¶¶ 307, 319.

and Martinović had filed their appeal briefs prior to the issuance of the *Stakić* Appeal Judgement, they did not have the benefit of the Appeals Chamber's views on the relationship between deportation under Article 5(d) and forcible transfer under Article 5(i). As a result, in the *Naletilić and Martinović* appeal, the Prosecution contended that the Trial Chamber erred in law by holding that deportation required the transfer of persons across state borders in order to distinguish it from forcible transfer.

The Appeals Chamber dismissed this ground of appeal, stating that this case did not provide an occasion to define the elements of deportation as a crime against humanity under Article 5(d) of the Statute because the indictment did not include charges under that article.[111] The Appeals Chamber was also of the view that, whether deportation encompassed a border element was not relevant for the purposes of deportation under Article 5(h) because acts of forcible displacement were equally punishable as underlying acts of persecution whether or not a border had been crossed.[112] Although the Appeals Chamber found that the Trial Chamber had erred in law on this point, it left Naletilić and Martinović's convictions undisturbed because they had been found responsible for persecutions through the underlying acts of forcible transfer.[113]

Judge Schomburg, the presiding judge in the *Stakić* trial, who had since been elevated to the Appeals Chamber, dissented from the holding of the majority and took the opportunity to express his views on the issue. Judge Schomburg, recalling his dissent in the *Krnojelac* Appeal Judgement, first expressed his difference with the majority that there was no need to define deportation in the context of persecution under Artricle 5(h) of the Statute.[114] He then examined various sources of international law, such as the Judgement of the Nuremberg Tribunal, the Nuremberg successor trials, and the International Law Commission's Commentary to Article 18 of the Draft Code of Crimes Against the Peace and Security of Mankind of 1996—finding that none of them required the cross-border transfer of victims.[115] Judge Schomburg emphasised that the question of whether or to what extent deportation required transfer across a border did not affect the principle of *nullum crimen sine lege* because forced displacement constituted a crime under international law whether it occurred within or without a state or across its borders.[116]

It was not only for legal reasons but also for political and moral ones that Judge Schomburg expressed his view that a cross-border requirement should not be judicially inserted into the crime of deportation. Taking up the torch

111 *Naletilić and Martinović* Appeal Judgement, ¶¶ 148, 152, 154.

112 *Id.* ¶ 154.

113 *Id.*

114 *Naletilić and Martinović* Appeal Judgement, Separate and Partially Dissenting Opinion of Judge Schomburg, ¶¶ 3-9.

115 *Id.* ¶¶ 10-15.

116 *Id.* ¶ 17.

from Judge Shahabuddeen in his dissenting opinion in the *Stakić* appeal, Judge Schomburg articulated the reasons for his views:

> Labelling alone does not suffice to establish or prove elements of a crime. However, it is equally clear that criminal law is not an abstract figure, but a (societal) reaction to specific threats to or violations of fundamental values. Exactly for this reason, this Tribunal was established to punish the crime of "ethnic cleansing" in the context of the armed conflicts in the former Yugoslavia, *inter alia*, by way of getting rid of other ethnic groups. Sticking to a formal definition of a "cross-border" transfer requirement for deportation does not mirror the events that took place in the former Yugoslavia. Moreover, this could result in no convictions at all being made for deportation, although "ethnic cleansing" included what was commonly perceived as large-scale deportation of civilians.
>
> A definition of deportation to be employed by the Tribunal has therefore to take into account social developments in a globalized world and should not be based on a formalistic-historical understanding of jurisprudence, conventions, studies or the like, which have themselves not taken the stance that deportation requires transfer of persons across State borders to the exclusion of transfer within the territory of a State. Instead, at stake are the legal values protected by the crime of deportation: the right of every person to stay in his or her home place, to live and socialize in his or her community, and to receive protection. In modern times, such protection may be guaranteed and granted in return for duties which an individual has as being "part" not only of a "State", but also of another entity exercising authority over a certain territory.[117]

Judge Schomburg asserted that his approach was consistent with a focus on human beings and their fundamental rights, which the Tribunal had advanced from its inception, rather than an approach focused on traditional state sovereignty.[118] According to Judge Schomburg, "[t]he growing importance of human rights militates against an unjustifiably narrow interpretation of the crime of deportation in the sense of covering displacement across *de jure* borders only."[119]

It should be noted that Judge Schomburg's approach to the issue of cross-border tranfer is also consonant with Anne-Marie Slaughter's observations that traditional, Westphalian notions of states' rights have had, in our modern era, to evolve into a more integrated approach to sovereignty issues:[120] this concept has been referred to as "interdependence sovereignty".[121] Judge Schomburg's concep-

117 *Id.* ¶¶ 18-19.

118 *See Prosecutor v. Tadić*, Case No. IT-94-1-AR-72, Decision on the Defence Motion for Interlocutory Appeal on Jurisdiction, 2 October 1995, ¶ 97.

119 *Naletilić and Martinović* Appeal Judgement, Separate and Partially Dissenting Opinion of Judge Schomburg, ¶ 29.

120 *See* Anne-Marie Slaughter, *Sovereignty and Power in a Networked World Order*, STAN. J. INT'L L. 283, 283-85 (2004).

121 STEPHEN KRASNER, SOVEREIGNTY: ORGANIZED HYPOCRISY 3 (1999).

tualisation and underlying reasoning is also reminiscent of Judge Shahabuddeen's concern that the majority of the Appeals Chamber in *Stakić* was construing the issue too narrowly and not taking the realities of actual transfers into account.

In respect of the *actus reus* element of forcible displacement, Judge Schomburg observed that the Security Council had included deportation in the list of crimes against humanity in Article 5 of the Statute of the Tribunal, but decided not to include forcible transfer. As a result, Judge Schomburg reasoned that "[i]t is hard to imagine that Article 5(d) of the Statute was originally intended to cover forced displacement of civilians only if it occurred via internationally recognized borders while any other conduct was to fall under the residual clauses of Article 5(h) and/or (i) of the Statute." Such a formalistic interpretation would be seriously out of step with the reality on the ground during the armed conflicts of the former Yugoslavia and would, in the words of Judge Schomburg, "miss the point."[122]

e. The Milošević Generals Trial

The case of *Prosecutor v. Milutinović et al.*, otherwise known as the "Milošević Generals Trial," was the original Kosovo case against Slobodan Milošević and his co-defendants Milan Milutinović, Nikola Šainović, and Dragoljub Ojdanić, who were all indicted together for crimes committed in Kosovo during the NATO bombing campaign during the summer of 1999, the first armed conflict in which NATO had ever been engaged. After Milošević's case was severed from the multi-accused trial so that he could be tried alone,[123] Milošević's co-defendants were tried later, from 2006 to 2009, in their own trial, along with three other defendants who were joined to the case: Nebojša Pavković, Vladimir Lazarević, and Sreten Lukić.[124] As a result, the *Milutinović et al.* case was essentially the Kosovo case without Milošević and was about the forcible displacement

122 *Naletilić and Martinović* Appeal Judgement, Separate and Partially Dissenting Opinion of Judge Schomburg, ¶¶ 22–25. Judge Schomburg concluded by expressing his view that the *mens rea* for deportation required that the perpetrator intends to *permanently* displace an individual. In order to support this view, he looked to, *inter alia*, the ICRC Commentary to the Geneva Convention IV and the *Krnojelac* Appeal Judgement. *Naletilić and Martinović* Appeal Judgement, Separate and Partially Dissenting Opinion of Judge Schomburg, ¶ 33.

123 *Prosecutor v. Milošević, Milutinović, Ojdanić, Šainović, and Stojilković*, Case No. IT-99-37-PT, Substituted Decision on Motion to Amend Indictment, 5 September 2002.

124 Vlajko Stojiljković took his own life on 13 April 2002, and Vlastimir Đorđević was severed from the trial proceedings because he was still at-large at the commencement of the trial. *See Prosecutor v. Milutinović et al.*, Case No. IT-05-87-PT, Order Replacing Third Amended Joinder Indictment and Severing Vlastimir Đorđević, 26 June 2006.

of almost the entire Kosovo Albanian population from the province of Kosovo by the army of the Federal Republic of Yugoslavia and police forces of Serbia.[125]

In articulating the elements of the crime of forcible displacement, the Trial Chamber followed the pronouncements of the Appeals Chamber in setting forth the *actus reus* of "forcible displacement" as (1) the displacement of persons by expulsion or other coercive acts, (2) from an area in which they are lawfully present, (3) without grounds permitted under international law. The *mens rea* for the offence was said to be the intent to displace, permanently or otherwise, the victims within the relevant national border (as in forcible transfer) or across the relevant national border (as in deportation).[126]

Having evaluated the evidence, the Trial Chamber found that the manner in which the Yugoslav Army and the Serbian Ministry of the Interior dealt with the Kosovo Liberation Army

> was often heavy-handed and involved indiscriminate violence and damage to civilian persons and property, further exacerbating rather than ameliorating the situation in Kosovo. The consistent eye-witness accounts of the systematic terrorisation of Kosovo Albanian civilians by the forces of the FRY and Serbia, their removal from their homes, and the looting and deliberate destruction of their property, satisfies the Chamber that there was a campaign of violence directed against the Kosovo Albanian civilian population, during which there were incidents of killing, sexual assault, and the intentional destruction of mosques. It was the deliberate actions of these forces during this campaign that caused the departure of at least 700,000 Kosovo Albanians from Kosovo in the short period of time between the end of March and beginning of June 1999.[127]

The Trial Chamber ultimately convicted five of the six accused for these crimes, either through their commission of them through participation in a joint criminal enterprise or by aiding and abetting the crimes.[128] In this case, where the massive displacement of almost the entire population of a province was at issue, there was evidence of both transfers across the national borders with neighbouring states and transfers within Kosovo itself. The Trial Chamber took the approach of exhaustively analysing the transfers on a crime site by crime site basis, after which it concluded that both crimes—deportation and forcible transfer—had been committed throughout the province of Kosovo.

The Trial Chamber made this finding despite the fact that one of the main thrusts of the defence's case was that it was not the forces of the FRY and Serbia

125 *See generally* TIM JUDAH, KOSOVO, WAR AND REVENGE (2002) (providing a good review of the conflict in Kosovo).

126 *Prosecutor v. Milutinović et al.*, Case No. IT-05-87-T, Judgement, 26 February 2009, vol. 1, ¶ 164.

127 *Id.* vol. 2, ¶ 1178.

128 *Id.* vol. 3, ¶¶ 1208-12.

that displaced the Kosovo Albanian population, but rather that the Kosovo Albanians had fled Kosovo out of fear of the NATO bombing. This was thus an important issue for the Chamber to confront: was the NATO bombing of the FRY and Serbian forces, which was intended to stop the displacement, in fact the cause of the Kosovo Albanians' flight? After all, the massive displacements temporally coincided with the bombing campaign: in the first week of the NATO bombing, over 300,000 Kosovo Albanians had crossed into Albania or Macedonia; by 6 April, that number doubled; and by 1 May, it reached 715,158.[129] The Trial Chamber, however, looked to the evidence of the many witnesses who appeared before it to give eye-witness accounts of the displacements and concluded that they had given a consistent account that, in the few weeks between 24 March and the beginning of June 1999, fear reigned in towns and villages across Kosovo, not because of the NATO bombing, but rather because forces of the FRY and Serbia deliberately expelled Kosovo Albanians from their homes in all 13 municipalities included in the indictment, either by ordering them to leave, or by creating an atmosphere of terror in order to effect their departure. Moreover, as they fled their homes, they were robbed, mistreated, and otherwise abused by the forces of the FRY and Serbia. The men were separated from women and children and then sometimes killed, vehicles of Kosovo Albanians were stolen or destroyed, their houses were deliberately set on fire, money was extorted from them, and they were forced to relinquish their personal identity documents.[130] In the words of one of the perpetrators who gave evidence for the Prosecution:

> all of us who took part in that operation, found it, if I can say, unpleasant to expel women, children, elderly persons and invalids. I know the KLA pretty well and I've not seen a single woman of 70 years old or a child or anybody in the KLA, people like that cannot be fighters and terrorists. Or people in wheelchairs. But we expelled them all from the baby in the cradle to the elderly people in wheelchairs and that's the problem that I have today.[131]

The Trial Chamber was indeed mindful of the fact that, in parts of Kosovo, some Kosovo Albanians may have left their homes because NATO was bombing targets close by.[132] However, this did not prevent the Chamber from finding that the NATO bombing was not the primary reason for the huge exodus from the province;[133] rather, it was the campaign of violence visited upon the Kosovo Albanian civilian population by the forces of the FRY and Serbia that caused the

---

129 *Id.* vol. 2, ¶ 1150.

130 *Id.* vol. 2, ¶ 1156.

131 *Id.* ¶ 1172.

132 *Id.* ¶ 1175.

133 *Id.* ¶ 1176.

departure of at least 700,000 Kosovo Albanians from Kosovo in the short period of time between the end of March and the beginning of June 1999.[134]

The armed conflict in Kosovo in the summer of 1999 is an example of the blurred lines of modern day warfare. It began with an insurgency, burgeoned into an internal armed conflict, and then exploded into an international war. Faced with such a complicated set of facts, and also with the responsibility of making its findings beyond a reasonable doubt, it is notable that the Trial Chamber decided that the evidence demonstrated a clear pattern of forcible displacement, rather than metaphorically throwing up its hands and concluding that there were too many co-factors in respect of the displacement to draw any reliable conclusions. The *Milutinović et al.* Trial Judgement is therefore an example for other courts, both international and domestic, that are trying to steer their way through the fog of complex, modern warfare in order to assess whether an accused is individually and criminally responsible for the forcible displacement of people in a time of war.

f. General Principles Emerging from the ICTY's Adjudication of Forcible Displacement

The foregoing examination of the ICTY's case law in respect of forcible displacement shows how the Tribunal's understanding of the crime of forcible displacement has developed over the past ten years. Through the adjudication of actual cases with complex sets of fact patterns, the Tribunal has added to the body of law that can be drawn upon for the creation of a uniform and truly international understanding of the definition of the crime of forcible displacement. Although the ICTY has not answered all of the questions in this area of the law and there is still much uncertainty even within the institution as to the contours of the crimes, the following conclusions may be gleaned from the ICTY experiment:

Genuine choice. In respect of deportation as a crime against humanity, the forcible displacement of persons must be by expulsion or other coercive acts from an area in which they are lawfully present. In other words, the displacement must be involuntary.[135] It is the absence of genuine choice that renders the displacement unlawful.[136] Where the circumstances of the displacement make purported consent of no value, genuine choice cannot be inferred from the fact that consent was expressed; henceforth, an apparent consent induced by force or threat of force cannot be held to be genuine consent.[137] The Chambers of ICTY have inferred

134 *Id.* ¶ 1178.

135 *Brđanin* Trial Judgement, ¶ 543; *Simić et al.* Trial Judgement, ¶ 125.

136 *Krnojelac* Appeal Judgement, ¶ 229; *Blagojević and Jokić* Trial Judgement, ¶ 596; *Brđanin* Trial Judgement, note 3, ¶ 543.

137 *Krnojelac* Appeal Judgement, note 2, ¶ 229. The *Krnojelac* Appeals Chamber held that "the prohibition against forcible population displacements therefore aims at safeguarding the right and aspiration of individuals to live in their communities and

a lack of genuine choice from threatening and intimidating acts intended to deprive persons of the ability to exercise their free will, such as the shelling of civilian objects, the burning of civilian property, and the commission of—or the threat to commit—other crimes "calculated to terrify the population and make them flee the area with no hope of return".[138] Genuine choice may be vitiated by the "threat of force or coercion, such as that caused by fear of violence, duress, detention, psychological oppression or abuse of power … or by taking advantage of a coercive environment."[139] The vulnerability of the victims can also be a factor in determining whether their displacement was unlawful.[140]

Lawful presence. The element involving whether the victims are lawfully present in the place whence they are displaced has only been dealt with significantly in one ICTY case. The Trial Chamber in *Popović et al.* held that lawful presence does not equate to lawful residence. It may be that the ICTY will further develop this element of the *actus reus* in subsequent cases if the issue arises. Due to the limited life span of the ICTY, it is possible, if not likely, that further elaboration on the element of lawful presence will be left to other international courts to examine, such as the ICC.

Displacement not permitted under international law. In respect of the requirement that the displacement not be permitted under international law, it is important to acknowledge that a civilian population can be evacuated for its security or for imperative military reasons.[141] A lawful displacement can often be discerned from an unlawful one by determining whether "persons thus evacuated [are] transferred back to their homes as soon as the hostilities in the area in question have ceased."[142] In this way, the unlawful use of an evacuation as a pretext to forcibly dislocate a population and seize control over a territory can be detected.[143] For example, in the *Krstić* case, the Chamber held that the grounds upon

homes without outside interference." *Krnojelac* Appeal Judgement, ¶ 218; *Milošević* Rule 98 *bis* Decision, ¶ 69; *Simić et al.* Trial Judgement, ¶ 125; *Brđanin* Trial Judgement, ¶ 596; *Krnojelac* Appeal Judgement, ¶ 229 (holding that "even in cases where those displaced may have wished—and in fact may have even requested—to be removed, this does not necessarily mean that they had or exercised a genuine choice").

138 *Krnojelac* Appeal Judgement, ¶ 126; *see Milutinović et al.* Trial Judgement, vol. 2, ¶ 1178.

139 *Simić et al.* Trial Judgement, ¶ 125.

140 *Blagojević and Jokić* Trial Judgement, ¶ 596.

141 *See Blagojević and Jokić* Trial Judgement, note 3, ¶ 597; *Brđanin* Trial Judgement, ¶¶ 556-600; Commentary to Additional Protocol II to the Geneva Conventions of 1949, at 1473.

142 *Brđanin* Trial Judgement, ¶ 556.

143 *Blagojević and Jokić* Trial Judgement, note 3, ¶ 597. *See* Commentary to Additional Protocol II to the Geneva Conventions of 1949, at 1473.

which people were evacuated from their homes in Srebrenica were not permitted under international law because the people were not returned to their homes when combat activities in the area in question had stopped.[144] As stated by the Chamber, "[t]he evacuation was itself the goal and neither the protection of the civilians nor imperative military necessity justified the action."[145] The *Naletilić & Martinović* Trial Chamber considered that the torching of houses after their owners had been forcibly displaced was evidence that the transfer in question was not a lawful evacuation.[146]

In the context of grave breaches of the Geneva Conventions, which are criminalised under Article 2 of the ICTY Statute, the Trial Chamber in *Naletilić & Martinović* noted that Geneva Convention IV does not prohibit evacuations and transfers motivated by the security of the population or imperative military reasons; however, evacuations are only provisional measures and cannot be effected through coercion.[147] Also in the context of Article 2 of the ICTY Statute, the *Naletilić and Martinović* Chamber looked to the Commentary to Geneva Convention IV for the proposition that an unlawful deportation or transfer could be either from occupied territory or within occupied territory, provided that the victims were in the hands of the occupying power.[148]

Permanency of removal. In respect of whether the displacement is effected with the intent that the removal of the persons be permanent, the Chambers of the ICTY have taken differing views. In the case law predating the *Stakić* appeal, Chambers found that displacement required an element of permanency in relation to the intention of the perpetrator,[149] be it deportation or forcible transfer.[150] For example, in relation to whether the displacement was intended to be permanent, the *Brđanin* Trial Chamber considered the fact that people's homes, businesses, and religious buildings were destroyed and the fact that people's property had been confiscated or relinquished without compensation.[151] If a perpetrator does not take steps to facilitate the return of displaced persons removed via lawful evacuations, this can go to show an intent to permanently displace those

144 *Krstić* Trial Judgement, ¶ 525.

145 *Id.* ¶ 526.

146 *Naletilić and Martinović* Trial Judgement, ¶ 526; *Simić et al.* Trial Judgement, ¶ 127; *Naletilić and Martinović* Trial Judgement, ¶ 523.

147 *Naletilić and Martinović* Trial Judgement, ¶¶ 518-19, note 1357; *see* Article 49 of Geneva Convention IV; Commentary to Geneva Convention IV, at 280.

148 *Naletilić and Martinović* Trial Judgement, ¶¶ 219, 221, 521, note 6; *see* Commentary to Geneva Convention IV, at 60.

149 *Brđanin* Trial Judgement, ¶ 545; *Simić et al.* Trial Judgement, ¶ 134; *Stakić* Trial Judgement, ¶ 687; *Naletilić and Martinović* Trial Judgement, ¶ 520.

150 *See Naletilić and Martinović* Trial Judgement, ¶ 520; *Simić et al.* Trial Judgement, ¶¶ 132-34; *Brđanin* Trial Judgement, ¶ 545.

151 *Brđanin* Trial Judgement, ¶ 555.

persons.[152] Moreover, the voluntary return of displaced persons does not necessarily mean that the perpetrator did not intend to displace them permanently.[153]

However, these holdings of the Trial Chambers have effectively been overruled by the Appeals Chamber in its judgement in the *Stakić* appeal wherein it was held that a perpetrator can be convicted for the crime of forcible displacement where he only intended the displacement of persons to be temporary.[154] The significance of this reversal is of limited significance, however, due to the fact that real-world examples of forcible displacement rarely involve the intent to remove persons from an area, only to then move them back into that same area.

Cross-border requirement. In respect of the requirement that the displacement be across a national border, the general trend of the jurisprudence of the Tribunal has been that displacement across a national boundary constitutes deportation and displacement within a national boundary constitutes forcible transfer.[155] It has also been held that people can be deported across *de facto* boundaries. However, although a majority of the Appeals Chamber has held that what constitutes a *de facto* border can only be determined on a case by case basis, this majority has also held that a constantly changing front line cannot constitute a *de facto* border. In doing so, the Appeals Chamber has restricted the crime of deportation and relegated intra-state transfers to a residual crime against humanity known as "other inhuman acts", and this has had the effect of adding elements to the crime of "forcible transfer" that are not needed to be proved for deportation. The ultimate premise upon which the distinction created by the Appeals Chamber on this issue rests is that the destination is determinative of the crime, rather than the fact that the victims have been removed from their homes. Judges Shahabuddeen and Schomburg, in their *tour de force* dissenting opinions in *Stakić* and *Naletilić & Martinović*, respectively, have demonstrated why there are sound reasons against adopting such an approach. It also may be that the historical reality of humanity's record of forcible displacement of people during both peace and wartime lends support to the view that the crime of forcible displacement should be defined not by the destination whither people are displaced, but rather by the fact that people are uprooted from their homes.

Nevertheless, the relegation of intra-state displacements to "other inhumane acts" under Article 5(i) of the ICTY Statute, rather than characterising them as "deportations" under Article 5(d), has become entrenched jurisprudence at the ICTY. The Appeals Chamber in the *Krajišnik* case, faced with an alleged

---

152 *Blagojević and Jokić* Trial Judgement, ¶ 601.

153 *Id.* ¶ 601; *Naletilić and Martinović* Appeal Judgement, Separate and Partially Dissenting Opinion of Judge Schomburg, ¶ 33.

154 *Stakić* Appeal Judgement, ¶¶ 304-19.

155 *See, e.g., Milošević* Rule 98 *bis* Decision, ¶ 79; *Prosecutor v. Krnojelac*, Case No. IT-97-25-T, Judgement, 15 March 2002, ¶ 474; *Krnojelac* Appeal Judgement, ¶ 129; *Simić et al.* Trial Judgement, ¶ 129; *Brđanin* Trial Judgement, ¶ 540; *Blagojević and Jokić* Trial Judgement, ¶ 595; *Krstić* Trial Judgement, ¶ 531; *Krstić* Appeal Judgement, ¶ 521.

error regarding the threshold of seriousness required for forcible transfer as other inhumane acts, reiterated that acts of forcible transfer *may be* sufficiently serious as to amount to other inhumane acts, citing its prior holding in the *Stakić* Appeal Judgement.[156] The logical inference from this statement is that there could be a displacement within a state's border that is not serious enough to rise to the level of a crime against humanity. A Trial Chamber is therefore required to examine if the specific instances of forcible transfer in the case before it were sufficiently serious to amount to "other inhumane acts", an examination which is apparently not required if it is dealing with a cross-border transfer. Because the Trial Chamber in *Krajišnik* made no such finding, the Appeals Chamber found that it had erred, but then went on to hold that the error did not invalidate the Trial Judgement because the gravity requirement was satisfied in the present case because "the acts of forcible transfer were of similar seriousness to the instances of deportation, as they involved a forced departure from the residence and the community, without guarantees concerning the possibility to return in the future, with the victims of such forced transfers invariably suffering serious mental harm".[157]

Therefore, the fears of Judges Shahabuddeen and Schomburg have already begun to manifest themselves. Relegating intra-state transfer to the residual crime against humanity of "other inhumane acts" is based upon the premise that the seriousness of cross-border transfer is inherent (and therefore does not have to be independently proved), but that intra-state transfer is not so inherently serious (and therefore has to be proved). But such a doctrinal structure is a-historical in that international borders are relatively recent geopolitical constructs: we have seen from the historical examples in chapter two that, prior to the Westphalian epoch, whether a transfer was across an international boundary or not was of little significance, especially to those who were being displaced. Moreover, whether a transfer is charged as a deportation under Article 5(d) of the ICTY Statute or as "other inhumane acts" under Article 5(i), in both cases the crime is committed in the context of a widespread or systematic attack upon a civilian population because they are both crimes against humanity. The question thus arises of how an intra-state transfer committed in the context of a widespread or systematic attack upon a civilian population *cannot* be considered inherently serious. It should also be acknowledged that an intra-state transfer can be *more* serious than an extra-state transfer and *vice versa*, depending upon the facts of the case, because the seriousness of the transfer does not turn upon whether the victims are forced across an international boundary. Such a legally formalistic approach could even lead to unwarranted acquittals in instances where the "seriousness" of a transfer is indeed high but not necessarily the same as the other crimes enumerated in Article 5. This is especially the case when one considers that—as held in the *Stakić* Trial Judgement and later confirmed in the *Krajišnik* Appeal Judgement—there is no legal requirement in respect of the crime of deportation

156 *Prosecutor v. Krajišnik*, Case No. IT-00-39-A, Judgement, 17 March 2009 (*Krajišnik* Appeal Judgement), ¶ 330 (citing *Stakić* Appeal Judgement, ¶ 317).

157 *Id.* ¶ 331.

"that a minimum number of individuals must have been forcibly transferred for the perpetrator to incur criminal responsibility" because this would be "tantamount to negating the protective effect of the prohibition against deportation."[158]

A further difficulty is that the distinction created between inter-state and intra-state transfers may not be applicable to displacements under Article 2 of the ICTY Statute, which criminalises grave breaches of the Geneva Conventions of 1949. Article 2(g) prohibits "unlawful deportation or transfer … of a civilian" during an international armed conflict. Article 49 of Geneva Convention IV provides that "[i]ndividual or mass forcible transfers, as well as deportations of protected persons from occupied territory to the territory of the Occupying Power or to that of any other country, occupied or not, are prohibited, regardless of their motive." Therefore, an unlawful deportation or transfer under Article 2(g) must be within an occupied territory or from an occupied territory, as was stated in the *Naletilić & Martinović* Trial Judgement.[159] It can be seen that transfers within and without occupied territory are treated the same by Geneva Convention IV and Article 2(g) of the ICTY Statute; in other words, one is not treated as more serious than the other. The treatment of deportation as inherently more serious than forcible transfer (as "other inhumane acts") in Article 5 of the Statute is therefore out of alignment with the plain text of Article 2 of the Statute, as well as Article 49 of Geneva Convention IV. Moreover, there is no apparent basis for treating a forcible transfer within an occupied territory during an international armed conflict (an Article 2 grave breach of the Geneva Conventions of 1949) as inherently more serious that a forcible transfer within a state in the context of a widespread or systematic attack upon a civilian population (an Article 5 crime against humanity).

As a final matter, it may be that the distinction in refugee law between a "refugee" and an "internally displaced person" has subtlety affected the ICTY's analysis of the crime of forcible displacement and the creation of the inter-state and intra-state dichotomy. Refugee law has traditionally distinguished between a person who has been forced from his or her country of nationality and a person who has been forced from his or her home within the borders of the state of nationality; and, the reason for this distinction is grounded in the fact that refugee law is concerned with the rights of persons after a displacement has already occurred and the fact that the nationality of the person in question and the state where that person finds him- or herself is relevant to those rights. States have the right to regulate their borders, as a basic function of their sovereignty. Such an entrenched and formulaic division could, mistakenly, be analogised to events not only after a displacement, but also before or during one. However, when it comes

158 *Stakić* Trial Judgement, ¶ 685; *Krajišnik* Appeal Judgement, ¶ 309. The *Krajišnik* Appeals Chamber even went so far as to hold—correctly—that the displacement of a limited number of victims or even a single victim could constitute a crime against humanity, provided that it was part of a widespread or systematic attack directed against a civilian population. *Krajišnik* Appeal Judgement, ¶ 309.

159 *Naletilić and Martinović* Trial Judgement, ¶ 521.

to the crime of forcible displacement, the rights of the persons concerned are not those of refugees and IDPs, who have already been displaced, but rather the rights of all persons to remain undisturbed in their homes. These rights do not turn upon the nationality or the location of the victim: they are of universal concern and applicability. The application of the refugee-IDP distinction is therefore inapposite to the crime of forcible displacement, which should not suffer a different characterisation based upon whether the displacement is accomplished inside or outside of a state's international boundaries.

* * *

Although ICTY was not—and was never intended to be—a comprehensive solution to the armed conflicts spread across the Balkans, it was, and still is, an important component in an array of post-conflict mechanisms brought to bear upon the situation. ICTY is nothing less than a bold experiment in international criminal law: at the time, no one knew what the consequences of Security Council Resolution 827 would be. The Tribunal has enabled the forcible displacements of several armed conflicts to be placed under the magnifying glass of judicial scrutiny and has advanced a "system" of international law through the development of legal standards applicable to the age-old phenomenon of forcible displacement. ICTY has provided a unique opportunity for the international community to define the elements of forcible displacement, not in an academic vacuum, but rather in relation to actual factual events. This can, however, be a double-edged sword: the development of law according to specific factual scenarios is a normal sociological process, but it can also lead to general statements of the law that do not hold true for all factual cases.

With this caveat, it seems relatively settled that, according to a majority of the ICTY Appeals Chamber, forcible displacement is the removal of persons by expulsion or other coercive acts, from an area in which they are lawfully present, without grounds permitted under international law. In the case of deportation, the removal must be across a *de jure* state border or, in certain circumstances, a *de facto* border. In the case of forcible transfer, the removal must take place within national boundaries. The perpetrator, in order to be individually criminally responsible, must intend to displace, permanently or otherwise, the victims within the relevant national border (as in forcible transfer) or across the relevant national border (as in deportation).[160] Issues relating to these general legal elements will no doubt be developed for as long as cases continue to be adjudicated in international and domestic courts, but the above seem to have captured the essential definition of what is meant by deportation and forcible transfer. Perhaps as important as defining these elements is ICTY's contribution to the rule of law and the fight against impunity through its actual assignment of criminal responsibility to those who have committed these crimes. The ICTY has also achieved progress in solidifying the legal principle underlying the prohibition of forcible

160 *Stakić* Appeal Judgement, ¶¶ 278, 317; *Milutinović et al.* Trial Judgement, vol. 1, ¶ 164.

displacement: "the right and aspiration of individuals to live in their communities and homes without outside interference."[161]

2. The Rwanda and Sierra Leone Tribunals

a. *The Special Court for Sierra Leone*

The experience of the Special Court for Sierra Leone is an interesting counterpoint to the extensive examination of the ICTY in respect of the crime of forcible displacement. In the wake of the protracted civil war that raged in Sierra Leone in the 1990s, the Special Court for Sierra Leone, a hybrid tribunal, was created jointly by the Government of Sierra Leone and the United Nations. It has jurisdiction over individuals who bear the greatest responsibility for serious violations of international humanitarian law and Sierra Leonean law that were committed on the territory of Sierra Leone since 30 November 1996.

Although Article 2(h) and (i) of the Statute of the Special Court would appear to encompass forcible transfer as persecution and other inhumane acts, respectively, none of the indictments charge forcible transfer. Consequently, there is no case-law on this crime from the Special Court, nor is there any on deportation. Perhaps a reason for this is that the conduct underlying the indictments at the Special Court has been charged as crimes other than forcible transfer. In general, the perpetrators of crimes during the armed conflict in Sierra Leone did not have the transfer of civilians as a goal in itself; rather, displacement was a "side-effect" of the abduction of civilians from their homes for other purposes, primarily diamond mining, farming, military training, forced marriages, and service as child soldiers. It would appear that the prosecutorial strategy was to charge this conduct as enslavement, other inhumane acts (forced marriage), and child recruitment rather than as forcible transfer. Similar choices of prosecutorial discretion have also been a feature of the sister-tribunal of ICTY, the International Criminal Tribunal for Rwanda, which will be examined next.

b. *The Interational Criminal Tribunal for Rwanda*

The United Nations International Criminal Tribunal for Rwanda (ICTR) was created by the United Nations Security Council the year after ICTY and in response to the mass genocide that occurred in Rwanda during the summer of 1994.[162] ICTR—considered to be the sister-tribunal of ICTY due to its legal and structural similarities—was established for the prosecution of persons responsible for genocide and other serious violations of IHL committed in the territory of Rwanda between 1 January and 31 December 1994.[163] ICTR's mandate also

161 *Krnojelac* Appeal Judgement, ¶ 218.

162 Security Council Resolution 955, S/Res/955 (8 Nov. 1994).

163 ICTR Statute, articles 1, 7; *Nahimana et al. v. Prosecutor*, Case No. ICTR-99-52-A, Judgement, 28 November 2007, ¶ 309.

permits it to deal with the prosecution of Rwandan citizens responsible for violations of IHL committed in the territory of neighbouring states during the same period (*ratione loci*).[164] Although ICTR has only a one-year temporal jurisdiction (*ratione temporis*), unlike ICTY's jurisdiction that has no formal end date, the Statute of ICTR otherwise bears a close resemblance to that of ICTY and criminalises genocide (Article 2), crimes against humanity (Article 3), and violations of article 3 common to the Geneva Conventions of 12 August 1949 for the Protection of War Victims and of Additional Protocol II thereto of 8 June 1977 (Article 4). In respect of crimes against humanity, ICTR has the power to prosecute persons responsible for deportation and inhuman acts, among other crimes, when they are committed as part of a widespread or systematic attack against any civilian population upon national, political, ethnic, racial, or religious grounds.

ICTR has not yet had the opportunity to deal with deportation as a crime against humanity in its cases. The forcible displacement of people in Rwanda, however, has been addressed, at least to some extent, as a general legal matter in respect of the *actus reus* for the crime of genocide.[165] In the case of *Prosecutor v. Akayesu*, the accused, a Rwandan citizen, was at the time of his crimes the mayor of Taba commune, Prefecture of Gitarama.[166] The Trial Chamber found that Akayesu had participated in a meeting on 18 April 1994 between members of the interim government and the *bourgmestres* in Murambi, Gitarama. It was after this meeting that Akayesu not only did not attempt to prevent the killing of Tutsis in the commune of Taba, but also participated in and even ordered killings there.[167] The Trial Chamber ultimately convicted Akayesu of multiple counts of genocide, direct and public incitement to commit genocide, and crimes against humanity in the forms of murder, extermination, rape, torture, and other inhumane acts.[168] The Trial Chamber sentenced Akayesu for each of the counts for which he was convicted, including three sentences to life in prison.[169] The Appeals Chamber dismissed Akayesu's appeal in its entirety and affirmed his sentence.[170]

In setting out the law in the Judgement, the *Akayesu* Trial Chamber briefly mentioned forcible displacement in the context of genocide. The Trial Chamber held that one of the ways of perpetrating a genocide was by deliberately inflicting on the target group conditions of life calculated to bring about its physical

---

164 ICTR Statute, articles 1, 7; *Prosecutor v. Kamuhanda*, Case No. ICTR-99-54A-T, Judgement, 22 January 2004, ¶ 4.

165 It should also be mentioned that factual scenarios involving the forcible displacement of people during the genocide in Rwanda feature in many other ICTR Judgements, but that forcible displacement has not been charged in these or other ICTR cases.

166 *Prosecutor v. Akayesu*, Case No. ICTR-96-4-T, Judgement, 2 September 1998 (*Akayesu* Trial Judgement), ¶¶ 1, 48-77.

167 *Id.* ¶¶ 183-93.

168 *Id.* section 8 (verdict).

169 *Id.* Sentencing Hearing, 2 October 1998.

170 *Prosecutor v. Akayesu*, Case No. ICTR-96-4-A, Judgement, 1 June 2001, section 5 (disposition).

destruction in whole or in part, which is specifically enumerated in the ICTR Statute.[171] The Trial Chamber then went on, however, to construe this language to mean methods of destruction by which the perpetrator does not immediately kill the members of the group, but by which, ultimately, the perpetrator seeks their physical destruction. Such methods were held to include, *inter alia*, subjecting a group of people to a subsistence diet, *systematic expulsion from homes*, and the reduction of essential medical services below minimum requirements.[172] However, due to the content of the indictment, which lacked allegations of systematic expulsion from homes, the Chamber did not have the opportunity to apply this pronouncement of the law to a concrete factual scenario.

In *Prosecutor v. Musema*, the accused was the director of the Gisovu Tea Factory in Kibuye prefecture; he was also a member of the "*conseil préfectorial*" in Byumba Préfecture and of the Technical Committee in the Butare Commune.[173] During the trial, he took the stand in his own defence and testified that, on 6 April 1994, a plane transporting Rwandan President Juvénal Habyarimana crashed upon its approach to Kigali airport in Rwanda and that it was soon thereafter that attacks and killings of civilians began throughout Rwanda. In the days following the plane crash, he witnessed massacres, the destruction of houses, and the displacement of people from Kigali. As Musema traveled between Kigali and Gitarama during the time of the massacres, he saw individuals manning roadblocks and many bodies along the roadsides. At the roadblocks, people were separated according to the ethnicity that was indicated on their identity cards.[174]

In setting forth the law, the Trial Chamber followed the same approach as *Akayesu*, holding that one of the methods of deliberately inflicting upon a group conditions of life calculated to bring about its physical destruction in whole or in part was the *systematic expulsion from homes*.[175] However, as with *Akayesu*, the *Musema* indictment did not charge the accused with forcible displacement, but rather focused upon Musema and employees of the Gisovu Tea Factory participating in massive attacks upon groups of Tutsi refugees. In the end, Musema was convicted of genocide by causing serious bodily and mental harm to members of the Tutsi ethnic group and extermination as a crime against humanity.[176]

In *Prosecutor v. Rutaganda*, the accused was the former second vice-president of the youth wing of the *Interahamwe* militia.[177] The Prosecution charged him

---

171 ICTR Statute, article 2(2)(c).

172 *Akayesu* Trial Judgement, ¶¶ 505-06.

173 *Prosecutor v. Musema*, Case No. ICTR-96-13-T, Judgement, 27 January 2000, ¶ 16.

174 *Id.* ¶¶ 359-61.

175 *Id.* ¶ 157.

176 *Id.* ¶¶ 884-968, Section 7 (verdict). Musema's conviction for rape as a crime against humanity was reversed by the Appeals Chamber, but his sentence of life imprisonment was affirmed. *See Prosecutor v. Musema*, Case No. ICTR-96-13-A, Judgement, 16 November 2001, ¶¶ 193-94.

177 *Prosecutor v. Rutaganda*, Case No. ICTR-96-3-T, Judgement, 6 December 1999 (*Rutaganda* Trial Judgement), ¶ 52.

with genocide, extermination, and murder for the killings of approximately 4,000 persons at the *École Technique Officielle* (ETO) and at a gravel pit in Nyanza.[178] In the indictment, the Prosecution alleged that the survivors of the ETO school massacre were "forcibly transferred" to the gravel pit.[179] The Prosecution, however, did not include a forcible displacement charge in the indictment.

After having assessed the evidence of the several witnesses who were called by the parties to give evidence regarding these alleged crimes, the Trial Chamber made factual findings upon "the refugee situation at the ETO, the attack by the *Interahamwe* following the departure of United Nations Assistance Mission for Rwanda (UNAMIR) troops, *the diversion of refugees heading towards Amahoro stadium to Nyanza*, and the massacre of refugees by soldiers and the *Interahamwe* which took place at Nyanza."[180] The Chamber found that several thousand people had fled their homes in order to seek refuge at the ETO from 7 to 11 April 1994 because troops of the UNAMIR were there. However, armed members of the *Interahamwe* congregated outside the ETO and surrounded it. Hutus were then separated from Tutsis. After UNAMIR troops abandoned those remaining at the ETO on 11 April, the *Interahamwe*, along with members of the Presidential Guard, began their assault upon the Tutsis taking refuge there. Using grenades, guns, machetes, and clubs, they killed a large number of Tutsis.[181] The Trial Chamber then made findings of fact that clearly constituted forcible displacement:

> Many of the refugees who escaped or survived the attack at ETO headed in groups towards the Amahoro Stadium, where they thought they would be safe as it was under [Rwandan Patriotic Front] control. These groups were stopped en route by soldiers, gathered together near the Sonatube factory and diverted, having been told that Colonel Rusatila had ordered them to Nyanza where their safety would be ensured. Some women were taken forcibly from the group and subsequently raped. Flanked on both sides by *Interahamwe*, approximately 4,000 refugees were then forcibly marched to Nyanza. Along the way, these refugees were abused, threatened and killed by soldiers and by the *Interahamwe* surrounding them, who were armed with machetes, clubs, axes, and other weapons.[182]

Thus, the survivors of the massacre at the ETO were forcibly displaced, killed, and raped. The Trial Chamber then went on to find that the refugees, when they arrived at Nyanza (still on 11 April), were corralled by the *Interahamwe* to a location at the base of a hill, at the top of which were armed soldiers. They

178 *Id.* at 8-9.

179 *Prosecutor v. Rutaganda*, Case No. ICTR-96-3-T, Indictment, ¶ 15.

180 *Rutaganda* Trial Judgement, ¶ 292 (emphasis added).

181 *Id.* ¶ 299.

182 *Id.* ¶ 301.

were therefore now surrounded by both *Interahamwe* and soldiers. Hutus were again separated from the Tutsis.[183] Then, in the late afternoon, the *Interahamwe* and soldiers began their slaughter of the refugees by lobbing grenades into their midst and by gunning them down. The attack began in the late afternoon and continued into the evening. After the grenade detonations and the shooting, the soldiers instructed the *Interahamwe* to continue killing whomever remained alive, and the *Interahamwe* did so with clubs and other weapons. Some of the girls, rather than being killed immediately, were separated from the rest, raped, and then killed. After finishing off as many of the refugees as they could manage, the *Interahamwe* departed at 11:00 p.m. and returned the next day (12 April), in order to finish off the job and collect any loot they could find. According to the findings of the Trial Chamber, approximately 200 people survived the massacre.[184]

Rutaganda took the stand in his own defence and testified that, on 11 April 1994, he witnessed "a mass exodus from the city, with many people on foot and others in vehicles." He, however, denied ever being at the ETO compound. The Trial Chamber gave no credence to his denials.[185] Based upon the evidence of eye-witnesses that Rutaganda brought *Interahamwe* reinforcements to Nyanza and directed the *Interahamwe* into position around the group of refugees directly before the attack began, the Trial Chamber found that Rutaganda "was present and participated in the forced diversion of refugees to Nyanza and that he directed and participated in the attack at Nyanza."[186] However, despite these findings, which included facts of forced displacement, the Trial Chamber only convicted Rutaganda of extermination and not deportation or transfer of the victims: the Trial Chamber would not have been permitted to convict Rutaganda of forcible displacement because, while extermination was an underlying offence charged in the indictment, forcible displacement was not.[187] He was sentenced to life in prison.[188]

The events at issue in the foregoing cases are representative of the other atrocities that were committed during the genocide in Rwanda, and the unimaginably

183 Apparently, the separation at the ETO was not entirely successful.

184 *Rutaganda* Trial Judgement, ¶ 302.

185 *Id.* ¶ 290.

186 *Id.* ¶¶ 303-04.

187 The Trial Chamber acquitted Rutaganda of murder as a crime against humanity for these events because it already had convicted him of extermination as a crime against humanity for the same events, in order to avoid cumulative convictions. *Rutaganda* Trial Judgement, ¶¶ 419-27. The Trial Chamber also acquitted Rutaganda of murder as a violation of Article III Common to the Geneva Conventions (*Rutaganda* Trial Judgement, ¶¶ 434-45, section 6, p. 163), but the Appeals Chamber reversed these acquittals and convicted him of these charges. *Prosecutor v. Rutaganda*, Case No. ICTR-96-3-A, Judgement, 26 May 2003, ¶¶ 556-85, section 14, at 168. The Appeals Chamber affirmed Rutaganda's life sentence. *Id.* ¶¶ 586-92, section 14, at 168.

188 *Rutaganda* Trial Judgement, ¶¶ 446-73, section 7, at 173.

horrific and tragic patterns of the crimes committed in Rwanda include forcible displacement. During the Rwanda genocide, there were both displacement within the national borders and displacement of people across Rwanda's national borders into neighbouring countries. The question thus arises of why there is an absence of forcible displacement convictions in ICTR cases. The proximate and legally technical cause of this phenomenon is that the ICTR Prosecutor—unlike the ICTY Prosecutor—chose not to charge the behaviour of the perpetrators as forcible displacement, more specifically as either deportation and inhuman acts as crimes against humanity, or even as a means of effectuating genocide. Rather, the indictments have focused upon murder, extermination, and rape. Even where Chambers have acknowledged that deliberately inflicting upon the target group conditions of life calculated to bring about its physical destruction in whole or in part—as the *actus reus* of genocide—can include the systematic expulsion from homes, the convictions have again been for genocide perpetrated through murder and extermination, rather than through forcible displacement. Again, this is due to the fact that a Trial Chamber can only convict an accused for a crime that was alleged in the indictment.

Delving more deeply into the substantive reasons for the procedural issues relating to charging practices of the ICTR Prosecutor, namely, the choice not to charge forcible displacement in cases where such a charge would seem to possess evidentiary support, there may be a valid reason for such a choice. It may be a matter of means versus ends. In the context of the multiple armed conflicts of the former Yugoslavia during the 1990s, the fact patterns, while certainly including mass killings, also included mass expulsions. In many situations in the former Yugoslavia, the perpetrators would have been able to kill a large number of people, but they chose instead to simply displace them in order to alter the ethnic balance of a specifically defined geographic region. In these situations, the displacement was the ultimate end to be achieved: in other words, the perpetrators' primary objective seemed to be—in the words of Judge Shahabuddeen—to simply "get rid of them"[189] and not necessarily to kill them. In Kosovo in 1999, it was even explicitly concluded that the aim of the criminal activity was to displace, rather than kill, the Kosovo Albanian population: the mass killings in many instances were but a means to instill fear and panic in the population in order to drive them out of the province.

By contrast, the criminal activity in Rwanda seems to follow the opposite pattern. The displacement of people from their homes seems to have been the means by which to more efficiently effect the killing of the Tutsis, who fled their homes in order to seek refuge in churches, for example. Or, they were displaced and herded onto hilltops. Typically, the Hutus were then separated from the Tutsis or Tutsi sympathizers, and then the killing would commence. In this sense, although the crime of forcible displacement was certainly committed as a matter of fact, such displacement reasonably can be considered to be overshadowed by the subsequent, horrific acts that followed and that resulted in

189 *Stakić* Appeal Judgement, Dissenting Opinion of Judge Shahabuddeen, ¶ 70.

the deaths of the victims. Such an interpretation of the conflict is discussed by William Schabas, who has observed that, "when the extremists responsible for the ethnic cleansing of Tutsi over several decades realized that their measures had been ineffective, and that the return of Tutsi refugees was ensured by the 1993 Arusha Accords, … their intent was transformed into one bent to destruction, not expulsion."[190] The relationship between displacement and murder is also a subject upon which Jean-Marie Henckaerts postulates as follows: "[o]n the one hand, ethnic cleansing seems to be aimed at removing people from a certain area, not really at annihilating them. On the other hand, the commission of the barbarous acts of which ethnic cleansing consists seems to indicate that the cleanser may also wish to annihilate the group".[191] Viewed in this manner, the conflict in Rwanda in the summer of 1994 can reasonably be characterised as one of genocide, rather than forcible displacement; and, the ICTR Prosecutor's choice to forego displacement charges and to instead focus upon murder, extermination, and rape—as genocide, crimes against humanity, or violations of common article 3 of the Geneva Conventions—is an understandable one: charging every single possible crime in an indictment can lead to unwieldy cases. This was the case in the *Slobodan Milošević* trial, which ended in the death of the accused before the trial could be completed, in part due to the fact that the Prosecution insisted on charging Milošević with thousands of crimes and the fact that the Appeals Chamber required that the Trial Chamber try all three indictments in a single, Sisyphean trial.[192] At some point, international tribunals need to decide which is more important: charging an accused with each and every offence that may have been committed, or actually obtaining verdicts on some, but not all, of the offences.

An "over-charged" indictment is also often evidence of a weak case and/or an inexperienced prosecutor. A Prosecutor should know his or her case and the evidence underlying it and be able to specify the charges therein with enough detail and precision; otherwise, valuable court time can be lost in trying to prove or defend against unnecessary surplusage contained within an indictment. Criminal trials are not about the encyclopedic categorisation of each and every crime for which an accused may have responsibility, and it must be kept in mind that there are constraints upon a trial, such as the limited life span of human beings and the finite financial resources devoted to the proceedings by the international community. It very well may be the case that, if the ICTR Prosecutor had chosen to charge forcible displacement as well as killings, some of the trials

190 William Schabas, *Symposium: Universal Jurisdiction: Myths, Realities, and Prospects: Problems of International Codification – Were the Atrocities in Cambodia and Kosovo Genocide?* 35 New Eng. L. Rev. 287, 295 (2001).

191 Jean-Marie Henckaerts, Mass Expulsion in Modern International Law and Practice 164 (1995).

192 *Prosecutor v. Slobodan Milošević*, Case Nos. IT-99-37-AR73, IT-01-50-AR73, IT-01-51-AR73, Reasons for Decision on Prosecution Interlocutory Appeal from Refusal to Order Joinder, 18 April 2002.

may have taken much longer and not come to a conclusion. It therefore is more prudent for a prosecutor to focus upon some of the worst crimes or upon a representative selection of the total number of crimes, so that a verdict can be rendered, than to expect too much from the criminal process and end up with an uncompleted case. Historians have their place in this process as well, and can always use the judgements of international courts in creating, according to their academic discipline, a more comprehensive account of the conflict and the crimes that were perpetrated therein. In this sense, the lack of convictions for forcible displacement at the International Criminal Tribunal for Rwanda should not be viewed as an indication that this crime was not committed during the conflict there in 1994, nor should it be interpreted as an indication that the crimes are unimportant in the Rwanda context. Rather, when the criminal activity is viewed in the broader context of the genocide that was perpetrated there, the displacement of the Tutsi population understandably takes on a secondary significance to that population's subsequent extermination.

3. The International Criminal Court

Before discussing the crime of forcible displacement in the Rome Statute of the International Criminal Court, it first will be helpful to explore the jurisdictional parameters that will apply to the commission of the crime before the ICC. The jurisdiction of the ICC is somewhat unique. Unlike that of the ICTY, it is neither concurrent with domestic courts, nor does it exercise primary jurisdiction over them; rather, the ICC operates in accordance with the principle of complementarity, which encourages investigation and prosecution by local authorities but provides for the intervention of the Court in limited circumstances. This innovative type of jurisdiction was created by the states that negotiated the Rome Statute, the multi-national treaty that established the functions, jurisdiction, and structure of the ICC.

Traditionally, a state had two options when crimes were committed: the state could extradite the perpetrator to another state that was willing to prosecute him, or the state could prosecute the perpetrator for the crimes in its own courts: *aut dedere aut iudicare*. States now have a third option—complementarity.[193] Under this principle, states do not lose their primary jurisdiction over genocide, crimes against humanity, and war crimes—as long as those states are willing and able to prosecute the perpetrators in their own courts. Although this sounds like concurrent jurisdiction, it is not. The starting point for the system of complementarity is to define situations in which the ICC will be able to exercise its jurisdiction. According to Articles 12 through 16 of the Rome Statute, the ICC may exercise jurisdiction over a case in three situations. First, the Security Council may refer a "situation" using its powers under Chapter VII of the UN

193 *See generally* Nicola Piacente, *Addressing the Impunity Gap Through Cooperation*, *in* International Criminal Justice, Law and Practice from the Rome Statute to Its Review 241 (Roberto Bellelli, ed.) (2010).

Charter, regardless of where or by whom the crimes in question were committed. This option has been used in the cases of Darfur and Libya. Second, a situation may be referred to the Prosecutor by a country that has ratified the Rome Statute, as has occurred in the cases of Uganda, the Democratic Republic of Congo, and the Central African Republic. Third, the Prosecutor may initiate an investigation on his own, but may only pursue it with the approval of the Pre-Trial Chamber. The Prosecutor sought such permission for the first time in November 2009 with respect to Kenya.[194] Therefore, except in the case of a Security Council referral, the ICC will be able to exercise jurisdiction only over crimes committed by nationals of countries that have ratified the Rome Statute or crimes committed on the territory of countries that have ratified the Rome Statute.

Article 17 makes it clear that the ICC does not have jurisdiction in basically three situations. The first situation is where the case is not of sufficient gravity to justify further action by the Court. The second situation is where the person concerned has already been tried for the conduct in question.[195] The third situation is where the case is being—or has been—dealt with by a state that has jurisdiction over it. However, where the state is unwilling or unable to genuinely carry out the investigation or prosecution, the ICC may have jurisdiction. When the Court is deciding whether a state is unwilling to prosecute, it takes into account whether the proceedings were or are being undertaken for the purposes of shielding the person concerned from criminal responsibility. The Court will also consider whether there has been an unjustified delay in the proceedings and whether the proceedings were—or are not being—conducted in an independent or impartial manner. When the Court is deciding whether a state is unable to prosecute, it takes into account whether the state, due to the total or substantial collapse or unavailability of its national judicial system, is unable to obtain the accused or the necessary evidence or is otherwise unable to carry out the proceedings. The states that have referred situations to the ICC have expressed various reasons for why they are unable to prosecute domestically, such as ongoing insecurity, the complexity of the case, and the passage of time.[196]

---

194 Human Rights Watch, *ICC: Prosecutor Seeks OK on Kenya Inquiry*, 26 November 2009, http://www.hrw.org/en/news/2009/11/26/icc-prosecutor-seeks-ok-kenya-inquiry.

195 Article 12(2)(a)(i) of the 1996 Draft Code on Crimes Against Peace and Security of Mankind, which states that "an individual may not be tried again for a crime of which he has been finally convicted or acquitted by a national court", but then lists several exceptions, including prosecution by an international criminal court if "the act which was the subject of the judgement in the national court was characterized by that court as an ordinary crime and not as a crime against the peace and security of mankind."

196 *See* Press Release, *ICC Office of the Prosecutor, Prosecutor Opens Investigation in the Central African Republic*, 22 May 2007, http://www.icc-cpi.int/menus/icc/press%20and%20media/press%20releases/2007/prosecutor%20opens%20investigation%20in%20the%20central%20african%20republic?lan=en-GB (complexity); International Center for Transitional Justice, *Germain Katanga and Mathieu*

Turning to the subject-matter jurisdiction of the ICC to prosecute the crime of forcible displacement, the Rome Statute prohibits unlawful deportation and forcible transfer as a crime against humanity under Article 7(1)(d) and as a war crime under Article 8(2)(a)(vii). Sudanese President Omar Hassan Ahmad Al Bashir has been charged with three counts of genocide; five counts of crimes against humanity, including one count of forcible transfer; and two counts of murder. The developments in the *Al Bashir* case will no doubt shed additional light upon the manner in which the ICC intends to prosecute forcible transfer under the Rome Statute. However, the impact of the ICTY experiment can already be seen upon the work of the ICC.

Unlike the ICTY, which developed the elements for forcible displacement over a number of years, the elements of both deportation and forcible transfer at the ICC were set forth at the beginning of the Court's life in a document entitled "Elements of Crimes". According to the ICC, the perpetrator must have deported or forcibly transferred, without grounds permitted under international law, one or more persons to another state or location, by expulsion or other coercive acts. The victim or victims must have been lawfully present in the area whence they were so deported or transferred. The perpetrator must have been aware of the factual circumstances that established the lawfulness of such presence.[197] The fact that the ICC has adopted many of the ICTY's definitions for the elements of forcible displacement demonstrates the lasting legacy that the work of the ICTY has had in this area of international criminal law.

Ngudjolo Chui Face Justice at the ICC, http://www.ictj.org/static/Factsheets/ICTJ_DRC_KatangaChuiTrial_fs2010_en.pdf (ongoing insecurity, passage of time).

197 *See* International Criminal Court, Elements of Crimes, http://www.icc-cpi.int/NR/rdonlyres/9CAEE830-38CF-41D6-AB0B-68E5F9C82543/0/Element_of_Crimes_English.pdf. In addition, the conduct must have been committed as part of a widespread or systematic attack directed against a civilian population; and, the perpetrator must have known that the conduct was part of or intended the conduct to be part of a widespread or systematic attack directed against a civilian population. These are almost identical to the last two general requirements for a crime against humanity under ICTY jurisprudence.

Chapter Five

Shifting the Displacement Paradigm from Compartmentalisation Towards Inclusion

The death of dogma is the birth of reality.[1]

A survey of the scholarly literature on the subject of forcible displacement provides several key insights into modern thinking on the subject. Scholarship on the subject has increased dramatically in volume since the early 1990s, yet forcible displacement is no new phenomenon. What then accounts for this intensification of interest? The most likely explanation, given the content and timing of this new wave of scholarship, is that the atrocities committed in the former Yugoslavia in the 1990s renewed a general concern over the practice of forcible displacement, particularly in the context of ethnic cleansing. Not since World War II had images and accounts of forcible displacement been so widely distributed. The combination of technology, the involvement of the UN and NATO, and the visual shock of the atrocities committed drew broad international coverage from nearly the beginning of the conflict. A survey of the major newspapers in the West shows fairly steady coverage of the conflict in the former Yugoslavia in the early 1990s, as well as the Security Council's creation of the ICTY in 1993 and the ensuing work of the ICTY.[2]

A perusal of the extensive body of scholarly work relating to forcible displacement reveals that views on certain issues are remarkably divergent and the academic treatment of others is in an incipient stage and thus not yet comprehensive. Scholars have honed in on discrete aspects or sub-topics of forcible displacement, leaving behind tracts that are rich in detail, but a landscape that is largely incomplete. Scholarly literature on the subject thus mirrors the legal treatment of forcible displacement in that both are in their infancy and require maturation and development. This chapter presents an overview of the literature on forcible displacement, considering the primary contexts in which forcible displacement is considered and the dominant academic debates within those contexts. Each debate takes a different approach in attempting to uncover solutions to the phenomenon of forcible displacement, which has been with us for a long time with no indications of abating. But it may be that any approach that is too specialised

1 Immanuel Kant, quoted in Rufus K. Noyes, Views of Religion 524 (1906).

2 It is to be noted that the scholarship and news survey of the authors is limited by language. The authors consulted a number of newspapers from English, French, and Spanish-speaking countries, although the scholarly literature discussed in this chapter is primarily in English.

will carry with it inherent flaws, whereas a comprehensive and consistent understanding of forcible displacement may be a more successful strategy for combating the crime.

There are five context-specific areas in which forcible displacement can be readily identified: internal displacement and the human rights of internally displaced persons (IDPs), refugees and refugee law, ethnically-motivated displacement, displacement in particular countries or conflicts, and development-induced displacement. It would be overly simplistic to assert that all literature on forcible displacement is exclusively confined to these five areas or that these five areas are wholly discrete. Nevertheless, considering these areas and the primary academic debates within them elucidates current thinking on forcible displacement, so that future directions for continued research can be explored.

1. The Debate upon IDP Protection

The subject of internal displacement and its causes and consequences has received a great deal of attention in recent years.[3] With 26 million IDPs in the world,[4] internal displacement is a topic of waxing concern among the international community, including among scholars and NGOs such as the Internal Displacement Monitoring Centre.[5]

At the center of the normative debate is the question of whether the provisions available in existing human rights and humanitarian law instruments provide sufficient protection and assistance to IDPs or whether additional measures are needed in order to effectively respond to the situation. Wading through the vast body of literature on IDPs, one can discern roughly three points of contention. The first concerns the adequacy of the UN's Guiding Principles on Internal Displacement (Guiding Principles), a non-binding set of principles that the UN has urged states to adopt in their domestic legislation. Some argue that the Guiding Principles fill the void in respect of the protection of IDPs, while others point out that the Guiding Principles are non-binding and considered "soft law" at best. The second, related debate considers the need to adopt binding legal

---

3 For a look at three of the seminal books on the issue of internal displacement, see Roberta Cohen & Francis Mading Deng, Masses in Flight: The Global Crisis of Internal Displacement (1998); Thomas G. Weiss & David A. Korn, Internal Displacement: Conceptualization and Its Consequences (2006); Caught Between Borders: Response Strategies of the Internally Displaced (Marc Vincent & Birgitte Refslund Sorenson, eds., 2001).

4 UNHCR Press Release, *UNHCR Annual Report Shows 42 Million People Uprooted Worldwide*, 16 June 2009, http://www.unhcr.org/4a2fd52412d.html.

5 For a recent and comprehensive analysis of internal displacement by country, see Internal Displacement Monitoring Centre, *Internal Displacement: Global Overview of Trends and Developments in 2009*, http://www.internal-displacement.org/8025708F004BE3B1/(httpInfoFiles)/8980F134C9CF4373C1257725006167DA/$file/Global_Overview_2009.pdf.

instruments specifically addressing IDPs. The third and final position taken by scholars aims at finding preventive solutions to displacement.

The literature evaluating the sufficiency of the Guiding Principles is expansive. Hannah Entwislet is of the view that, despite the fact that the Principles are soft-law, they have been "surprisingly influential in shaping how countries and international organizations regard and treat internally displaced populations".[6] Thomas Weiss generally commends the Guiding Principles, but advocates for centralisation of UN responsibility for IDPs and greater operational capabilities.[7] Many UN agencies themselves have published material addressing the gap in protection for internally displaced persons.[8] Francis Deng, whose team authored the Guiding Principles, has continually written about their efficacy, defending his team's decision to draft the Guiding Principles rather than to adopt a new convention for IDPs.[9] Yet, others maintain that "the Guiding Principles ... do not really fill any legal gap; they simply state and interpret existing norms."[10] Due to the non-binding nature of the Guiding Principles and the fact that they principally address the rights of IDPs *ex post facto*, a number of commentators have attempted to devise more preventive solutions to the problem of internal displacement, as well as displacement across international borders.

Some scholars and practitioners believe that, at the very least, the UN should undertake to implement an early warning system, requiring the UN to monitor situations likely to lead to displacement. Scholars differ in opinion over the steps the UN would take once a state of affairs progressed past the point of potential prevention to a situation of mass displacement. Proposals range from imposing military and economic sanctions on a country that does not heed warnings[11] to full-scale humanitarian intervention. The principal of humanitarian intervention and its corollary, the principal of non-intervention, have been examined in-depth

6 Hannah Entwisle, *Racing Cascades: The Normative Development of the U.N. Guiding Principles on Internal Displacement*, 19 GEO. IMMIGR. L.J. 369, 371 (2005).

7 Thomas G. Weiss, *Internal Exiles: What Next for Internally Displaced Persons?* 24 THIRD WORLD QUARTERLY 429, 442 (Jun. 2003) (generally commending the Guiding Principles but advocating centralisation of UN responsibility for IDPs and greater operational capabilities).

8 *See, e.g.*, NO REFUGE: THE CHALLENGE OF INTERNAL DISPLACEMENT, OFFICE FOR THE COORDINATION OF HUMANITARIAN AFFAIRS 73–90 (2003) (containing an informative section on the protection of internally displaced persons and the applicability of international law, including the Guiding Principles).

9 *See generally* Francis Deng, *A Decade in Human Rights Law: International Response to Internal Displacement: A Revolution in the Making*, 11 HUM. RTS. BR. 24, 27 (2004); Francis Deng, *The UN and the Protection of Human Rights: The Global Challenge of Internal Displacement*, 5 WASH. U. J.L. & POL'Y 141 (2001).

10 Michael Barutciski, *Tensions Between the Refugee Concept and the IDP Debate*, 3 FORCED MIGRATION REVIEW 13 (Dec. 1998). Note that Barutciski asserts that existing legal instruments adequately address the needs of IDPs from a legal standpoint.

11 *See, e.g.*, Corinne E. Lewis, *Dealing with the Problem of Internally Displaced Persons*, 6 GEO. IMMIGR. L.J. 693, 717 (1992).

by numerous commentators. Alan Dowty and Gil Loescher are among those who assert that the principal of non-intervention, which has long been recognised as a central tenet of international relations, is not applicable to situations of massive displacement because states producing refugees and IDPs lose the privilege of asserting non-intervention by causing or failing to prevent involuntary migrations that impact other states. In the words of Dowty and Loescher, any state "that forces its people to flee or takes actions that compel them to leave in a manner that threatens regional peace and security has in effect international-ized its internal affairs, and provides a cogent justification for policymakers elsewhere to act directly upon the source of the threat."[12]

A significant group of commentators has proposed the adoption of entirely new legal instruments to address forcible displacement. Nearly forty years ago, Arthur Helton was among the first scholars to propose such an instrument. Helton's idea did not gain much following at the time. In the 1990s, however, there was a renewed interest among scholars in the creation of a treaty preventing mass displacement. In an influential article, Jack Garvey wrote that situations of mass displacement required consideration as a matter of inter-governmental obligation. Garvey explained that "mass exodus is a matter of international legal responsibility, not just a violation of human rights ideals that states can denigrate on the basis of national sovereignty."[13] Paul Freedman, on the other hand, viewed forcible displacement not only as an issue of responsibility of the state creating refugee and IDP situations, but also as the responsibility of the international community, an idea in which the principal of humanitarian intervention finds its roots. Freedman suggested the adoption of a "Treaty on Massive Displacement," which would apply to both IDPs and refugees crossing international borders.[14] Freedman's envisioned treaty would clarify and confirm the responsibility of the international community to intervene in situations creating mass displacement and would permit situations of mass forcible displacement to be referred directly to the Security Council.[15]

The international community is still wrestling with the dilemma of IDPs, and the literature on IDPs exhibits a variance of opinions over the best approach to take to address IDP issues. The proposals set forth by the scholars discussed in this section are progressive increments forward: the scholarship on IDPs forms part of the solution and is an important component of creating a culture primed for more effective remedial action. Yet, only a handful of scholars, such as Garvey and Freedman, have addressed IDPs from within a broader context of forcible displacement, rather than confining their proposals to IDP-specific situations.

12 *See* Alan Dowty & Gil Loescher, *Refugee Flows and International Action,* 21 International Security 43, 59 (1996).

13 *See* Jack I. Garvey, *Toward a Reformulation of International Refugee Law*, 26 Harv. Int'l L.J. 483, 496 (1985).

14 *See generally* Paul Freedman, *International Intervention to Combat the Explosion of Refugees and Internally Displaced Persons,* 9 Geo. Immigr. L.J. 565 (1995).

15 *Id.* at 598–99.

Attention to this area should not be limited to IDPs, but should also address the needs of those who are displaced across international boundaries but who do not fall within the scope of the Refugee Convention, a topic considered below.

2. The Debate upon the Revitalisation of Refugee Law

The refugee law community has debated the need to revise the current refugee regime for years. In the 1990s, scholars vigorously argued over whether there was a need to "overhaul" the entire refugee law system.[16] Proposals such as that of scholar James Hathaway to implement a regional system of "burden-sharing"[17] or that of Satvinder Juss, who advocated the inclusion of refugee law within the broader framework of immigration law,[18] were met with ardent criticism.[19] A related and ongoing debate has focused more specifically on whether the legal regime governing refugees should be expanded to encompass protection of other types of forcibly displaced persons that do no fit within the purview of the Refugee Convention, such as IDPs or individuals who have fled their countries of origin due to reasons other than the grounds for persecution identified in the Refugee Convention.

A number of scholars defend the need to maintain a distinct and separate legal regime for the protection of refugees meeting the Refugee Convention definition.[20] Writing over a decade ago, Michael Barutciski argued that extending the refugee law regime to internally displaced persons would be "detrimental" to those currently falling within the protections of refugee law.[21] Barutciski emphasised that the protections afforded by the Refugee Convention—namely, the principle of *nonrefoulement* for individuals who have been persecuted and

---

16 *See, e.g.*, Peter H. Schuck, *Refugee Burden Sharing: A Modest Proposal*, 22 Yale J. Int'l L. 243 (1997); Joan Fitzpatrick, *Flight From Asylum: Trends Toward Temporary "Refuge" and Local Responses to Forced Migrations*, 35 Va. J. Int'l L. 13 (1994) (discussing the effectiveness of temporary asylum schemes as a partial reform of refugee law).

17 James C. Hathaway, *Making International Refugee Law Relevant Again: A Proposal for Collectivized and Solution-Oriented Protection*, 10 Harv. Hum. Rts. J. 115, 117-18 (1997).

18 *See generally* Satvinder Juss, *Toward a Morally Legitimate Reform of Refugee Law: The Uses of Cultural Jurisprudence*, 11 Harv. Hum. Rts. J. 311, 343-44 (1998) (arguing that "State responses to refugees cannot realistically change unless they are tied to state responses to immigration as a whole").

19 *See* Deborah Anker, Joan Fitzpatrick, & Andrew Shacknove, *Crisis and Cure: A Reply to Hathaway/Neve and Schuck*, 11 Harv. Hum. Rts. J. 295, 298 (1998) (asserting that "[t]he context in which refugee crises of various origins unfold is too complex and unpredictable for one over-arching structural cure").

20 *See, e.g.*, Francois Bugnion, *Refugees, Internally Displaced Persons, and International Humanitarian Law*, 28 Fordham Int'l L.J. 1397, 1410 (2008).

21 Michael Barutciski, *Tensions Between the Refugee Concept and the IDP Debate*, 3 Forced Migration Review 11 (Dec. 1998).

the provision of social and economic services to those granted asylum—had no logical application to individuals displaced within their countries.[22] He further argued that the rights of IDPs were already adequately addressed within the rubric of international human rights law and international humanitarian law, including humanitarian intervention.[23]

Nearly ten years later, in addressing the "scholarly shift away from 'refugee studies' in favour of 'forced migration studies'," James Hathaway echoed the view that the specific set of individuals covered by the Refugee Convention must continue to be distinguished from other displaced individuals, including IDPs.[24] Hathaway presented two justifications for his position. The first concerned the grounds for discrimination provided for in the Refugee Convention:

> As bad as it clearly is for anyone to face human rights abuse, refugee status is a recognition of the special imperative to respond to the needs of persons in flight from risk prompted by discrimination—the prohibition of which is the most central human rights commitment of the international community. Simply put, refugees are persons who are seriously at risk because of who they are or what they believe. Refugees are therefore doubly deserving: not only is the risk they have fled profoundly serious, but their exposure to such risk is based on characteristics which are either unchangeable (like race or nationality) or so fundamental that they should not have to be renounced in order to be safe (like religion or political opinion).[25]

The second justification propounded by Hathaway concerned the geographical restrictions of the Refugee Convention: "[t]he restriction of refugee status to persons who have left their own country is logical because it defines a class of persons to whom the international community can, as a matter of practicality, undertake to provide an unconditional response."[26]

The views of both Barutciski and Hathaway have prompted criticism. In a 1999 article, Bonaventure Rutinwa asserted that Barutciski's view was flawed for several reasons.[27] First, Barutciski erroneously assumed that the same protections afforded to refugees under the current regime would be afforded to IDPs

---

22 *Id.* at 12 ("[T]he kinds of rights granted to refugees would not make sense for displaced persons who are still in their country of origin. Refugee rights include basic socio-economic entitlements that allow them to survive in a foreign country where they do not have citizenship rights. These rights would be redundant if granted to citizens in their own states.").

23 *Id.* at 13.

24 *See generally* James C. Hathaway, *Forced Migration Studies: Could We Agree Just to "Date"?*, 20 J. Refugee Stud. 349 (2007).

25 *Id.* at 352.

26 *Id.* at 353.

27 *See* Bonaventure Rutinwa, *How Tense is the Tension Between the Refugee Concept and the IDP Debate?* 4 Forced Migration Review 29 (1999).

by their own governments under any proposed expansion of the law to address IDPs; IDP advocates, however, were not asking for the exact same treatment of IDPs as refugees, but rather were seeking to engage international protection for IDPs.[28] Second, the reasons for which the drafters of the Refugee Convention limited its scope to persons crossing external borders, including the hesitance to interfere with state sovereignty, had become obsolete, particularly in the current climate of humanitarian intervention.

Roberta Cohen articulated similar criticisms. While Cohen did not advocate that refugees and IDPs be considered as one and the same for purposes of the law, she took pains to explain that IDPs and refugees share certain characteristics.[29] First, Cohen pointed out that IDPs in conflict situations have often fled persecution and discrimination, just like refugees.[30] Second, IDPs, like refugees, may be in need of international protection in spite of the fact that they remain within the territory of their country of habitual residence because "protection for IDPs in civil wars or other situations of internal strife cannot be assigned to the very authorities that may have been the cause of their persecution and displacement in the first place."[31] Moreover, many governments, even if they wish to protect IDPs, lack the resources and capacity.

Each of these arguments has its own merit and shares the concern over the fact that there are categories of forcibly displaced individuals who currently fall within different protection regimes, which are based either on the reason behind their forcible displacement or the location to which they are displaced, or both. If one takes a step back from the after-the-fact displacement, however, and instead focuses on the *act* of displacement itself, it becomes clear that all forcibly displaced individuals have something in common: they were displaced against their will and made to leave their homes. Protection of individuals once the act of displacement has taken place is integral to adequately responding to the entire phenomenon of forcible displacement; and, in that context, there may be reason to distinguish between individuals' protection needs based on certain criteria. The international community must continue to focus on the underlying causes of forcible transfer and the potential methods of *preventing* displacements that ultimately lead to the need to provide protections for the victims of this crime in the first place. The scholarship on refugee law is therefore key to understanding the international protection system and constitutes an essential analytical step required to address the situation of forcible displacement.

28 *See id.* at 30.

29 *See generally* Roberta Cohen, *Response to Hathaway*, 20 J. Refugee Stud. 370 (2007).

30 *Id.* at 371.

31 *Id.*

3. Displacement as an Element of Ethnic Cleansing or Genocide

The third major thematic basis in which forcible displacement is considered is within the context of genocide and ethnic cleansing. The primary debate concerns whether forcible displacement for ethnic reasons, without the specific intent to destroy the group, constitutes ethnic cleansing only, or whether it does or should constitute genocide.

There is no consensus on what constitutes ethnic cleaning. A workable definition, provided by the Security Council's Commission of Experts on Violations of Humanitarian Law, is "rendering an area ethnically homogenous by using force or intimidation to remove persons of given groups from the area."[32] The drafters of the Genocide Convention, after vigorous debate, rejected a proposal to include a provision to the effect that forcible transfer of a population for ethnic reasons constitutes genocide.[33] Their rejection, however, was not a definitive answer to the question, and scholars continue to debate the issue.[34] The debate is significant for our purposes because it illuminates the challenge in prosecuting the crime of forcible displacement.

William Schabas, who advocates that ethnic cleansing and genocide are wholly separate, explains his view as follows:

> The genocidaire seeks to kill individuals with the intent to destroy the group to which they belong, in whole or in part. Herein lies the fundamental difference with ethnic cleansing, which generally involves killing, but with the intent to effect forced migration from a territory. The ultimate consequence may be the same: the ethnically cleansed group, deprived of its linguistic, cultural, economic and political infrastructure may well cease to exist as a result of such forced migration.... The ethnic cleanser may become frustrated, of course, and evolve into a related but distinct species, the genocidaire. This is what happened in Rwanda, when the extremists responsible for the ethnic cleansing of Tutsi over several decades realized that their measures had been ineffective, and that the return of Tutsi refugees was ensured by the 1993 Arusha Accords.

32 *Letter Dated 9 February 1993 from the Secretary-General Addressed to the President of the Security Council*, at 55, Annex No. 1, U.N. Doc. S/25274 (9 Feb. 1993).

33 *See* John Quigley, *State Responsibility for Ethnic Cleansing*, 32 U.C. Davis L. Rev. 341, 350 note 47 (1999) (summarising the responses of the delegates at the drafting conference of the Genocide Convention to the question of whether to include mass expulsion as a means of genocide in Article 2 of the Genocide Convention).

34 For a helpful discussion of the debate, see Linnea D. Manashaw, *Genocide and Ethnic Cleansing: Why the Distinction? A Discussion in the Context of Atrocities Occurring in Sudan*, 35 Cal. W. Int'l L.J. 303 (2005).

> When they realized the ineffectiveness of mere ethnic cleansing, their intent was transformed into one bent to destruction, not expulsion.[35]

However, a number of other scholars take the view that ethnic cleansing should be considered a means of genocide because the intent to forcibly displace a population out of ethnic motivations *is* equivalent to intending to destroy a group based upon the ethnicity, religion, or race of a group of people.[36] Jean-Marie Henckaerts, author of the seminal book *Mass Expulsion in International Law*, considers the idea that ethnic cleansing could amount to genocide:

> It is not entirely self-evident that mass forcible expulsions, deportations of civilians and the uprooting of civilians in general, the destruction or *de facto* expropriation and/or confiscation of property as part of an ethnic cleansing campaign constitute acts of genocide. On the one hand, ethnic cleansing seems to be aimed at removing people from a certain area, not really at annihilating them. On the other hand, the commission of the barbarous acts of which ethnic cleansing consists seems to indicate that the cleanser may also wish to annihilate the group .... As with all claims of genocide, proof of the intent to destroy is crucial in this case.[37]

Schabas' position on this issue is at odds with the jurisprudence of the ICTY, which clearly holds that forcible displacement can be a means by which genocide is perpetrated, a position that seems to accord with the reality of conflicts in which people are forcibly displaced. It is not only the extermination of a group of people, but also their forcible displacement that has historically had the effect of seriously disrupting, or even destroying, the cultural identity of that group. The fact that members of a displaced group may survive and carry on their culture in

---

35 William Schabas, *Symposium: Universal Jurisdiction: Myths, Realities, and Prospects: Problems of International Codification – Were the Atrocities in Cambodia and Kosovo Genocide?* 35 New Eng. L. Rev. 287, 295 (2001).

36 *See, e.g.*, John Quigley, *Repairing the Consequences of Ethnic Cleansing*, 29 Pepp. L. Rev. 33, 34 (2001) (opining that "[a]cts of ethnic cleansing may constitute genocide, if the elements defined in the Genocide Convention are present"); Jennifer Trahan, *Why the Killing in Darfur Is Genocide*, 31 Fordham Int'l L.J. 990, 1002, 1020-21 (2008) (arguing that displacement in deplorable conditions could be considered as an attempt to destroy); Micol Sirkin, *Expanding the Crime of Genocide to Include Ethnic Cleansing: A Return to Established Principles in Light of Contemporary Interpretations*, 33 Seattle Univ. L. R. 489, 521 (2010) (stating "if a policy of ethnic cleansing is more than just discriminatory, and also intends to destroy, then ethnic cleansing is more appropriately categorized as a form of genocide"); Natan Lerner, *Ethnic Cleansing, in* War Crimes in International Law, 156-57 (Y. Dinstein & M. Tabory, eds., 1996) (explaining that ethnic cleansing could be interpreted as the intent element of the crime of genocide).

37 Jean-Marie Henckaerts, Mass Expulsion in Modern International Law and Practice 164 (1995).

a different form does not mean that the displacement did not succeed in destroying the group of people as they existed prior to the displacement.

4. Case Studies of Conflict-Related Displacement

The fourth context in which forcible displacement is treated in scholarly literature focuses upon either geographic or conflict-specific situations. Along with work upon internal displacement, this is perhaps the most frequent setting in which forcible displacement is considered. Due to the sheer volume of works of this type, it is difficult to firmly delineate any conclusions regarding these areas of scholarly and practical endeavour. However, a survey of these materials does yield the observation that there exists an overwhelming focus on "after the fact" analysis, despite the academic discipline of the author. Attempts to understand the causes of the displacement and the potential for prevention are rare, although there are exceptions.

There are two broad themes that appear in case studies. First, there are numerous works focusing upon humanitarian intervention. These analyses tend toward the descriptive, following a general pattern of tracing the origins of a conflict, the resulting displacement caused by the conflict, and the ensuing efforts to contain the crisis and to adequately provide for the needs of individuals afflicted by the conflict. The case studies predominately exhibit an affinity for institutional responses upon the ground, piecing together the actions of various UN agencies, task forces, the International Committee for the Red Cross, and other international organisations. Where applicable, government responses are considered as well.

A case study of Burundi, for example, considers the institutional response and capacity to assist displaced individuals within Burundi.[38] A case study on the Karen refugees from Burma similarly details the responses of the Royal Thai Government to the thousands of refugees living on the Thai side of the Thai-Burmese border and evaluates the efforts of UNHCR and NGOs to meet the basic human needs of the refugees.[39] Dozens of similar studies focus upon displaced persons in the countries that constituted the former Yugoslavia, Iraq, Colombia, Afghanistan, Sudan, and Southeast Asia.[40]

---

38 *See generally* CATCHING FIRE: CONTAINING FORCED MIGRATION IN A VOLATILE WORLD (Nicholas Van Hear & Christopher McDowell, eds., 2006).

39 *See generally* Helen K. Brooks, *Burmese Refugees in Thailand: The Provision of Humanitarian Relief to Karen Refugees on the Thai-Burmese Border*, *in* CONFLICT AND DISPLACEMENT: INTERNATIONAL POLITICS IN THE DEVELOPING WORLD (Andrzej Bolesta, ed., 2004).

40 *See, e.g.*, IRAQ'S DISPLACEMENT CRISIS: THE SEARCH FOR SOLUTIONS (Marion Couldrey & Tim Morris, eds., 2009); JOSEPH SASSOON, THE IRAQI REFUGEES: THE NEW CRISIS IN THE MIDDLE EAST (2009); FORCED MIGRATION IN THE SOUTH ASIAN REGION: DISPLACEMENT, HUMAN RIGHTS, AND CONFLICT RESOLUTION (Omprakash Mishra, ed., 2004); INTERNAL DISPLACEMENT IN SOUTH ASIA:

A second dominant issue in case studies is that of durable solutions in post-conflict settings. The major categories of these solutions include resettlement to third countries, integration into the country of asylum, and voluntary repatriation or, for the internally displaced, voluntary return to one's home. An informative piece by Mulenga Nkula, for example, juxtaposes the attempts to find durable solutions in Mozambique and Kosovo, challenging the current view that repatriation and reintegration are "the most desirable durable solution to the refugee problem by most host states in the post cold war era."[41] Other case studies consider repatriation and reintegration in Afghanistan,[42] Sri Lanka,[43] and Myanmar,[44] among others.

The case studies that consider forcible displacement are much-needed additions to the corpus of literature on forcible displacement. They provide key, credible, and "real-world" insights into the successes and failures of governmental and institutional responses to the needs of refugees and internally displaced persons and the advantages and disadvantages of different approaches to ameliorating the situations. The detailed analyses contained in these case studies are of the utmost importance for the international community in creating institutional frameworks that adequately provide for assistance to displaced persons.

5. Development-Induced Displacement

A final thematic category, development-induced displacement, has only recently received attention from legal scholars, and even that attention has been rather limited.[45] Development-induced displacement consists of the forcible movement

---

THE RELEVANCE OF THE UN'S GUIDING PRINCIPLES (Paula Banerjee, ed., 2005); DEVELOPMENT AND DISPLACEMENT: WOMEN IN SOUTHEAST ASIA (Glen Chandler, Norma Branson, & Jan Branson, eds., 1998).

41 *See* Mulenga Nkula, *Refugees and Durable Solutions: The Case of Mozambique and Kosovo*, *in* FORCED MIGRATION AND THE CONTEMPORARY WORLD: CHALLENGES TO THE INTERNATIONAL SYSTEM 187-206 (Andrzej Bolesta, ed., 2003).

42 *See generally* Edward R. McClesky, *Repatriation and Reintegration in Afghanistan: The Role of Demilitarisation*, *in* FORCED MIGRATION AND THE CONTEMPORARY WORLD: CHALLENGES TO THE INTERNATIONAL SYSTEM 207-20 (Andrzej Bolesta, ed., 2003); Peter Marsden, *Afghanistan's Complex Forced Migration*, *in* CATCHING FIRE: CONTAINING FORCED MIGRATION IN A VOLATILE WORLD (Nicholas Van Hear & Christopher McDowell, eds., 2006).

43 *See generally* Didier Bertrand, *The Forced Repatriation of Tamil Asylum Seekers from European Countries to Sri Lanka and Their Reintegration Process*, *in* FORCED MIGRATION IN THE SOUTH ASIAN REGION: DISPLACEMENT, HUMAN RIGHTS AND CONFLICT RESOLUTION 264-88 (Omprakash Mishra, ed., 2004).

44 *See generally* Chowdhury R. Abrar, Repatriation of Roningya Refugees (presented at UNCHR Conference in Sri Lanka in 1995).

45 A related topic that is beyond the scope of this book involves displacement caused by environmental factors. For a helpful analysis of the subject, see RICHARD BLACK, REFUGEES, ENVIRONMENT AND DEVELOPMENT (1998).

of persons from their homes due to development projects such as the building of dams, roads, and other infrastructure, as well as the exploitation of natural resources in mining and oil projects, to name just a few examples. Such displacement can be direct, such as when a government orders individuals to abandon their land to provide space for the development project, or it can be indirect, usually occurring when the development project has secondary effects rendering the surrounding area uninhabitable.

The literature on development-induced displacement reflects a broader sense that the international community has not yet directly addressed the problem of development-induced displacement, let alone fashioned a solution. Development-induced displacement can pose more conceptual challenges than displacement caused by armed conflict. First, who is responsible for development-induced displacement: the state or the private corporations often responsible for initiation of development projects? Second, should development-induced displacement be treated differently depending upon whether the displacement is caused directly by the state as part of a policy or regulation relating to development project or whether the displacement is caused indirectly as a consequence of hazardous conditions from development projects or the economic changes brought about by those projects?

Beyond questions of state responsibility, there is a broader and more pressing question that neither the UN nor scholars have successfully tackled, which is what legal framework should be applied to development-induced displacement in the first place. Legal scholars and social scientists long took the view that development-induced displacement was somehow a different creature from conflict-induced displacement. Over twenty years ago, in a 1990 article, Michael Cernea wrote, "There is a visible, yet in my opinion hardly justified, dichotomy within the social science literature on displaced populations: a literature on refugees coexists side by side with a literature on development-caused involuntary resettlement. The two literatures do not usually speak to one another."[46] Cernea's comment resonates: although scholars, the UN, and NGOs are increasingly taking a "rights-based approach" to development-induced displacement, the academic discussion on development-induced displacement remains largely isolated from broader discussions of coerced population movements, including discussions of internally displaced persons and refugees. Moreover, opinions differ as to which substantive rights are at issue when it comes to development-induced displacement. There is even uncertainty in respect of the proper terminology that should be used for development-induced displacement, which has often been referred to

46 Michael Cernea, *Internal Refugee Flows and Development Induced Population Displacement*, 3 J. Refugee Studies 320, 323 (1990).

as "forced eviction"[47] and "planned displacement"[48]—nomenclature that tends to have the effect of distinguishing it from other forms of displacement.

Recently, scholars, practitioners, and various UN entities have begun to situate development-induced displacement within the human rights framework, a topic which is further discussed in the next chapter. The movement towards inclusion of development-induced displacement is by no means a uniform effort undertaken by the international community, however. In fact, a number of scholars continue to consider development-induced displacement to be a purely domestic issue that does not and should not entail questions of international human rights law.

The multitude of attempts to frame the issue of development-induced displacement is indicative of the international community's lack of a coordinated approach to the epidemic phenomenon of development-induced displacement. Moreover, framing development-induced displacement as an indigenous rights issue is not sufficient because it does not include the thousands of non-indigenous groups that are displaced by development projects. The literature on development-induced displacement merely reinforces the conclusion that a comprehensive approach must be taken to *all forms* of involuntary displacement and to the *prevention* of displacement before it happens.

* * *

Scholars and practitioners have been engaged in a process of hunting oscillations for a number of years, as they have attempted to analyse, define, and ultimately adapt the concept of forcible displacement to a plethora of situations in which the crime is committed. But there is a critical lack of consistency in approaching the subject, which mirrors the broader jurisprudential debate in the international courts and tribunals regarding the prosecution of crimes of displacement. At the heart of the debate is the conceptual problem of identifying the contours of the crime of forcible displacement. For example, the crime of forcible displacement in the context of armed conflict is not uniformly defined in the existing law. There are other forms of displacement, such as development-induced displacement, in relation to which there is no common consensus regarding whether they in fact constitute crimes. Differing views exist upon whether internal displacement is an internal problem to be solved by states themselves without international intervention or whether humanitarian intervention is justified in such situations. These issues are still at the centre of active debates, despite the prodigious body of academic literature that has striven to examine them.

---

47 *See* Brant McGee, *The Community Referendum: Participatory Democracy and the Right to Free, Prior and Informed Consent to Development*, 27 Berkeley J. Int'l L. 570, 572 (2009) (discussing the right to "free prior and informed consultation" and its implementation through the use of community referenda).

48 *See* Shivani Chaudry, *Development-induced Displacement and Forced Evictions*, 41 Stud. Transnat'l Legal Pol'y 591 (2010).

Solutions to the problem of forcible displacement tend to be confined to specific contexts, often within the five thematic categories identified above. The result is that authors writing on internal displacement are debating whether to reform the Refugee Convention, while authors writing on development-induced displacement may confine their analysis to the need to reform housing and land rights at the domestic level. Still other authors considering conflict-specific situations of forcible displacement attempt to discern durable solutions from an interdisciplinary and operational vantage point. It may be that all of these scholars and practitioners are dealing with issues that are more interconnected than they think, with the result that a more integrated approach could yield exponential gains.

Somewhat surprisingly, much of the literature devoted to forcible displacement largely ignores the concept of individual responsibility for the crime. Aside from the debate over ethnic cleansing as a potential means of genocide, there is little to no discussion of the applicability of international criminal law to forcible displacement. However, the blossoming corpus of jurisprudence from the international courts on the crime of forcible displacement has recently begun to remedy this oversight.

The divergent approaches to scholarship on forcible displacement echo the wide-ranging efforts within the international community to combat various situations of displacement. Such a splintered approach is not the most effective means of proceeding and diverts resources and efforts away from the need to comprehensively address forcible displacement in a practical and interdisciplinary manner. The right to stay in one's home is a fundamental human right that can be violated in a variety of ways—limited only by the human imagination for cruelty. The right needs to be protected in all instances, regardless of the motivations of the perpetrators, for the effect is the same. Approaches that are too narrow are to be dealt with skeptically, and it may be that a broader vantage point is warranted, as well as an approach that focuses upon prevention through the potential liability of states and, perhaps even more importantly, that which drives the actions of any state—the individual. The various strands of the academic debate must be carefully considered and then braided together into a durable cord that is sturdy enough to cope with the immense problem of forcible displacement: and this cord should take the shape of a new convention on forcible displacement.

Chapter Six

Broadening the Concept of Forcible Displacement to Include Development-Induced Displacement

In all affairs it's a healthy thing now and then to hang a question mark on the things you have long taken for granted.[1]

In addition to the vast numbers of people forced to flee their homes because of armed conflict and human rights violations, there are millions of individuals that are involuntarily displaced for a different reason: economic development, usually in the form of the construction of large-scale infrastructure projects.[2] Similar to those displaced by armed conflict and human rights violations, individuals displaced by development suffer from the loss of their homes and livelihoods, the dispersal of their communities, and the physical and psychological damage associated with other types of involuntary displacement.

Historically, those displaced by conflict and human rights violations have been considered in a separate category than those displaced by development projects, whose rights have been largely relegated to the realm of internal affairs. Recently, scholars, practitioners, NGOs, and the United Nations have begun to situate the plight of individuals displaced by development within the rubric of international human rights law. The question is whether it is justified on a legal and political level to "combine" approaches to development-induced displacement and other types of displacement, given their differences.

The first section of this chapter provides an introduction to development-induced displacement. The second section examines the mounting consensus that development-induced displacement should be considered within a human rights framework in conjunction with other types of forcible displacement. The third section endeavours to provide an overview of some development projects and corresponding resettlement schemes in Asia, Africa, and Latin America, the three regions where development-induced displacement affects the largest numbers of individuals.

The last two sections consider the applicable institutional and international legal frameworks that may be capable of addressing development-induced dis-

1 Bertrand Russell, 1872-1970, Author and Mathematician.

2 Michael M. Cernea, *Development-induced and Conflict-induced IDPs: Bridging the Research Divide*, Forced Migration Review, Special Issue, at 25-27 (December 2006), http://www.fmreview.org/FMRpdfs/BrookingsSpecial/15.pdf (reporting that approximately 15 million people are displaced due to development projects each year); Norwegian Refugee Council, *The Number of Displaced Persons Increases*, 16 June 2010, http://www.nrc.no/?did=9492731.

placement. Because various actors in the area of international law have only relatively recently attempted to grapple with development-induced displacement as a human rights issue for which states are responsible, the legal framework is incomplete. In the past, development-induced displacement has sometimes been addressed in the realm of indigenous rights, but many of the displaced do not belong to indigenous groups. Several soft law instruments have initiated the process of codifying human rights norms pertaining to development-induced displacement, although only one legal instrument, the African Union Convention for the Protection and Assistance of Internally Displaced Persons in Africa (Kampala Convention), has gone so far as to transmogrify these norms into binding obligations upon states. Apart from the Kampala Convention, which is only applicable to African states, there is no binding legal document that squarely identifies development-induced displacement as a state responsibility or that places the onus upon states to prosecute those who carry out development-induced displacement in a manner that does not take into account human dignity and human rights.

1. Development and Its Costs

Development, as the authors refer to it in this chapter, entails major projects to develop infrastructure, harness energy, and extract land resources. The most common projects involve the construction of dams, irrigation canals, and bridges; the building or expansion of transport routes; and large-scale extraction of natural resources such as minerals and oil. The nature and size of development projects can vary, as can the number of persons such projects displace; the numbers of persons displaced per project frequently reaches the thousands and sometimes millions.[3] In addition to physically displacing persons, development projects interfere with the livelihoods of many who do not inhabit land appropriated for development projects, but who depend upon it for activities such as farming, fishing, and collecting raw materials. The World Bank and other international lending institutions recognise both physical displacement and interference with livelihoods as compensable losses.

Of the many types of development projects that contribute to displacement, the two that cause the greatest costs to human populations in terms of displacement are dam construction and transport projects.[4] Dams are useful for a number

3 The Three Gorges Dam in China, for example, displaced an estimated 1.3 million. *See* chapter two.

4 For example, the World Bank carried out a comprehensive study of involuntary resettlement required by the projects it funded, finding that 63% of displacement was due to dam construction, while 23% was due to building transport corridors. *See* World Bank, *Resettlement and Development: The Bankwide Review of Projects Involving Involuntary Resettlement 1986–1993*, at 8, (1996), http://www.wds.worldbank.org/external/default/WDSContentServer/WDSP/IB/1996/03/01/000009265_3980728143956/Rendered/PDF/multi_page.pdf.

of reasons, including irrigation purposes, generation of hydroelectric power, and prevention of floods. The phenomenon of global warming has resulted in the generation of hydroelectric power becoming increasingly critical. Although dams have been used for thousands of years, the construction of large dams has increased exponentially in the last century—from approximately 5,000 in 1949 to more than 45,000 by the year 2000.[5] The World Commission on Dams has reported, "The impacts of dam-building on people and livelihoods—both above and below dams—have been particularly devastating in Asia, Africa and Latin America, where existing river systems supported local economies and the cultural way of life of a large population containing diverse communities."[6] China and India have constructed approximately 57% of all large dams, which have resulted in the displacement of tens of millions of people.[7]

Transport projects, such as the construction of highways and railroads, also cause large-scale displacements due to their size and the fact that they tend to be located in areas of high population density. For example, the Liaoning Urban Transport Project in China, funded by the World Bank, involved the widening of roadways and the construction of expressways, tramways, and busways in three different cities, which required the relocation of 16,000 people and affected another 16,000 in other material ways.[8]

A third major contributor to development-induced displacement, but one that has received far less attention from the international community, is mining and the extraction of resources. No estimates of the numbers of displaced persons from mining are available, although the Indian experience with mining, which displaced 2.55 million persons between 1950 and 1990, may be representative of the magnitude.[9]

Regardless of the type of project that causes displacement, people who are forced from their homes due to development can be affected in similar ways, suffering a range of emotional, physical, and socio-economic harm. Sociologist and World Bank economist Michael Cernea has developed a list of eight factors that contribute to the impoverishment and overall decline in the well-being of indi-

5 World Commission on Dams, *Dams and Development: A New Framework for Decision-making*, at 8 (November 2000), http://www.dams.org//docs/report/wcdreport.pdf.

6 *Id.*

7 From 1950-1990, estimates for the numbers of displaced persons due to dam construction in India and China range from 26 to 58 million people. *Id.*

8 World Bank, *Project Appraisal Document on a Proposed Loan in the Amount of US$150.0 Million to the People's Republic of China for the Liaoning Transport Project*, at 20, http://www-wds.worldbank.org/external/default/WDSContentServer/WDSP/IB/1999/04/06/000094946_99032505555610/Rendered/PDF/multi_page.pdf.

9 Theodore E. Downing, *Avoiding New Poverty: Mining-Induced Displacement and Resettlement*, at 3 (commissioned by the International Institute for Environment and Development) (2002), *commdev.org/files/1376_file_Avoiding_New_Poverty.pdf* (discussing the overall impact of mining on displacement).

viduals who are displaced by development, which includes landlessness, joblessness, homelessness, marginalisation, increased morbidity, food insecurity, loss of access to common property, and social disarticulation.[10] Many, if not all, of these factors are common to any type of displacement, whether it be development-induced or conflict-induced, which provides a valid basis for the consideration of development-induced displacement within the framework of international human rights law, a topic considered in the next section.

2. The Inclusion of Development-Induced Displacement within the Human Rights Law Discourse

Until recently, one of the most common approaches to development-induced displacement, and one adopted by several UN entities, including the World Bank,[11] was to treat development-induced placement as an issue of indigenous rights.[12] Within the indigenous rights approach, scholars and practitioners focused upon the right to land,[13] the right to culture, and the right to self-determination. A number of scholars and practitioners also supported the view that indigenous land rights were best protected by the "right to free prior and informed consent"[14] (FPIC) (also termed "free prior and informed consultation"). Some of these scholars and practitioners continue to argue that FPIC is an emerging legal norm[15] that encompasses the right of indigenous persons to consent to development practices that will impact their land and potentially result in their

10 Cernea defines food insecurity as "calorie-protein intake levels below the minimum necessary for normal growth and work." "Social dis-articulation" refers to "[t]he dismantling of communities' social organization structures, the dispersion of informal and formal networks, associations, societies, etc. …". Michael M. Cernea, *Understanding and Preventing Impoverishment from Displacement: Reflections on the State of Knowledge*, 8 J. Refugee Studies 245, 251 (1995).

11 For a discussion of the United Nation's approach to development and indigenous rights, see *Universal Rights or a Universe unto Itself? Indigenous Peoples' Human Rights and the World Bank's Draft Operational Policy 4.10 on Indigenous Peoples*, 17 Am. U. Int'l L. Rev. 527, 613-19 (2002).

12 *See, e.g.*, Dean E. Cycon, *When Worlds Collide: Law, Development and Indigenous People*, 25 New Eng. L. Rev. 761 (1991) (exploring the relationship between development and indigenous rights).

13 *See, e.g.*, Lillian Aponte Miranda, *The Indigenous Rights Movement in Other Contexts: The U'Wa and Occidental Petroleum: Searching for Corporate Accountability in Violations of Indigenous Land Rights*, 31 Am. Indian L. Rev. 651 (2006-2007).

14 Lisa J. Laplante and Suzanne A. Spears were among the first scholars to advocate the free prior and informed consent (FPIC) approach as a means of solving disputes between indigenous communities and corporations and governments engaging in development projects, in *Out of the Conflict Zone: The Case for Community Consent Processes in the Extractive Sector*, 11 Yale H.R. & Dev. L.J. 69 (2008).

15 International Labour Organisation Convention C107, Indigenous and Tribal Population Convention, art. 12, 26 June 1957, http://ilolex.ilo.ch:1567/scripts/;

relocation. However, others dispute the efficacy of FPIC as a means to protect indigenous land rights.[16]

Another group of scholars and practitioners have viewed development-induced displacement as a domestic problem, meriting wholly domestic solutions. Many of the case studies of development-induced displacement thus focus upon the capability of domestic apparatuses to address the situation of individuals displaced within national borders by assessing domestic resettlement and rehabilitation programmes.[17] The massive nature and extent of development projects in India, for example, have prompted a number of critiques of India's lack of national resettlement and rehabilitation programme.[18] Other scholars have evaluated resettlement and rehabilitation programmes in African countries.[19] Regardless of the country considered, these scholars focus upon specific, domestic cases, generally limiting recommendations to the improvement and expansion of domestic operational initiatives aimed at after-the-fact displacement. And such approaches may indeed be the most appropriate for these situations.

While the approaches to the legal framework of development-induced displacement discussed are still advocated by some scholars and practitioners, there is a recent and notable trend, led by the United Nations and a variety of NGOs, of viewing development-induced displacement as an international human rights issue, and thus as a matter for which both the international community and states are responsible. The writings of Michael Cernea provided much of the impetus towards this movement: for over two decades, Cernea has urged that, by considering development-induced displacement within the same academic rubric as other forms of displacement, scholars could "broaden and refine their conceptualisations by exploring similarities and differences between their sets of variables. Politically, they could influence the public arena stronger by mutually reinforcing their policy

---

International Labour Organisation Convention C169, art. 16(2) (27 June 1989); United Nations Draft Declaration on the Rights of Indigenous Peoples, art. 10.

16 *See* Connie Chan, *Response: Lisa J. Laplante & Suzanne A. Spears, Out of the Conflict Zone: The Case for Community Consent Processes in the Extractive Sector*, 11 Yale H.R. & Dev. L.J. 117, 119 (2008) (arguing that, although "indigenous peoples' participatory rights have been recognized in various emerging human rights standards, the extent to which these rights are rigorously captured by binding treaty obligations or rules of customary international law remains controversial at best").

17 *See, e.g.*, Shyam K. Upadhyaya and Karuna Sharma, Displacement, Resettlement, and Rehabilitation Issues in Hydropower Projects (2004) (considering resettlement policies and experiences of countries with displacement caused by hydropower projects).

18 *See, e.g.*, Gautam Appa and Girish Patel, *Unrecognised, Unnecessary and Unjust Displacement – Case Studies from Gujarat, India*, *in* Understanding Impoverishment: The Consequences of Development-Induced Displacement (1996); Manish Kumar Verma, Development, Displacement and Resettlement (2004).

19 *See, e.g.*, Véronique Lassailly-Jacob, *Land-Based Strategies in Dam-Related Resettlement Programmes in Africa*, *in* Understanding Impoverishment: The Consequences of Development-Induced Displacement (1996).

advocacy and operational recommendations."[20] Of late, development-induced displacement has also been addressed by entities within the United Nations, including those whose mandates cover internally displaced persons and indigenous rights. Walter Kälin, the former Representative of the Secretary-General on the Human Rights of Internally Displaced Persons (a position now titled the Special Rapporteur on the Human Rights of Internally Displaced Persons), recently included a section on persons that are internally displaced by development in his final report to the Human Rights Council in January 2010, noting that

> [t]he stereotypical image of internally displaced persons—reinforced by media reports—remains that of people who flee conflict areas and end up destitute in camps or collective shelters. The reality is far more complex. Every year more people are displaced by natural disasters and development projects than by conflict and violence.[21]

Kälin advocates that development-induced displacement should be included as one of the "major challenges" to be tackled at an international level and advises both states and international actors to "[r]ecognize, protect and assist all internally displaced persons in accordance with the Guiding Principles on Internal Displacement, including … people evicted in the context of development."[22]

The Human Rights Council, to whom the Rapporteur on the Human Rights of Internally Displaced Persons reports, and one of the foremost entities addressing violations of human rights within the UN system, is also devoting new attention to development-induced displacement. In 2000, the Human Rights Commission appointed a Special Rapporteur on Adequate Housing; and, in 2001, it appointed a Special Rapporteur on the Situation of Human Rights and Fundamental Freedoms of Indigenous People.[23] The mandates of both Rapporteurs include reporting on persons displaced by development.[24] The Human Rights Council intensified its scrutiny of development-induced displacement in 2007, when it adopted a set of guidelines addressing forced displacement

20 Michael M. Cernea, *Development-induced and Conflict-induced IDPs: Bridging the Research Divide*, Forced Migration Review, Special Issue , at 25-27 (December 2006), http://www.fmreview.org/FMRpdfs/BrookingsSpecial/15.pdf.

21 *See generally* Report of the Representative of the Secretary-General on the Human Rights of Internally Displaced Persons, Walter Kälin, Human Rights Council, U.N. Doc A/HRC/13/21 (5 January 2010), http://www2.ohchr.org/english/bodies/hrcouncil/docs/13session/A-HRC-13-21.pdf.

22 *See id.*

23 *See* W. Courtland Robinson, *Risks and Rights: The Causes, Consequences, and Challenges of Development-Induced Displacement*, Brookings Institution – SAIS Project on Internal Displacement, http://www.brookings.edu/fp/projects/idp/articles/didreport.pdf (discussing the United Nations entities involved in development-induced displacement).

24 *See id.*

caused by development. The guidelines begin by noting that "[f]orced evictions share many consequences similar to those resulting from arbitrary displacement, including population transfer, mass expulsions, mass exodus, ethnic cleansing and other practices involving the coerced and involuntary displacement of people from their homes, lands and communities."[25] The Guidelines, which are based upon an earlier set of Guidelines drafted by the Sub-Commission on Prevention of Discrimination and Protection of Minorities (now referred to as the Sub-Commission on the Promotion and Protection of Human Rights), squarely ground development-induced displacement within the framework of international human rights law and upon the prohibition of forcible transfer encompassed in several international conventions.

The African Commission of Human and Peoples' Rights has effectuated this doctrinal shift by considering those displaced by development and those displaced by other human rights violations within the same creedal category. Bahame Tom Nyanduga, the African Commission's Special Rapporteur on Refugees, Asylum Seekers, IDPs, and Migrants in Africa, is tasked with considering the situation of *all* of the displaced, not only those displaced by conflict or individualised persecution and has emphasised the need for the Commission to address development-induced displacement, citing it as one of the factors that will contribute substantially to an increase in the already high number of displaced persons in Africa.[26] Balakrishnan Rajagopal, a long-time advocate of viewing development-induced displacement from an international law perspective, argues that there is no "internal theory" within human rights discourse that requires the two types of transfers to be viewed separately and that drawing such a distinction "reflects the dominant understandings of the role of the state in the economy."[27] He has observed that it is anomalous to consider "the mass deportation of 1.5 million people from Phnom Penh by the Khmer Rouge in 1975 [as a] crime against humanity, while the mass eviction/deportation of 33 million development refugees from their homes due to development projects such as dams, by the Indian Government, is simply seen as the 'social cost' … of development."[28]

The increasing involvement of the United Nations in development-induced displacement reflects a potential turning point in the "dominant understanding of the role of the state" and an opportunity for states and non-state actors to rethink development-induced displacement. Given that development-induced displacement and other forms of displacement have many of the same effects

25 Report of the Special Rapporteur on adequate housing as a component of the right to an adequate standard of living, Miloon Kothari, Human Rights Council, U.N. Doc A/HRC/4/18 (5 February 2007).

26 Report of Commissioner Bahame Tom Nyanduga, Special Rapporteur on Refugees, Asylem [sic] Seekers, IDPs and Migrants in Africa for the Period November 2008 – May 2009, ¶ 6, http://www.law.georgetown.edu/idp/docs/EN/2086-EN.pdf.

27 Balakrishnan Rajagopal, International Law from Below: Development, Social Movements and Third World Resistance 195 (2003).

28 *Id.*

upon the displaced, the convergence of these heretofore doctrinally separate phenomena could be a watershed event in how displacement is treated by domestic and international authorities.

3. Regions Affected

Development-induced displacement is most common in developing countries that are engaged in large-scale projects to increase and improve their economies and domestic infrastructures. Because development projects are dependent upon significant monetary funds, they are most common in countries that possess the resources to pay for such projects or in countries that are seen to be "stable" enough, both financially and politically, to be attractive to foreign investors and to international lending institutions, such as the World Bank.

Many Asian countries fit this description, where widespread displacement and failed resettlement schemes are well-documented. Asian countries account for the greatest amount of development-induced displacement in the world, and Asian Development Bank-financed projects account for approximately 100,000 to 150,000 displaced persons in Asia alone.[29] Moreover, many countries in Asia do not have domestic policies in place to govern development-induced displacement or are only now in the process of developing such policies. For example, India, Sri Lanka, and Pakistan have draft policies which have not yet been fully adopted by their governments, while Indonesia, Vietnam, Laos, the Maldives, Bhutan, and Nepal have no policy for rehabilitation or income compensation.[30] Other countries, such as China, have relatively comprehensive development policies, but less than strict implementation of those policies.[31]

India's record with development-induced displacement is one of the most well-documented, with scores of books and articles discussing the massive development projects that have become part and parcel of the Indian government's activity in this area. Large-scale projects were first undertaken by the government in the 1930s and marked the beginning of the trend in India to build large dams.[32] As of 2003, it was estimated that approximately 16.4 million people had been displaced in India due to irrigation and hydroelectric power projects alone,

29 Eric Johnston, *Large-scale ADB Projects Draw Criticism*, THE JAPAN TIMES, 8 May 2007, http://search.japantimes.co.jp/cgi-bin/nn20070508a5.html.

30 Brooke McDonald, Michael Webbter, & Duan Yuefang, *Involuntary Resettlement as an Opportunity for Development: The Case of Urban Resettlers of the Three Gorges Project, China*, 21 J. REF. STUDIES 82, 85 (2008) (providing an overview of resettlement policies in Asia).

31 The first formal policy in China was adopted in 1991, titled "Regulations on Compensation for Land Acquisition and Resettlement for the Construction of Large and Medium-sized Water Conservancy and Hydroelectric Projects". A number of laws and regulations were added over the years, resulting in a relatively comprehensive legal regime. *See id.*

32 *See* D.C. SAH, INVOLUNTARY MIGRATION 15 (2003).

while another 2.5 million were displaced by mines, and 1.25 million by industrial projects.[33] For many decades, development-induced displacement was governed by the Land Acquisition Act of 1894, which provided only monetary compensation to individuals who were expelled from their land under the principle of eminent domain. Monetary compensation was awarded based upon records of individual ownership, which resulted in the exclusion from the compensation scheme of communities that did not subscribe to individual ownership of land.[34] Despite some regional efforts in India to implement more comprehensive resettlement policies, some displaced individuals have remained homeless for years, and the involvement of various actors causes delays in compensation.[35] For example, the Sardar Sarovar Project, which is part of the Narmada Valley Development Project, entailed the construction of over 100 dams along the Narmada river in northwestern India, the biggest of which was the Sardar Sarovar Dam. Upon the completion of the dam's construction in 2007, tens of thousands of families had been displaced.[36] The resettlement schemes for the displaced involved uneven compensation and land distribution, resulting in the return of many families to the areas where they previously lived that, while not inundated, were not habitable due to concerns having to do with safety and hygiene.[37]

India's neighbor, Pakistan, has similar experiences with development and likewise has no national resettlement policy in place to provide standards for the displacement and consequent resettlement and compensation of the displaced.[38] Eighty-one dams have been built in Pakistan since 1947,[39] and there are similari-

---

33 *See* Mahendra P. Lama, *IDPs in India*, *in* DISPLACED WITHIN HOMELANDS: THE IDPS OF BANGLADESH AND THE REGION 159 (Chowdhury R. Abrar & Mahendra P. Lama, eds., 2003).

34 *See* D.C. SAH, INVOLUNTARY MIGRATION 44 (2003) (discussing the flaws of the compensation scheme under the 1894 Land Acquisition Act).

35 In the case of the Pong Dam built in 1975, 21,000 displaced families have not yet received the land they were promised at the time of displacement. *See* Mahendra P. Lama, *IDPs in India*, *in* DISPLACED WITHIN HOMELANDS: THE IDPS OF BANGLADESH AND THE REGION 159 (Chowdhury R. Abrar & Mahendra P. Lama, eds., 2003).

36 *See India Finishes Controversial Dam*, BBC NEWS, 1 January 2007, http://news.bbc.co.uk/2/hi/south_asia/6222079.stm (noting that an estimated 35,000 individuals were displaced by the dam's construction).

37 *See* Supriya Garikipati, *Consulting the Development-Displaced Regarding Their Resettlement: Is There a Way?* 18 J. REFUGEE STUDIES, 340, 341-42 (2005).

38 While the 1894 Land Acquisition Act and its amendments provide some guidance upon compensation, it is not adequate because there is no comprehensive resettlement policy. Atta ur Rehman Sheikh, *Pakistan: Development and Disaster*, *in* INTERNAL DISPLACEMENT IN SOUTH ASIA 79-81 (Banerjee, Chaudhury, & Das, eds., 2005) (concluding that the "key issue in development-induced displacement [in Pakistan] is the absence of national resettlement policy and a law that can address the problems of fair and timely compensation, rehabilitation, restoration of livelihood and participation of affected communities in the decision making at all stages of the project").

39 *Id.*

ties between the treatment of displaced persons in both Pakistan and India. In the late 1960s, for example, the Mangla Dam in the Kashmir region was built, causing between 5,000 and 30,000 displacements.[40] Many of the displaced were sent to the provinces of Punjab and Sindh, but as of 2005 were still not given the lands promised to them.[41] Another group was sent by the government to the Jhang and Khushab districts, but continues to be denied ownership of the land that was allotted for its resettlement, which has no electricity or drinking water.[42]

Another major dam project undertaken in the 1960s, the Tarbela Dam, produced similar results. The dam's construction inundated 120 villages and displaced 96,000 individuals. Many of the displaced persons either were never given access to the land they were promised or were not able to assume ownership of those lands because of poor land conditions or because they were ousted by communities already living there.[43] An investigation by the World Bank, which funded the Tarbela Dam, found that litigation was still pending for 2,100 different families, three and a half decades after the dam was constructed.[44] While the World Bank funded the project, it was not ultimately responsible for compensating these individuals and lacked authority to enforce compensation schemes.[45]

In general, the development projects in Africa and the corresponding numbers of the displaced are less staggering than those in Asia, although countries of the African continent are increasingly engaging in massive-scale development projects[46] and the legal framework for addressing the needs of the displaced are largely nonexistent or undeveloped. Bahame Tom Nyanduga of the African Commission of Human and Peoples Rights has stated that the legal framework in many African countries in respect of compensation for development-induced displacement is inadequate in addressing long-term concerns of the livelihood of populations that are uprooted by mining companies and foreign investors.[47] Most

40 *Id.* (noting that the official statistic provided by the government of Pakistan was 5,000 displaced persons, while other estimates reached as high as 30,000).

41 *Id.* at 66.

42 *Id.*

43 *Id.* at 68.

44 *Id.* at 68-69.

45 The World Bank served only as the "Administrator" of the funds, which were obtained from numerous lenders, including several European countries. *See* Project Completion Report, Pakistan, Tarbela Dam Project, at 25, 15 Sept. 1986, http://www-wds.worldbank.org/external/default/WDSContentServer/WDSP/IB/1999/07/27/000009265_3960924202616/Rendered/PDF/multi_page.pdf.

46 For additional information on recent large-scale development projects in Africa and the corresponding numbers of the displaced, see Michael Cernea, *African Involuntary Population Resettlement in a Global Context*, World Bank Research Papers (1997), http://www-wds.worldbank.org/servlet/WDSContentServer/WDSP/IB/1997/02/01/000009265_3980728144037/Rendered/PDF/multi_page.pdf.

47 Report of Commissioner Bahame Tom Nyanduga, Special Rapporteur on Refugees, Asylem [sic] Seekers, IDPs and Migrants in Africa for the Period November 2008 –

academic research on development-induced displacement in Africa has focused upon displacement due to the construction of dams, although there are several studies on other types of project-induced displacement, such as mining. With respect to development-induced displacement, reports indicate delays in the payment of cash compensation, resettlement to land where conditions lead to a lower quality of life, and failure to compensate individuals who do not hold official land titles, such as pastoralists.[48]

The case of the World Bank-funded Antananarivo Plain Project in Madagascar is illustrative. The project was intended to improve the drainage and irrigation systems of the city of Antananarivo and the Antananarivo Plain, with projections of the displacement of 6,000 individuals. The actual number of displaced individuals turned out to be 12,000 persons, double of what was estimated. It is not uncommon for resettlement plans to underestimate the numbers of the displaced, particularly given the complexities in determining which individuals will be negatively affected by development projects in ways other than physical displacement.[49]

Many of those who were displaced by the Antananarivo Plain Project sustained losses in their earnings and living conditions. The majority of the uprooted families ultimately were forced to find their own housing—in spite of the fact that the government set aside allotted plots of land—because the land lacked housing, electricity, and running water.[50] Most of the proposed programmes to assist the displaced with food, shelter, and healthcare failed, largely due to a breakdown of coordination among NGOs and local government and an inability to implement the initial resettlement programme approved by the World Bank.[51] The failure of the resettlement strategy was also attributed to a lack of ownership or consensus among the various government entities, NGOs, and international funding institutions.[52]

May 2009, ¶ 6, http://www.law.georgetown.edu/idp/docs/EN/2086-EN.pdf.

48 Chris de Wet, *Risks and Opportunities Relating to Dam-Induced Resettlement*, *in* Displacement Risks in Africa: Refugees, Resettlers and Their Host Population 263 (Itaru Ohta & Yntiso D. Gebre, eds., 2005) (discussing dam-related resettlement).

49 In the Antananarivo Plain Project, 2,341 households, constituting approximately 12,000 individuals, were ultimately displaced by the project. Paul Francis, *Involuntary Resettlement in Urban Development: Plan, Performance and Outcome in the World Bank-funded Antananarivo Plain Project, Madagascar*, 12 J. Refugee Studies 180, 187 (1999).

50 *Id.* at 193.

51 *Id.* at 187 (opining that "lack of consultation, lack of security of tenure, and the caprices of the political and administrative process doomed the attempts to support house construction and provide social services and income generation activities for displaced households").

52 *Id.* at 196.

The Lesotho Water Highlands Project provides another example of the consequences of the current lack of an international legal framework to govern development-induced displacement. It is the largest development project ever undertaken in Africa. The project consists of a series of dams and tunnels that will reroute water from the Senqu/Orange River in Lesotho to South Africa.[53] Like most major development projects, a multitude of private and public actors are involved, including four different international lending institutions. The project is also being built in phases, and the World Bank recently published an independent assessment of one of these phases, which exhibited concerns related to the resettlement policy. The report found that there were delays in payment of compensation and that greater institutional capacity was needed to both implement and monitor the resettlement process.[54]

In Latin America, the construction of dams and other water-related projects similarly accounts for a substantial portion of those dislocated by development-induced displacement. The Inter-American Development Bank financed 140 different dam-related projects between 1960 and 1999, 80% of which were located in Argentina, Chile, Brazil, Colombia, and Venezuela.[55] In the period from 1970 to 1997, dams were the most frequent cause of displacement and resettlement among the Inter-American Development Bank's projects, affecting over 240,000 people, followed by urban development projects, transportation-related projects, and other water-related projects, such as sanitation and irrigation systems.[56] This number only represents the projects funded by the Inter-American Development Bank, which tends to fund smaller-scale projects than certain other institutions, such as the World Bank.

One of the more well-known cases of dam-related development-induced displacement is that of the Yacyretá Hydroelectric Project, undertaken by both Argentina and Paraguay in the late 1980s and financed in part by the World Bank. The project involved the construction of two large dams, which created a reservoir that flooded approximately 1,650 square kilometers, including 500 hectares of land where cities and towns were located. The initial estimate of dis-

53 *See* W. Courtland Robinson, *Risks and Rights: The Causes, Consequences, and Challenges of Development-Induced Displacement*, Brookings Institution – SAIS Project on Internal Displacement, http://www.brookings.edu/fp/projects/idp/articles/didreport.pdf (providing a brief discussion of the Lesotho Project and its likely effects on displaced populations).

54 Project Performance Assessment Report, Lesotho, Highlands Waster Project, Phase 1B and Community Development Support Project, at 41, Independent Evaluation Group (World Bank), 4 May 2010, http://lnweb90.worldbank.org/oed/oeddoclib.nsf/DocUNIDViewForJavaSearch/ABA84CCADDF5E8CC8525775E006CDDD4/$file/Lesotho%20Highlands%20Water%20Project-Phase%201B.pdf.

55 Luis García, Diego Rodríguez, & Lorena Rossi, *Dams, Development, and the Environment in Latin America and the Caribbean: Some Experiences of the Inter-American Development Bank*, at 5-6, Inter-American Development Bank, http://idbdocs.iadb.org/wsdocs/getdocument.aspx?docnum=359614.

56 *Id.* at 17.

placed persons was 33,000, although it soon became clear that this was an underestimation: by 1992 the number of displaced persons had already reached 42,000, before the project was completed. An independent investigation by a panel hired by the World Bank found that the resettlement programme failed to consider satisfactory alternative housing sites and to take adequate action to restore income earning capacity and generally provided inadequate oversight of the resettlement project. The panel also found that there were major delays in resettlement, which "brought substantial costs and serious hardships to the affected populations."[57]

Although the Brazilian government has constructed dams to generate hydroelectric power and reduce the country's dependence upon other types of energy such as petrochemicals,[58] Brazil lacks a formal resettlement policy, and resettlement schemes are developed on an *ad hoc* and case-by-case basis.[59] The Itaparica Dam, which was planned by the state energy agency in the 1970s, created a reservoir in 1988 that called for the resettlement of approximately 10,400 families to four new towns and 127 *agrovilas* divided into plots of land. As of 2001, the efforts to provide irrigation water to the families were still ongoing.[60] Left without irrigation and with non-arable plots of land, many of the displaced, who depended upon farming for their livelihoods, have been left with no alternative methods of supporting themselves.[61] The main advocate for the displaced was the farming syndicate, while the actor with the primary responsibility for resettlement was the state-run electrical agency.[62] The World Bank did not assist with funding the project itself, but only stepped in at a later time to fund the resettlement programme, which had already been partially structured by the electrical agency.[63]

57 World Bank, *Investigation Report, Paraguay – Reform Project for the Water and Telecommunications Sector (Loan No. 3842-PA): Argentina – SEGBA V Power Distribution Project (Loan 2854-AR)*, 24 February 2004, http://siteresources.worldbank.org/EXTINSPECTIONPANEL/Resources/FullInvestigationReport.pdf ("The Panel finds that supervision of resettlement by the Bank is inadequate in two important respects: a failure to ensure sound technical quality in the design, construction, and implementation of resettlement programs, and inadequate consultation with affected people.").

58 Anthony Oliver-Smith, Defying Displacement: Grassroots Resistance and the Critique of Development 113 (2010) (discussing Brazil's plan to build over 80 dams in order to avoid dependency on oil).

59 Involuntary Resettlement: Comparative Perspectives 110 (Robert Picciotto, Warran van Wicklin, & Edward Rice, eds., 2001) (noting that "federal and state implementing agencies continue to develop a resettlement strategy piecemeal, scheme-by-scheme").

60 *Id.* at 101.

61 *Id.* at 112 (noting that "[due to the inability to farm] [p]eople sit idle in some of the towns and agrovilas, and no organized attempt is being made to give them alternative productive employment").

62 *Id.* at 110.

63 *Id.*

4. Existing Institutional Protections

International and regional lending institutions have been at the forefront of efforts to provide a systematic, rights-based approach to development-induced displacement. The World Bank was the first international institution to develop such a policy in 1980.[64] The Asian Development Bank followed with a similar Development Policy in 1995, as did the Inter-American Development Bank in 1998. A number of countries have also adopted policies to govern the projects of their own national aid agencies; all 25 countries of the Organisation for Economic Cooperation and Development have adopted such policies, for example.

The World Bank's policy requires that those borrowing funds set forth a "resettlement plan" or "resettlement policy framework" before the World Bank will consider an overall appraisal of a project. The policy is applicable to projects that result in the involuntary taking of land that causes relocation or loss of shelter; the loss of assets or access to assets; the loss of income sources or means of livelihood, whether or not the affected persons must move to another location; or the involuntary restriction of access to legally designated parks and protected areas resulting in adverse impacts upon the livelihoods of the displaced persons. The borrowers must inform and consult with individuals who will be displaced as a result of the project and provide them with compensation, which is determined by the extent and type of losses that will be sustained. For example, those who will be physically displaced from their land are entitled to monetary assistance during the process of relocation, as well as housing and/or agricultural sites that are of an equivalent value in terms of location and productive potential. Where appropriate, the displaced are also entitled to compensation and support, including training and land preparation, for the time that is reasonably necessary for them to obtain their original standard of living. Finally, the World Bank Policy requires that, where indigenous peoples are to be displaced, they be resettled upon land that is "compatible with their cultural preferences", based upon consultation with the affected individuals. If the displaced do not wish to be resettled upon a particular piece of land or if resettlement on adequate lands is not possible, monetary compensation for lost assets is required.[65]

The Policy of the Asian Development Bank is similar, requiring borrowers to submit a resettlement plan to the Bank as part of its appraisal procedure. The Policy requires that resettlement plans include an appropriate combination of compensation, resettlement, and rehabilitation, as necessary to restore indi-

64 Can Compensation Prevent Impoverishment? Reforming Resettlement Through Investments and Benefit-Sharing 3, note 1 (Michael M. Cernea & Hari Mohan Mathur, eds., 2008).

65 *See* Operational Policy 4.12 – Involuntary Resettlement (updated March 2007), ¶¶ 3, 6, 9, 11-12, 22, http://web.worldbank.org/WBSITE/EXTERNAL/PROJECTS/EXTPOLICIES/EXTOPMANUAL/0,,contentMDK:20064610~menuPK:64701637~pagePK:64709096~piPK:64709108~theSitePK:502184,00.html.

viduals to their previous quality of life.[66] This includes provision of adequate land to individuals whose livelihoods are agriculturally-based or individuals who have close cultural ties to land, such as indigenous groups.[67] The Inter-American Development Bank Involuntary Resettlement Policy and the African Development Bank's Involuntary Resettlement Policy are also comparable to the World Bank Policy and the Asian Development Bank Policy,[68] requiring compensation, rehabilitation, and resettlement for the displaced and for those whose livelihoods are negatively affected by a project and emphasising the importance of adequately compensating groups with special, non-monetary ties to the land.[69]

Despite these institutional policies, reports of failed resettlement schemes are common. Most of the international lending institutions, such as the World Bank, commission independent panels to review implementation of institutional objectives, including whether resettlement schemes are effectively carried out. Many of these evaluations reveal that resettlement schemes either are not carried to fruition or that planned resettlement actions are in fact not feasible, due to such causes as the poor quality of land allocated for resettlement or the costliness of compensation schemes. The result is that many of the displaced suffer from impoverishment, loss of family and community structures, and homelessness—despite the efforts of lending institutions.

Despite the efforts of the World Bank and its fellow lending institutions to ensure that development proceeds in a socially responsible manner, they may

---

66 Asian Development Bank, Involuntary Resettlement, ¶ 38, August 1995 [hereinafter Asian Development Bank Involuntary Resettlement Policy], http://www.adb.org/documents/policies/involuntary_resettlement/involuntary_resettlement.pdf.

67 *Id.*

68 The African Development Bank in 1995 developed operational Guidelines on Involuntary Displacement and Resettlement for Bank financed projects and published its formal policy document in 2003. *See* African Development Bank Involuntary Resettlement Policy, February 2003 [hereinafter African Development Bank Policy], http://www.afdb.org/fileadmin/uploads/afdb/Documents/Policy-Documents/10000009-EN-BANK-GROUP-INVOLUNTARY-RESETTLEMENT-POLICY.PDF.

69 The Inter-American Development Bank Involuntary Resettlement Policy, for example, provides that rehabilitation and compensation packages must "take adequate account of intangible assets, especially non-monetary social and cultural assets and, particularly in the case of rural populations, of customary rights to land and natural resources." Inter-American Development Bank, Involuntary Resettlement Policy, http://www.iadb.org/en/about-us/involuntary-resettlement,6660.html. The African Development Bank states, "As far as possible, the project should avoid the destruction of cultural, religious and archaeological sites or provide alternative sites that are acceptable to the displaced persons and host communities and that have at least the same locational and productive advantages as the land which has been lost. In case of destruction of such sites, all attempts should be made to reconstruct them and to maintain the sense of community among settlers, and between settlers and their hosts." African Development Bank Policy.

not be in the best position to monitor displacement and resettlement schemes. Many of the flaws in resettlement programmes only become clear *ex post facto*, by which time the money loaned to finance the project has already been distributed and can no longer be used as leverage to ensure compliance. States are better placed to monitor and, where possible, prevent development-induced displacement under international legal standards, the subject of the following section.

5. International Instruments Prohibiting Development-Induced Displacement

Until the last decade, international law tended to consider development-induced displacement as a sub-topic of indigenous rights. The only binding Convention that directly addressed development-induced displacement was thus found in the International Labour Organisation's Convention 169 concerning Indigenous and Tribal Peoples in Independent Countries, which requires that indigenous communities be consulted in the creation and implementation of plans for economic development that will affect them and that such plans prioritise their well-being.[70] A different provision of the same Convention, not explicitly confined to situations of economic development, prohibits expulsion of indigenous and tribal peoples from their lands and provides that, where permanent removal of such persons is unavoidable, they must be

> provided in all possible cases with lands of quality and legal status at least equal to that of the lands previously occupied by them, suitable to provide for their present needs and future development. Where the peoples concerned express a preference for compensation in money or in kind, they shall be so compensated under appropriate guarantees.[71]

70 *See* International Labour Organisation Convention 169 Concerning Indigenous and Tribal Peoples in Independent Countries, art. 7 [hereinafter ILO Convention 169] ("1. The peoples concerned shall have the right to decide their own priorities for the process of development as it affects their lives, beliefs, institutions and spiritual well-being and the lands they occupy or otherwise use, and to exercise control, to the extent possible, over their own economic, social and cultural development. In addition, they shall participate in the formulation, implementation and evaluation of plans and programmes for national and regional development which may affect them directly. 2. The improvement of the conditions of life and work and levels of health and education of the peoples concerned, with their participation and co-operation, shall be a matter of priority in plans for the overall economic development of areas they inhabit. Special projects for development of the areas in question shall also be so designed as to promote such improvement. 3. Governments shall ensure that, whenever appropriate, studies are carried out, in co-operation with the peoples concerned, to assess the social, spiritual, cultural and environmental impact on them of planned development activities. The results of these studies shall be considered as fundamental criteria for the implementation of these activities.").

71 ILO Convention 169, art. 16.

In 2009, the African Union took an important step in respect of development-induced displacement that may have implications upon state responsibility for such displacement and may broaden protection to cover all types of people, rather than only indigenous people. This step was taken with the adoption of the African Union Convention for the Protection and Assistance of Internally Displaced Persons in Africa (Kampala Convention). Article 10 of the Kampala Convention specifically applies to internal displacement due to development projects. The article in full provides:

> 1. States Parties, as much as possible, shall prevent displacement caused by projects carried out by public or private actors;
> 2. States Parties shall ensure that the stakeholders concerned will explore feasible alternatives, with full information and consultation of persons likely to be displaced by projects;
> 3. States parties shall carry out a socio-economic and environmental impact assessment of a proposed development project prior to undertaking such a project.[72]

These provisions seem to reflect the "best practices" approach propounded by the World Bank and other international lending institutions and advances the legal framework applicable to development-induced displacement.

In addition to the Kampala Convention and ILO Convention 169, there are several human rights instruments that are broadly applicable to the rights of those displaced by development. These treaties include the International Covenant on Civil and Political Rights, encompassing the rights to freedom of movement and choice of residence; the Universal Declaration on Human Rights, containing the right to an adequate standard of life; and the International Covenant on Economic, Social and Cultural Rights, encompassing the rights to an adequate standard of living and to participate in cultural activity. In 1997, the Committee on Economic, Social and Cultural Rights—the United Nations treaty body that oversees the International Covenant on Economic, Social and Cultural Rights and clarifies the scope of the articles contained in the Covenant—adopted a General Comment on the right to adequate housing, which called upon states parties to refrain from carrying out forced evictions, including those evictions carried out in the name of

---

72 African Union Convention for the Protection and Assistance of Internally Displaced Persons in Africa (Kampala Convention), art. 10.

development[73] and to adopt and implement legislation prohibiting arbitrary forced evictions and penalising those responsible for illegal forced evictions.[74]

In addition to the above, there are two soft-law instruments of particular relevance. The first is the United Nations Guiding Principles on Internal Displacement, of which Principle 6 states that "[e]very human being shall have the right to be protected against being arbitrarily displaced from his or her home or place of habitual residence."[75] Principle 6 explicitly includes "cases of large-scale development projects, which are not justified by compelling and overriding public interests."[76] The Guiding Principles therefore provide a non-binding starting point for the precept that people should not be forced from their homes by development projects. The second soft-law instrument relating to development-induced displacement is a 2007 set of guidelines contained within a report of the United Nations Special Rapporteur on Adequate Housing to the Human Rights Council. These guidelines contain a list of state responsibilities and begin by noting that "[w]hile a variety of distinct actors may carry out, sanction, demand, propose, initiate, condone or acquiesce to forced evictions, States bear the principal obligation for applying human rights and humanitarian norms, in order to ensure respect for the rights enshrined in binding treaties and general principles of international public law." Among the state responsibilities listed are the obligations to "apply appropriate civil or criminal penalties against any public or private person or entity within its jurisdiction that carries out evictions in a manner not fully consistent with applicable law and international human rights

---

73 *See* Committee on Economic, Social and Cultural Rights, General comment No. 7, The right to adequate housing (art. 11.1): forced evictions, ¶ 7, 20 May 1997 ("Other instances of forced eviction occur in the name of development. Evictions may be carried out in connection with conflict over land rights, development and infrastructure projects, such as the construction of dams or other large-scale energy projects, with land acquisition measures associated with urban renewal, housing renovation, city beautification programmes, the clearing of land for agricultural purposes, unbridled speculation in land, or the holding of major sporting events like the Olympic Games.").

74 *See id.* ¶ 9 ("Such legislation prohibiting forced evictions should include measures which (a) provide the greatest possible security of tenure to occupiers of houses and land, (b) conform to the Covenant and (c) are designed to control strictly the circumstances under which evictions may be carried out. The legislation must also apply to all agents acting under the authority of the State or who are accountable to it. Moreover, in view of the increasing trend in some States towards the Government greatly reducing its responsibilities in the housing sector, States parties must ensure that legislative and other measures are adequate to prevent and, if appropriate, punish forced evictions carried out, without appropriate safeguards, by private persons or bodies. States parties should therefore review relevant legislation and policies to ensure that they are compatible with the obligations arising from the right to adequate housing and repeal or amend any legislation or policies that are inconsistent with the requirements of the Covenant.").

75 United Nations Guiding Principles on Internal Displacement, Principle 6(1).

76 *Id.* Principle 6(2)(c).

standards"; to "adopt appropriate legislative and policy measures to ensure the protection of individuals, groups and communities from evictions that are not in conformity with existing international human rights standards"; and to "fully explore all possible alternatives to eviction."[77]

These guidelines are still relegated to the realm of "soft law" and therefore are not binding upon states; however, the appearance of development-induced displacement on the agenda of the UN, both the Guiding Principles and the guidelines in the report of the UN Special Rapporteur on Adequate Housing to the Human Rights Council, are an indication that development-induced displacement is increasingly being considered as a human rights issue that must be addressed by states curbing their own actions and the actions of those under their legal jurisdiction in order to reduce adverse impacts upon the livelihoods of persons dislocated by development-induced displacement. The inclusion of a provision related to development-induced displacement in the Kampala Convention, which is binding upon ratifying African states, is further evidence of an emergent consensus that development-induced displacement is a type of displacement that states have the responsibility to prevent.

* * *

Until now, international and regional lending institutions have borne the primary responsibility for regulating development-induced displacement and resettlement projects, which has led to varying standards and inconsistent implementation of resettlement plans, where such resettlement plans exist. However, the UN and other international actors have progressively called for development-induced displacement to be considered within the rubric of human rights, which entails state involvement and potential liability. The Kampala Convention is an important step towards formal recognition of state responsibility for development-induced displacement.

The specific examples of development-induced displacement discussed within this chapter demonstrate that the lack of a centralised, domestic authority responsible for resettlement has frequently led to a situation where no single actor is ultimately accountable for the protection of the rights of the displaced. As Michael Cernea has observed, "[n]ational governments are best placed to prevent or at least reduce, through farsighted planning, some of the causes and at least some of the effects of planned displacement."[78] The World Bank has noted:

77 Report of the Special Rapporteur on Adequate Housing as a Component of the Right to an Adequate Standard of Living, Miloon Kothari, ¶¶ 11, 22, 38, Human Rights Council, U.N. Doc A/HRC/4/18, 5 February 2007. The provisions provided in the text were chosen for their pertinence to the present chapter. The document contains a number of other provisions that would be useful to promote and protect the right to one's home and to encourage state prevention of development-induced displacement.

78 Michael M. Cernea, *Internal Refugee Flows and Development-Induced Population Displacement*, 3 Journal of Refugee Studies 320, 336 (1990).

> Resettlement works when governments want it to work. The main way governments express their commitment to good resettlement is by creating adequate institutional capacity, defined as the synergy between policy, organizations, and resources. Where Borrowers do not genuinely concur with the Bank's resettlement policy objectives from the outset, resettlement is generally not carried out well, regardless of the number of covenants, follow-up supervision missions, or the frequency of Bank threats to suspend disbursements.[79]

Some states have implemented legislation or adopted policies to govern development-induced displacement and resettlement, but there are other states where no such legislation or policies exist or where the implementation of such policies is pursued in an *ad hoc* manner.

As suggested by Walter Kälin, development-induced displacement should be accorded a higher level of importance in the international community's agenda and should be treated as an act entailing state and, where applicable, individual responsibility. Moreover, it should be treated as part of every state's responsibility to prohibit and prevent acts of forcible displacement that are contrary to the principles of international law. When a state considers that a large-scale development project justifies a displacement due to "compelling and overriding public interests", it must be carried out in a way that is consistent with agreed-upon standards and principles of responsible resettlement.

It is probable that it will take some time before the panoply of state obligations pertaining to development-induced displacement is adopted in binding form. The reality is that development projects occupy an important position in domestic economic growth schemes and that states are reluctant to undertake binding obligations that may interfere with their economic development. The rights and corresponding state responsibilities involving development-induced displacement will therefore require an incremental approach, the first step of which is to codify state responsibility to prevent development-induced displacement where possible, to carry out development resettlement schemes responsibly, and to prosecute individuals who do not comply with the law applicable to a particular development project being undertaken. In addition, any international convention on the prevention and punishment of the crime of forcible displacement should define the crime in such a way so that development-induced displacement can come within the compass of the prohibition against the forcible displacement of people from their homes.

79 *See* World Bank, *Resettlement and Development: The Bankwide Review of Projects Involving Involuntary Resettlement 1986-1993*, at 8, (1996), http://www.wds.worldbank.org/external/default/WDSContentServer/WDSP/IB/1996/03/01/000009265_3980728143956/Rendered/PDF/multi_page.pdf.

Chapter Seven

A Contemporary Domestic Case Study: Forcible Displacement in Colombia

Oh what a tangled web we weave ....[1]

This chapter seeks to demonstrate both the problems inherent in the modern construction of international law governing forcible displacement and the need to create an international legal framework that can pragmatically address the crime of forcible displacement in the many forms it takes. The analysis proceeds against the backdrop of the prolonged situation of forcible displacement in Colombia. The Colombian situation is axiomatic of the need to reconceptualise our current approach to both prosecuting and preventing forcible displacement. After nearly half a century of violent conflict involving widespread forcible displacement, and with no end in sight, it is increasingly clear that neither the Colombian domestic legal framework nor the current regional or international legal regime is sufficiently equipped to confront the situation of forcible displacement in Colombia or to effectively prevent future forcible displacement there.

1. A Short History

With one of the highest numbers of displaced persons in the world, approximately three million persons,[2] and a complex, multi-actor conflict, with numerous co-factors, Colombia provides a tragic and yet instructive example of forced displacement in the context of modern war.

---

1 Sir Walter Scott, Marmion: A Tale of Flodden Field 169 (1893) (written in 1808).

2 Although estimates vary, the United Nations High Commissioner for Refugees places the number of internally displaced persons in Colombia at three million, 70% of whom come from rural areas. UNHCR, Colombia, http://www.unhcr.org/cgi-bin/texis/vtx/page?page=49e492ad6#. The three million figure was also cited by the Colombian Constitutional Court in Order of Compliance 218, 11 Aug. 2006, relating to the T-025 Judgement. Although the government reports a general trend of diminishing numbers of displaced persons, NGOs found that in 2008 alone approximately 380,000 individuals were displaced, representing an increase of 24.7% from 2007. *See Aumenta número de desplazados en 24%* (23 April 2009), Prensa.com, http://mensual.prensa.com/mensual/contenido/2009/04/23/hoy/mundo/1763824.asp (reporting the results of a study released by Consultoría para los Derechos Humanos y el Desplazamiento (Codhes), one of Colombia's larger NGOs concerned with internal displacement in Colombia).

The extensive internal displacement in Colombia stems from the protracted internal armed conflict that has raged in Colombia for over forty years. The Colombian armed conflict is one of the least understood and perhaps most complex civil wars of modern times. Moreover, the conflict has evolved since its beginning decades ago. A discussion of the origins of the conflict is therefore necessary in order to comprehend the large-scale forcible displacement carried out today by the guerilla and paramilitary groups.

Even pinpointing the beginning of the conflict is challenging, given its progressive nature over a relatively long period of time. Nevertheless, it is now generally accepted that the armed conflict at least in part grew out of a period of political turmoil known as "La Violencia," which lasted from approximately 1946 to 1957. La Violencia was a result of massive uprisings among rural Colombians who had latched onto populist politics and sought to assert their agrarian and property rights.[3] Many of these rural Colombians organised into guerilla groups claiming allegiance to the liberal party, endeavoring to overthrow what they viewed as a repressive conservative government.[4] The conservative government reacted violently, embarking upon a series of campaigns to murder, torture, and rape rural peasants.[5] A military junta soon overthrew the existing government, but the violence toward the rural population did not abate.[6] Over the entire period of La Violencia, at least two million individuals were forcibly displaced, and thousands were killed.[7]

The activities of La Violencia ended in 1957, when the military junta was overthrown and the conservatives and liberals together created a National Front under which the two parties were to divide power equally. The National Front led an uneasy and undemocratic[8] existence for the next few years. The leftist guerillas remained active in the countryside, a constant source of discomfort for the National Front, which repeatedly sought to stamp out the guerilla insurgencies.[9]

Boiled down to its simplest terms today, the armed conflict in Colombia contains three actors: the Colombian government; the paramilitaries; and the left-wing guerillas. Both paramilitaries and guerillas are the legacy of the violence that has plagued Colombia since the mid-20th century.

The left-wing guerilla groups, the largest of which is the Revolutionary Armed Forces of Colombia (FARC), organised themselves in the 1960s, build-

---

3 Forrest Hylton, Evil Hour in Colombia 42 (2006).

4 *Id.* at 39.

5 *Id.* at 43-45 (describing the violent reprisals carried out by Conservatives).

6 *Id.* at 46.

7 *Id.* at 39 (2006) (noting that "[s]ome 300,000 people, 80 per cent men, most of them illiterate peasants" were killed during La Violencia).

8 One scholar has characterised the National Front as a "semi-authoritarian parliamentary dictatorship". *Id.* at 54.

9 *Id.*

ing upon guerilla groups that had formed during La Violencia.[10] Today, the primary guerilla organisations are the FARC and the National Liberation Army (ELN). The FARC counts at least 9,000 members amongst its ranks and controls approximately a third of Colombia's territory, while the ELN has a smaller member base estimated to be between 2,200 and 3,000.[11] The guerillas are heavily involved in the drug trade and "tax" many of the farmers and other individuals involved in the growth and production of cocaine.[12] The guerillas are responsible for approximately 26.7% of cases of displacement registered under the national registration system in Colombia.[13]

The paramilitaries are right-wing groups that were initially formed in the 1980s to combat the guerilla groups.[14] Since 1997, they have been organised under an umbrella group, the United Self-Defense Groups of Colombia (AUC).[15] The AUC consists of approximately 6,000 to 8,000 members,[16] although there are estimates ranging much higher.[17] The AUC is also heavily involved in Colombia's drug trade.[18] Although the AUC and other paramilitary groups purport to protect civilians, they are in fact responsible for more incidents of displacement than the guerillas. Approximately 31.3% of registered displacement is attributed to the paramilitaries.[19]

---

10 Rafael Pardo, *Colombia's Two-Front War*, 79 Foreign Affairs No. 4, 64, 67 (Jul.-Aug. 2000), http://www.jstor.org/stable/pdfplus/20049809.pdf (noting that "[t]he armed bands were made up of the remnants of peasant groups that had rebelled against the government … (later gathered into FARC) and new groups promoted by Cuba").

11 Stephanie Hanson, *FARC, ELN: Colombia's Left-Wing Guerillas*, Council on Foreign Relations (19 Aug. 2009), http://www.cfr.org/publication/9272/.

12 The FARC earns a reported $300 million annually from its "taxes" and is estimated to be the wealthiest insurgent group in the world. *See Colombia's Most Powerful Rebels*, BBC News (19 Sept. 2003).

13 Luis Jorge Garay Salamanca, Fernando Barberi Gómez, & Clara Ramirez Gómez, *The Humanitarian Tragedy of Forced Displacement in Colombia* (15 Jan. 2011) (report), www.codhes.org.

14 June S. Beittel & Clare Ribando Seelke, *Colombia: Issues for Congress, Congressional Research Service* (7 Aug. 2009), http://www.fas.org/sgp/crs/row/RL32250.pdf (describing the origins of the Colombian armed conflict and its primary actors).

15 United Self-Defense Forces, GlobalSecurity.org (undated), http://www.globalsecurity.org/military/world/para/auc.htm.

16 *Id.*

17 The National Consortium for the Study of Terrorism and Responses to Terrorism, for example, estimates that there are upwards of 18,000 AUC members currently. *See* Terrorist Organization Profile: United Self-Defense Group of Colombia (undated), http://www.start.umd.edu/start/data/tops/terrorist_organization_profile.asp?id=126.

18 United Self-Defense Forces, GlobalSecurity.org (undated), http://www.globalsecurity.org/military/world/para/auc.htm.

19 Luis Jorge Garay Salamanca, Fernando Barberi Gómez, & Clara Ramirez Gómez, *The Humanitarian Tragedy of Forced Displacement in Colombia* (15 Jan. 2011) (report), www.codhes.org.

What ostensibly began as a war of political ideology is now a contest for territorial control and wealth. Both the guerillas and the paramilitaries vie for territorial control and power over coca manufacture and exportation. The extent of the government's involvement in the conflict—and in providing paramilitary support in particular—is much debated. The Colombian military officially disassociated itself from the paramilitaries in 1989, although several high profile cases involving government officials' links to the paramilitaries have come to light in recent years and the so-called "para-politica" scandal continues to unfold, in which more than fifty members of Congress have been accused of cooperating with the paramilitaries.[20] The most recent report of the UN Secretary-General has noted that there are currently ninety-three open cases of alleged paramilitary links against 268 members of Congress, and thirteen individuals have been convicted.[21]

2. Causes and Consequences

Walter Kälin, the Representative of the Secretary-General on the Human Rights of Internally Displaced Persons, has found that the situation with regard to displaced persons in Colombia is "one of the most serious in the world" and "affects most parts of the country."[22] Displacement in Colombia is pervasive and occurs throughout the conflict-ridden areas of the country. The vast majority of displacement in Colombia is internal, with individuals most often fleeing to cities such as Cali, Medellin, and Bogota.[23] Displacement across Colombia's national borders occurs as well, although less frequently, primarily into Ecuador, Venezuela, and Panama.[24] Regardless of their ultimate destination, the displaced suffer equal harm, including psychological trauma and sharp decreases in socioeconomic status. Poverty levels of IDPs in Colombia, for example, are similar to those of individuals displaced across national borders. Approximately 98.6% of

20 *See, e.g.*, Human Rights Watch, *Colombia: Paramilitary Leaders to Face Prosecution in US* (13 May 2008), http://www.unhcr.org/refworld/country,,HRW,,COL,,482d42251e,0.html (discussing the "parapolitics" scandal).

21 Annual Report of the United Nations High Commissioner for Human Rights and Reports of the Office of the High Commissioner and the Secretary-General, *Report of the United Nations High Commissioner for Human Rights on the Situation of Human Rights in Colombia*, Sess. 13, A/HRC/13/72 (4 Mar. 2010) [hereinafter 2010 High Commissioner for Human Rights Report], ¶¶ 32-33.

22 *See* Walter Kälin, *Report of the Representative of the Secretary-General on the Human Rights of Internally Displaced Persons, Mission to Colombia*, A/HRC/4/38/Add.3 (24 Jan. 2007), http://daccess-dds-ny.un.org/doc/UNDOC/GEN/G07/104/50/PDF/G0710450.pdf?OpenElement [hereinafter Kälin Report on IDPs], ¶ 9.

23 Internal Displacement Monitoring Centre, *Global Overview 2009* (May 2010), at 51, http://www.internal-displacement.org/8025708F004CE90B/(httpRegionPages)/54F848FB9440347280257 0A6005595DA?OpenDocument.

24 Internal Displacement Monitoring Centre, *Internal Displacement in the Americas* (May 2010), http://www.internal-displacement.org/8025708F004CE90B/(httpRegionPages)/54F848FB94403472802570A6005595DA?OpenDocument.

internally displaced families are below the poverty line in Colombia.[25] Poverty levels of forcibly displaced Colombians in Ecuador were equally serious, with 50% living in extreme poverty on less than one United States dollar per day, and 75% living on less than two United States dollars per day.[26]

Displacement in Colombia, whether cross-border or internal, takes place both on an individual level and on a mass level. It is difficult, however, to isolate the causes of the forcible displacement, as there are multiple co-factors in play. Some generalisations, however, can appropriately be made. Certainly the primary cause of displacement is the extreme violence carried out by the armed groups, which causes both direct and indirect displacements: civilians are caught in the cross-fire between the various armed actors, or the civilians are targeted by the armed actors and are the objects of extrajudicial killings, torture, massacres, and other human rights violations.[27] To give a sense of the magnitude of the violence, in 2008 alone, forty-two massacres were committed by the illegal armed groups.[28] The direct and indirect violence creates waves of involuntary migration as people leave their homelands in search of less danger-ridden areas. There is also widespread use of sexual violence, most often against women, which has specifically contributed to the involuntary displacement of thousands of women.[29]

The displacement pattern in Colombia tends to consist largely of individuals or single families fleeing over a period of time, rather than large collective dis-

---

25 Internal Displacement Monitoring Centre, *Colombia: New Displacement Continues, Response Still Ineffective* (3 July 2009), at 28, http://www.internal-displacement.org/8025708F004BE3B1/(httpInfoFiles)/5BCA28036BFAA8ADC12575E8005CBF23/$file/Colombia+-+July+2009.pdf.

26 Brandon Bloch, *Colombian Refugees in Ecuador: The Collateral Damage of a Drug War and an Insurgency*, Council on Hemispheric Affairs (Aug. 2009), http://www.coha.org/colombian-refugees-in-ecuador-the-collateral-damage-of-a-drug-war-and-an-insurgency/.

27 Note that 37% of registered displaced persons report that the paramilitaries were responsible for their displacement, while 29.8% attribute their displacement to the FARC. 1% reported that the Colombian military caused their displacement. *See* Proceso Nacional de Verificación de los derechos de la Población desplazada, Informe I de la Comisión de Seguimiento (31 Jan. 2008), at 32.

28 This statistic was provided by the Colombian government's human rights office. *See* Consultoría para los Derechos Humanos y el Desplazamiento (CODHES), Víctimas emergentes: desplazamiento, derechos humanos y conflicto armado en 2008, http://www.internal-displacement.org/8025708F004CE90B/(httpDocuments)/A12968300F7E4257C12575A500438DFC/$file/codhes+informa+n°+75.pdf [hereinafter CODHES 2008 Report on Displacement], at 5.

29 Statistics contained in a report issued by the Consejería Presidencial Para la Equidad de la Mujer, the Executive Agency responsible for promoting equality of women in Colombia, indicate that 64% of women experienced intimidation, often sexual, by illegal armed groups prior to becoming displaced. *See* CODHES 2008 Report on Displacement, at 16.

placements.[30] The Internal Displacement Monitoring Centre estimates that 89% of displacement in Colombia today takes place in this form, often referred to as displacement "*gota a gota*" or "drop by drop."[31] This individualised form of displacement is a result of the fact that different individuals will choose to leave at different times, depending upon how strongly they perceive the threat of violence to be. This is not to say that large collective displacements do not occur as well. In 2008 alone, armed groups caused eighty-two mass displacements, resulting in approximately 43,000 people fleeing their homes.[32] Displacement is also increasingly becoming a goal of armed actors, rather than a byproduct of generalised violence, and therefore taking a more direct form. The armed groups are known to specifically target entire communities and their lands in order to expropriate territory,[33] particularly in areas of the country that are rich in certain natural resources or that are strategically located along the drug trade route. Land fertile for growing coca and producing cash crops, such as bananas and palm oil, is highly coveted.[34] Since 2000, displaced persons have been forced to abandon approximately 5.5 million hectares of land, most of which has passed into the hands of the illegal armed groups or their supporters.[35] One study has found that landowners are four times more likely to have to flee their homes because they are violently targeted.[36] The armed groups force landowners to transfer title to

30 Donny Meertens, *Forced Displacement in Colombia: Public Policy, Gender and Initiatives for Reconstruction*, National University of Colombia, Colombia (June 2003), pum.princeton.edu/pumconference/papers/6-Meertens.pdf.

31 Internal Displacement Monitoring Centre, *Displacement Colombia: New Displacement Continues, Response Still Ineffective*, (3 July 2009), http://www.internal-displacement.org/8025708F004BE3B1/(httpInfoFiles)/5BCA28006BFAA8ADC12575E8005CBF23/$file/Colombia+-+July+2009.pdf, at 25.

32 CODHES 2008 Report on Displacement, at 4.

33 A study by the Internal Displacement Monitoring Centre, for example, concluded that "[f]orced displacement in Colombia is primarily a way to seize agricultural land from peasants and small farmers, and only to a lesser degree the unintended consequence of fighting between warring parties." *See* Internal Displacement Monitoring Centre, *Colombia: Government "Peace Process" Cements Injustice for IDPs* (30 June 2006), http://www.internal-displacement.org/8025708F004BE3B1/(httpInfoFiles)/2F1618E6C169F2EBC125719C002F6421/$file/Special%20Country%20Report%20Colombia.pdf, at 12.

34 Kälin Report on IDPs, ¶ 9.

35 CODHES 2008 Report on Displacement, at 3. The UN High Commissioner for Human Rights estimates that, in total, between 1.2 and 10 million hectares of land have been expropriated from subsequently displaced individuals. 2010 High Commissioner for Human Rights Report, ¶ 79.

36 Ana María Ibáñez & Carlos Eduardo Vélez, *Forced Displacement in Colombia: Causality and Welfare Losses* (June 2003), http://economia.uniandes.edu.co/content/download/9089/44052/file/Causes%20of%20displacement.AMI%20-%20CEV%20Iba%C3%83%C2%B1ez.pdf.

their land under duress or simply forge the necessary land titles.[37] Violence is also a method of control to deter local populations from collaborating with enemy armed groups and to punish them when they are suspected of collaborating. Civilians in drug producing areas must pay "taxes" to the armed groups from drug profits, the ultimate goal being territorial control and wealth.

There are two groups that are in particular danger of being targets of forcible displacement: women and indigenous persons. Women are targeted for a number of reasons.[38] Female property owners are vulnerable to expropriation of their land because they often do not possess documents proving ownership.[39] As mentioned above, armed groups also use sexual and generalised violence to displace women. Young girls have also been forced to leave their homes due to forced sexual relations with members of the illegal armed forces. A final reason for the disproportionate displacement of women is that many women leave their communities and move to urban areas in order to protect their children from forced recruitment by both the paramilitaries and guerillas.[40]

In addition to seeking out female victims, armed actors target indigenous and Afro-Colombian populations. The disproportionate number of indigenous and Afro-Colombian displaced persons is evident from a recent study conducted in conjunction with Colombia's Constitutional Court, which has expressed alarm at the situation of these individuals. The study revealed that, although indigenous persons comprise 3.4% of the total Colombian population, they make up 6.5% of the displaced population.[41] Likewise, Afro-Colombians, who make up 7.2% of the population, constitute 16.6% of the displaced population. The Constitutional Court has severely criticised the government's failure to ade-

37 Kälin Report on IDPs, ¶ 53.

38 For further analysis of the gendered dimension of displacement in Colombia, see *Violence and Discrimination Against Women in the Armed Conflict in Colombia*, Report, Inter-American Commission on Human Rights (18 Oct. 2006), http://www.cidh.oas.org/countryrep/ColombiaMujeres06eng/TOC.htm.

39 Land ownership by women has been historically rare. Despite legislative measures in favor of women owning land, the practice of male ownership to the exclusion of females has continued. Even those women who do own land often are not seen as legitimate landowners, as female ownership may be more "informal" because women do not have ownership records. *See* Guidelines for Comprehensive Care of Displaced Population with a Gender Differential Approach (translated from original Spanish title, *Directriz de Atención Integral a Población Desplazada con Enfoque Diferencial de Género*, by authors) (undated), http://www.mujercolombia.com/index.php?mode=publicaciones&pagina=3, at 18.

40 Kälin Report on IDPs, ¶ 15.

41 The armed actors responsible for displacement are primarily the paramilitaries and the FARC. 32% of displaced indigenous persons reported that they were displaced by the paramilitaries, 31.1% by the FARC, and 12.2% by other guerilla groups. *See* El desplazamiento forzado en el caso de las Comunidades Indígenas, XIV Informe de la Comisión de Seguimiento (12 Mar. 2009), at 9.

quately protect indigenous persons from displacement. In a 2009 decision, the Court stated the following:

> [Displacement of indigenous persons] is an emergency that is as serious as it is invisible …. While numerous groups are attacked, displaced and scattered through the national territory by the armed actors … the State and society continue to talk of their multicultural character, of its ethnic riches and distinct aspects of the national indigenous cultures. This contradiction between the reality and the generalized representation of this reality has surprised the Constitutional Court, not only for it inherent cruelty, but also by revealing an attitude of indifference to the horror the indigenous communities have had to go through ….[42]

Armed groups focus on indigenous communities for two reasons: first, groups such as the FARC operate in many of the areas where indigenous communities live; second, they perceive that indigenous communities are particularly vulnerable. As such, the armed groups use specific methods to target them, including occupation of schools and sacred places. Many displaced indigenous persons attribute their displacement to direct threats by armed groups.[43]

3. Limitations of the Current Structures

The inability of the Colombian government to effectively prevent forcible displacement and the power wielded by the armed actors make it unlikely that a purely domestic solution is possible.[44] At the same time, the international community stands at a loss as to what steps to take to lessen the human suffering

42 *See* Auto-004, Colombian Constitutional Court (26 Jan. 2009). The following is the original Spanish text: "[el desplazamiento de las personas indígenas] es una emergencia tan grave como invisible … [m]ientras que numerosos grupos indígenas son atacados, desplazados y desintegrados en todo el territorio nacional por los actores armados … el Estado y la sociedad colombianos continúan preciándose de su carácter multicultural, de sus riquezas étnicas y de distintos aspectos de las culturas indígenas nacionales. Esta contradicción entre la realidad y la representación generalizada de dicha realidad ha sorprendido a la Corte Constitucional, no sólo por su crueldad inherente, sino por revelar una actitud de indiferencia generalizada ante el horror que las comunidades indígenas del país han debido soportar en los últimos años – indiferencia que en sí misma es un menosprecio de los postulados constitucionales básicos que nos rigen como Estado Social de Derecho fundado en el respeto de la diversidad étnica y cultural."

43 *See id.* at p. 13 (noting that 42.5 % of indigenous displaced persons attribute their displacement to direct threats).

44 *See* Manuela Trindade Viana, *International Cooperation and Internal Displacement in Colombia: Facing the Challenges of the Largest Humanitarian Crisis in South America*, 10 SUR INT'L J. ON HUM RTS. 133 (2009) (describing the Colombian government's institutional inability to effectively combat or prevent internal displacement).

of civilians caught in the cross-fire. To date, the Security Council has never addressed the situation of internal displacement in Colombia, and the prosecutor of the International Criminal Court has refrained from officially opening an investigation into human rights violations in Colombia. A survey of the international legal framework as applied to the situation in Colombia is instructive in beginning to identify the structural weaknesses in the current legal regime governing forcible displacement.

a. International, Regional, and Domestic Law

There are a myriad of obligations relating to forcible displacement, discussed in chapter three, and Colombia has undertaken nearly all of these obligations, in addition to being subject to the Inter-American Court of Human Rights. Colombia is a party to all of the Geneva Conventions and their Additional Protocols, which prohibit the targeting and forced displacement of civilians during an armed conflict. The Geneva Conventions also mandate that states parties undertake to prosecute those responsible for gross violations of the Conventions.[45] Due to the internal nature of the conflict, Colombia is bound by its obligations pursuant to Additional Protocol II of the Geneva Conventions, which provides that "[c]ivilians shall not be compelled to leave their own territory for reasons connected with the conflict."[46] Moreover, Protocol II also prohibits targeting the civilian population for attack in addition to "[a]cts or threats of violence the primary purpose of which is to spread terror among the civilian popu-

45 *See* Geneva Convention [No. I] for the Amelioration of the Condition of the Wounded and Sick in Armed Forces in the Field, art. 49, 12 Aug. 1949, 6 UST 3114, 75 UNTS 31; Geneva Convention [No. II] for the Amelioration of the Condition of Wounded, Sick and Shipwrecked Members of Armed Forces at Sea, art. 50, 12 Aug. 1949, 6 UST 3217, 75 UNTS 85; Geneva Convention [No. III] Relative to the Treatment of Prisoners of War, art. 129, 12 Aug. 1949, 6 UST 3316, 75 UNTS 135; Geneva Convention [No. IV] Relative to the Protection of Civilian Persons in Time of War, art. 146, 12 Aug. 1949, 6 UST 3516, 75 UNTS 287 [hereinafter Geneva Conventions] ("The High Contracting Parties undertake to enact any legislation necessary to provide effective penal sanctions for persons committing, or ordering to be committed, any of the grave breaches of the present Convention .... Each High Contracting Party shall be under the obligation to search for persons alleged to have committed, or to have ordered to be committed, such grave breaches, and shall bring such persons, regardless of their nationality, before its own courts ....").

46 Protocol Additional to the Geneva Conventions of 12 August 1949, and relating to the Protection of Victims of Non-International Armed Conflicts (Protocol II), 8 June 1977, art. 17(2) [hereinafter Additional Protocol II to the Geneva Conventions]. Colombia acceded to Additional Protocol II on 14 August 1995.

lation."[47] Significantly, all of Colombia's armed actors are bound by Common Article 3, which prohibits, *inter alia*, violence and outrages to personal dignity.[48]

In addition to its obligations under international humanitarian law, Colombia is bound by its obligations under human rights conventions to which it is a party. In relation to the rights that are derogable, Colombia has an obligation to follow specific procedures if it chooses to temporarily suspend these rights.[49] Further, Colombia is a member of the Organisation of American States (OAS), the primary regional organisation of the Americas. Colombia has ratified all of the human rights instruments propounded by the OAS, including the American Convention on Human Rights, which creates the Inter-American Court of Human Rights and the Inter-American Commission on Human Rights.[50] As a member of the OAS, Colombia is bound by the decisions of the Inter-American Court.

---

47 Additional Protocol II to the Geneva Conventions, art. 13(2).

48 *See* Common Article III to the Geneva Conventions. Common Article III is unique in that it creates legal obligations for *all* parties to an internal armed conflict, and not just the government. *See* Colombia: the ICRC continues to support those affected by conflict, Operational Update, International Committee of the Red Cross (5 May 2005), http://www.icrc.org/eng/resources/documents/report/colombia-report-050505.htm (noting that "the provisions contained in common Article 3 are considered to be customary law and minimum standards to be implemented and respected by armed forces and organized armed groups alike"). Additional Protocol II to the Geneva Conventions and Common Article III both apply *automatically* where there is a *de facto* situation of internal armed conflict. *See* ICRC Commentary, Additional Protocol II to the Geneva Conventions, Part I: Scope of this protocol.

49 Colombia has ratified all of the major human rights instruments and their optional protocols. International Covenant on Economic, Social and Cultural Rights, ratified 29 Oct. 1969; ICCPR, ratified 29 October 1969; Optional Protocol to the International Covenant on Civil and Political Rights, ratified 29 October 1969; Convention on the Elimination of All Forms of Discrimination Against Women, ratified 19 Jan. 1982; Optional Protocol to the Convention on the Elimination of Discrimination Against Women, ratified 23 Jan. 2007; Protocol to Prevent, Suppress and Punish Trafficking in Persons, Especially Women and Children, ratified 4 Aug. 2004; Convention Against Torture and Other Cruel, Inhuman or Degrading Treatment or Punishment, ratified 8 Dec. 1987; Convention on the Elimination of All Forms of Racial Discrimination, ratified 2 Sept. 1981; Convention on the Rights of the Child, ratified 28 Jan. 1991; Optional Protocol to the Convention on the Rights of the Child on the Involvement of Children in Armed Conflicts, ratified 25 May 2005; Genocide Convention, ratified 27 Oct. 1959. The only treaty Colombia has not signed onto is the Optional Protocol to the Convention Against Torture and Other Cruel, Inhuman or Degrading Treatment or Punishment.

50 *See* American Convention on Human Rights, Art. 33, O.A.S. Treaty Series No. 36, 1144 U.N.T.S. 123, *entered into force* 18 July 1978. The American Convention on Human Rights was ratified by Colombia on 28 May 1973. The Court has the power to examine domestic legal provisions in the light of other international human rights obligations, such as those in CEDAW.

Although Colombia has ratified many pertinent international and regional human rights instruments, the UN Special Rapporteur on Forced Displacement has observed that "[a] clear gap [exists] between the policies decided in the capital Bogotá and their often ineffective implementation at the departmental and municipal levels."[51] For example, Colombia's Law 387 of 1997 is the cornerstone piece of legislation that establishes the framework for prevention of internal displacement and protection of IDPs. It calls for the creation of a "National Plan on Comprehensive Assistance to IDPs," which was established in 1998. Law 387 provides a fairly broad definition of an IDP:

> A displaced person is any person who has been forced to migrate within the national territory, abandoning his place of residence or customary economic activities, because his life, physical integrity, personal freedom or safety have been violated or are directly threatened as a result of any of the following situations: internal armed conflict, civil tension and disturbances, general violence, massive Human Rights violations, infringement of International Humanitarian Law, or other circumstances arising from the foregoing situations that drastically disturb or could drastically disturb the public order.[52]

Law 387 has been supplemented by additional legislation and Presidential decrees aimed at providing greater protection to IDPs and putting "early warning" systems in place in cases where displacement is anticipated.[53] Decree No. 250 of 7 February 2005 calls for the establishment of prevention plans at the municipal levels and requires a greater protective presence of the armed forces in conflict-ridden areas.[54] All of the laws call for provision of emergency humanitarian assistance, access to healthcare, and registration of IDPs.

In theory, Colombia's international obligations relating to forcible displacement and its implementing domestic legislation should lessen, if not prevent, instances of forcible displacement. In practice, it is not clear that the international legal regime has had a substantial effect in reducing instances of forci-

51 Kälin Report on IDPs, ¶ 27.

52 Law 387 of 1997, http://www.brookings.edu/~/media/Files/Projects/IDP/Laws%20and%20Policies/Colombia/Colombia_Law387_1997_Eng.pdf.

53 *See, e.g.*, Decree 2569 of 2000, http://www.brookings.edu/~/media/Files/Projects/IDP/Laws%20and%20Policies/Colombia/Colombia_Decreto2569_2000.pdf (in Spanish); Agreement No. 244 of 2003 Concerning the Subsidized Regime of the General System of Social Security in Health, http://www.brookings.edu/~/media/Files/Projects/IDP/Laws%20and%20Policies/Colombia/Colombia_AcuerdoNo244_2003.pdf; Decree No. 250 of February 7, 2005 Concerning the Adoption of a National Plan for Comprehensive Attention to the Population Displaced by Violence, http://www.brookings.edu/~/media/Files/Projects/IDP/Laws%20and%20Policies/Colombia/Colombia_DecretoNo250_2005.pdf (in Spanish).

54 *See id.*

ble displacement or in apprehending perpetrators of forcible displacement. Displacement continues to be employed as a war tactic, and armed groups are known to use civilians as human shields and to target civilian objects, both of which are violations of the Geneva Conventions.[55] Headquarters and posts are placed in the midst of civilian settlements, defying basic tenets of humanitarian law, which is intended to protect civilians to the extent possible during war.[56] The number of IDPs continues to grow, and the Constitutional Court has on at least two occasions, in 2004 and again in 2009,[57] pronounced that the government's repeated failure to provide displaced persons with adequate protection and care constitutes an "unconstitutional state of affairs".[58] The Constitutional Court has

55 *See, e.g.*, Protocol Additional to the Geneva Conventions, art. 51 ("The presence or movements of the civilian population or individual civilians shall not be used to render certain points or areas immune from military operations, in particular in attempts to shield military objectives from attacks or to shield, favour or impede military operations. The Parties to the conflict shall not direct the movement of the civilian population or individual civilians in order to attempt to shield military objectives from attacks or to shield military operations.").

56 For example, one armed group set up headquarters directly in the middle of a village, next to a primary school, and installed posts next to playgrounds and churches. *See* Kälin Report on IDPs, ¶ 18.

57 In a 2009 Decision, the Court stated that, "despite the achievements of certain rights, [the Government] has not yet succeeded in achieving a comprehensive and systematic progress in the enjoyment of all rights of the displaced population." (Original text: "a pesar de los logros alcanzados en algunos derechos, aún no se ha logrado un avance sistemático e integral en el goce efectivo de todos los derechos de la población desplazada."). *See* A-008 of 2009, http://www.corteconstitucional.gov.co/RELATORIA/Autos/2009/A008-09.htm. The Representative of the Secretary-General on the Human Rights of Internally Displaced Persons exhibited a similar sentiment with regard to the Colombian government's failure to adequately implement its policies on displaced persons, noting that he was "perturbed by the clear gap between the policies decided in the capital Bogotá and their often ineffective implementation at the departmental and municipal levels." *See* Kälin Report on IDPs, ¶ 27.

58 The Court stated, "[La Corte] concluye que por las condiciones de vulnerabilidad extrema en las cuales se encuentra la población desplazada, así como por la omisión reiterada de brindarle una protección oportuna y efectiva por parte de las distintas autoridades encargadas de su atención, se han violado tanto a los actores en el presente proceso, como a la población desplazada en general, sus derechos a una vida digna, a la integridad personal, a la igualdad, de petición, al trabajo, a la salud, a la seguridad social, a la educación, al mínimo vital y a la protección especial debida a las personas de la tercera edad, a la mujer cabeza de familia y a los niños. Esta violación ha venido ocurriendo de manera masiva, prolongada y reiterada y no es imputable a una única autoridad, sino que obedece a un problema estructural que afecta a toda la política de atención diseñada por el Estado, y a sus distintos componentes, en razón a la insuficiencia de recursos destinados a financiar dicha política y a la precaria capacidad institucional para implementarla. Tal situación constituye un *estado de cosas inconstitucional*." T-025, http://www.corteconstitucional.gov.co/relatoria/2004/T-025-04.htm.

also directed other branches of the Colombian government to confront the plight of the displaced, but with little apparent success.

b. The Inter-American Court of Human Rights

The Inter-American Court of Human Rights has encountered difficulties in ensuring that Colombia complies with its obligations to prevent and punish forcible displacement, as two important cases demonstrate. In neither case did the Colombian government fully investigate or prosecute those responsible for mass forced displacements, even subsequent to the Inter-American Court's explicit direction to Colombia to do so.

The Inter-American Court first considered forced displacement in Colombia in the Case of the "Mapiripán Massacre" v. Colombia in 2005. The case was particularly significant because it revealed the extent of the Colombian government's participation in war crimes, including forced displacement. The case concerned a massacre and forcible displacement carried out by more than one hundred paramilitaries of the AUC in 1997. The paramilitaries, in cooperation with the Colombian armed forces, entered the town of Mapiripán and remained for five days. During these five days, they terrorised the town and tortured, dismembered, and beheaded at least forty-nine people.[59]

The town of Mapiripán was an important drug center for the FARC guerilla group, and the AUC had launched a counter-operation to weaken the FARC's control of the area.[60] The attack was planned far in advance and with the assistance of the Colombian military, which outfitted the AUC, provided them with ammunition, and transported them from the airport to the town of Mapiripán.[61]

The events in Mapiripán caused the displacement of dozens of families, both within Mapiripán and in the surrounding area.[62] Of the 3,000 individuals that lived in the town, the majority fled. Although the Mapiripán case came before the Inter-American Court eight years after the massacre, the greater part of displaced persons remained displaced and expressed terror at the thought of returning to Mapiripán. Their fear was largely in response to the possibility of reprisals, as the vast majority of individuals responsible for the massacre were never investigated or prosecuted.[63]

59 Case of Mapiripán v. Colombia, Inter-American Court of Human Rights, ¶¶ 96.30-50.

60 *Id.* ¶¶ 96.25-28 ("In early 1997 the AUC held several meetings to organize their entry into the area of Mapiripán and the inhabitants of said municipality were declared to be military objectives by [a] paramilitary leader ..., because, 'according to him, a consolidated front of the insurgency was operating there, with absolute control of a territory appropriate for a complete cycle of drug trafficking, planting, processing, and trading.'").

61 *Id.* ¶¶ 96.25-28.

62 *Id.* ¶ 96.63.

63 *Id.* ¶¶ 165-89.

The Court held the Colombian government partially responsible for the crimes committed at Mapiripán due to its active participation in the events surrounding the massacre and its failure to protect the citizens.[64] It also found that the mass displacement constituted a violation of Colombia's obligations under Article 22 of the Inter-American Convention on Human Rights, encompassing the right to freedom of movement and the right to choose one's place of residence.[65]

A year later, the Inter-American Court heard the Ituango Case. The case involved massacres and the resulting forced displacement of dozens of individuals in two villages, La Granja and El Aro, both located in the Ituango municipality. Similar to the Mapiripán case, the massacres were carried out by paramilitaries, who accused the villagers of cooperation with the guerillas. The paramilitaries summarily executed dozens of people, destroyed dozens of houses by setting fire to them, and stole much of the livestock of the village inhabitants. Colombia's military police stood by passively while the events transpired.[66]

The Court stated that setting fire to the houses of the inhabitants was meant to "spread terror and cause … displacement, so as to gain territory in the fight against the guerilla in Colombia."[67] It found that the paramilitaries were responsible for the displacement of over one thousand people, many of whom were the owners of the razed homes.[68] Accordingly, the Court held that Colombia had again violated Article 22 of the Inter-American Convention on Human Rights. The Court also found that the government had failed to adequately prosecute and investigate those responsible for the crimes in Ituango.[69] First, the government did not open an official investigation into the massacre until three years after it

64 *Id.* ¶ 123 ("The Court has reached the conclusion that the international responsibility of the State has resulted from a set of actions and omissions by State agents and private citizens, conducted in a coordinated, parallel or linked manner, with the aim of carrying out the massacre. First of all, said agents collaborated directly or indirectly with the acts committed by the paramilitary, and secondly, they were remiss regarding their duty to protect the victims against said acts and regarding their duty to effectively investigate them, all of which has led to violations of human rights embodied in the Convention.").

65 *Id.* ¶ 189.

66 Case of Ituango, ¶¶ 126.26-40.

67 *Id.* ¶ 182.

68 *Id.* ¶¶ 216-18 ("It has been proved that the massacres that occurred in La Granja and El Aro, and also the damage suffered as a result of the theft of the livestock and the destruction of the property of the inhabitants, added to the fear of similar events recurring, the intimidation, and the threats received by some of them from the paramilitary group, led to the internal displacement of many families."). *Id.* ¶ 225.

69 The Court stated, "In the El Aro case, the authorities' delay and lack of diligence in the proceedings is evident, because more than eight years have elapsed since these events, in which dozens of civilians took part with the acquiescence and tolerance of the law enforcement bodies, and most of those responsible have not yet been investigated in any criminal proceedings. The Court observes that an operation of this

took place.[70] Second, of the more than twenty persons identified as the perpetrators in the La Granja massacre, only four were convicted, and only two of the four were imprisoned.[71] Likewise, of the thirty persons identified as perpetrators in the El Aro massacre, only seven were investigated and only three were convicted, one of whom was imprisoned.[72] The arrest warrants of the other two, both well-known paramilitary leaders responsible for numerous war crimes, were never executed.[73]

As of today, most of those responsible for the massacres and forced displacements of Mapiripán and El Aro/La Granja have not been apprehended. The principal planner of all of the massacres and a top paramilitary leader, admitted—as part of his amnesty agreement under the Justice and Peace Law—to planning the massacres with the help of the Colombian military; yet, the Colombian government agreed to his extradition to the United States for drug trafficking charges, foregoing the chance to prosecute him for crimes committed against Colombia's own people.[74] This move was denounced by the Inter-American Court, which called his extradition an impediment to the investigation and prosecution of grave crimes.[75]

As is the case with most human rights mechanisms, compliance in the Inter-American system rests generally on a state's good will to fulfill its treaty obligations. There is only one provision relating to enforcement of the Inter-American Court's decisions, which permits the Court to refer incidents of non-compliance to the General Assembly of the OAS.[76] It is not clear what the General Assembly is meant to do when alerted of non-compliance. Under the current system, the prosecution of Colombian nationals for forcible displacement could remain at a permanent standstill.

---

size could not have gone unnoticed by the authorities in the zone, and this has been acknowledged by the State in the proceedings before the Court." *Id.* ¶ 315.

70 Case of Ituango, ¶¶ 302-09.

71 *Id.*

72 *Id.* ¶¶ 310-25.

73 *Id.*

74 Inter-American Court of Human Rights, Press Release, *IACHR Expresses Concern About Extradition of Colombian Paramilitaries* (14 May 2008), https://www.cidh.oas.org/Comunicados/English/2008/21.08eng.htm.

75 *Id.*

76 American Convention on Human Rights, art. 65, O.A.S.Treaty Series No. 36, 1144 U.N.T.S. 123, *entered into force* 18 July 1978, *reprinted in* Basic Documents Pertaining to Human Rights in the Inter-American System, OEA/Ser.L.V/II.82 doc.6 rev.1 at 25 (1992) ("To each regular session of the General Assembly of the Organization of American States the Court shall submit, for the Assembly's consideration, a report on its work during the previous year. It shall specify, in particular, the cases in which a state has not complied with its judgments, making any pertinent recommendations.").

c. *The International Criminal Court*

Although the Inter-American Court of Human Rights has not yet been effective in protecting individuals subjected to forcible displacement, the possibility of supranational adjudication of the crimes of Colombian nationals remains a possibility, if a distant one.[77] Colombia is a party to the ICC,[78] although the ICC only officially obtained jurisdiction in August 2009 because of Colombia's exercise of the right of reservation under the Rome Statute, which allows ratifying parties to defer the ICC's exercise of jurisdiction for a period of seven years following ratification.[79]

The ICC can obtain jurisdiction over a case in three ways: the Security Council may refer a "situation" using its powers under Chapter VII of the UN Charter; a situation may be referred to the Prosecutor by a country that has ratified the Rome Statute; or the Prosecutor may initiate an investigation, but may only pursue it with the approval of the Pre-Trial Chamber.[80] It is not likely that the Colombian government would self-refer a case to the ICC, given that many of its own government officials are implicated in the crimes that have been committed in the context of the conflict. In addition, the Security Council has shown no indication of referring Colombia's case to the ICC. This leaves one option for obtaining jurisdiction over the crimes committed: the prosecutor must initiate an investigation. Due to Colombia's exercise of the right of reservation, the ICC Prosecutor only recently acquired the authority to investigate Colombia. However, the principal of complementarity will have to be respected in any exercise by the ICC of its jurisdiction over the crimes in Colombia.

As mentioned in chapter four, the principle of complementarity prevents the ICC from taking on a case unless the country that has jurisdiction over the crime at issue is "unwilling or unable genuinely to carry out the investigation or prosecution."[81] The Colombian government has adhered steadfastly to this principal and has on numerous occasions reminded the ICC of the principle of comple-

77 When the ICC first obtained jurisdiction over war crimes and crimes against humanity in Colombia in 2009, a number of human rights activists were hopeful that the ICC would prosecute individuals responsible for such crimes, and the Colombian newspapers reported widely on the possibility of the ICC's prosecution of Colombian nationals. *See CPI pone en aviso a grupos subversives y al propio Gobierno*, El Espectador, 30 Oct. 2009, http://elespectador.com/noticias/judicial/articulo169502-cpi-pone-aviso-grupos-subversivos-y-al-propio-gobierno.

78 Colombia signed the Rome Statute on 10 December 1998 and ratified it on 5 August 2002. International Criminal Court, Colombia, http://www.icc-cpi.int/Menus/ASP/states+parties/Latin+American+and+Caribbean+States/Colombia.htm.

79 Article 124 of the Rome Statute allows States Parties to decline to confer jurisdiction to the International Criminal Court for a period of seven years after ratification. *See* Rome Statute, art. 24.

80 *See id.* art. 13.

81 *Id.* art. 17(1)(a).

mentarity.[82] Recently, the Colombian delegation to the ICC made great efforts to demonstrate that Colombia is neither "unwilling" nor "unable" to prosecute its nationals who have committed war crimes, stating:

> [Colombia] renew[s] [its] determination to continue in the common effort to eradicate impunity, and in order to achieve that end … [has] made tremendous efforts … in the implementation of the Justice and Peace Law that has allowed the demobilization and prosecution of both the members of self-defense groups, as well as of guerilla groups. To that end, efforts have also been made in the institutional strengthening of the General Prosecutor and of the judicial apparatus.[83]

However, it is not clear whether these efforts amount to Colombia being willing and able to prosecute its nationals as required by the principle of complementarity. Colombia's former President attempted to promote efforts to prosecute forcible displacement, but was unsuccessful. His first term began in 2002, at which time he declared his intention to confront the situation of violence by cracking down on the illegal armed groups that controlled much of Colombia's territory.[84] He immediately declared a state of emergency[85] and passed several laws purporting to demobilise[86] paramilitary groups and to end impunity.[87] To carry out

82 International Criminal Court, Assembly of Sates [sic] Parties, Sixth Session, Statement by the Permanent Representative of Colombia to the UN (3 Dec. 2007), http://wwwold.icc-cpi.int/library/asp/Colombia_gd_en_statement_6th_asp.pdf.

83 *Id.* The Colombian Ambassador to the ICC also stated, "The ICC has no reason to investigate war crimes in Colombia as the country's courts are already doing so." *See ICC Warns Colombian Illegal Armed Groups and State It Will Prosecute*, Colombia Reports (30 Oct. 2009), http://colombiareports.com/colombia-news/news/6664-icc-warns-colombian-illegal-armed-groups-and-state-it-will-prosecute.html.

84 *Colombia's Rightists Back Talks With Marxists*, The New York Times (31 May 2002), http://www.nytimes.com/2002/05/31/world/colombia-s-rightists-back-talks-with-marxists.html?pagewanted=1 (discussing the former President's success in the 2002 elections).

85 *President Declares State of Emergency*, Los Angeles Times (12 Aug. 2002), \http://articles.latimes.com/2002/aug/12/world/fg-briefs12.2.

86 Demobilisation has been defined as "the process in which armed organizations (which may consist of government or opposition forces, or simply armed factions) decrease in size or are dismantled as one component of a broad transformation from a state of war to a state of peace that may involve the concentration, quartering, disarming, management, and licensing of former combatants with the incentive of compensation or other assistance to reenter civilian life." Lisa J. Laplante & Kimberly Theidon, *Transitional Justice in Times of Conflict: Colombia's Ley de Justicia y Paz*, 28 Mich. J. Int'l L. 49, 55 (2006).

87 The policy is embodied in a number of laws, beginning with Law 782 of 2002, which was followed by Decree 128 of 2003, Decree 4760 of 2005, and ending with Law 975 of 2005, better known as the "Justice and Peace Law." *See* Internal Displacement

the tasks of demobilisation, investigation, and prosecution, the government created a "Justice and Peace" unit in the national prosecutor's office, in addition to Justice and Peace Tribunals and a National Commission on Reconciliation and Reparation. Each of these entities was tasked with investigating the participation of those who come forward to confess crimes committed in the context of the armed conflict.[88]

Despite the government's efforts to prosecute individuals for war crimes, including forcible displacement, they have been criticised by Colombia's own Constitutional Court[89] and the Inter-American Commission on Human Rights.[90] The Special Representative on Displaced Persons, Walter Kälin, has noted that, rather than prosecuting the crime of forcible displacement independently, prosecutors thus far have merely considered forcible displacement as an accessory fact or "a simple consequence" of armed conflict.[91]

To date, there has not been a conviction under Law 975.[92] A new Unit of Displacement and Forced Disappearances was recently created within the office of the prosecutor in Colombia, but it remains to be seen whether this unit will be able to effectively investigate the thousands of cases currently under its super-

---

Monitoring Centre, *Colombia: Government "Peace Process" Cements Injustice for IDPs* (30 June 2006), http://www.internal-displacement.org/8025708F004BE3B1/(httpInfoFiles)/2F1618E6C169F2EBC125719C002F6421/$file/Special%20Country%20Report%20Colombia.pdf, at 14. The Justice and Peace Law is meant to regulate judicial investigation, procedures, and prosecution of members of illegal armed groups that participated in criminal acts. In return for an ex-combatant's agreement to demobilise, the law provides an "alternative sentence" that is far less stringent than Colombia's ordinary penal laws. *See* Lisa J. Laplante & Kimberly Theidon, *Transitional Justice in Times of Conflict: Colombia's Ley de Justicia y Paz*, 28 Mich. J. Int'l L. 49, 80 (2006).

88 *See* Inter-American Commission on Human Rights, *Statement by the Inter-American Commission on Human Rights on the Application and Scope of the Justice and Peace Law in Colombia* (1 Aug. 2006), https://www.cidh.oas.org/Pronunciamiento.8.1.06ENG.pdf.

89 In 2006, Colombia's Constitutional Court declared parts of the law to be unconstitutional. *See* Constitutional Court Decision C-370/06 (Dossier D-6032) (2006).

90 *See* Inter-American Commission on Human Rights, Follow-up on the Demobilization Process of the AUC in Colombia, Digest of Published Documents, at 45 (2004-2007), http://www.cidh.oas.org/pdf%20files/Colombia-Demobilization-AUC%202008.pdf ("The IACHR also observes that the institutional mechanisms created by the law to administer justice—in particular the Prosecutor's National Unit for Justice and Peace, composed of 20 prosecutors—lacks the strength necessary to undertake effectively the task of prosecuting thousands of massacres, selective executions, forced disappearances, kidnappings, tortures, forced displacement and usurpation of lands, amongst other crimes, committed by several thousand demobilized individuals during the many years that paramilitary structures have operated in Colombia.").

91 Kälin Report on IDPs, ¶ 81.

92 *See* 2010 High Commissioner for Human Rights Report, ¶ 81.

vision.[93] Meanwhile, there are numerous reports that demobilised persons are being allocated land that was seized illegally from displaced persons[94] and that the armed groups and military are "increasingly encroach[ing] upon" the lands of indigenous groups and Afro-Colombians.[95]

Despite an investigatory mission in August 2008 to Colombia, the ICC Prosecutor[96] thus far has only asserted that his office is engaged in a "preliminary" investigation of Colombia.[97] Since August 2008, the ICC Prosecutor has not taken further steps to open an official investigation. It must be acknowledged that, due to the principle of complementarity, which stems in part from the desire of states to guard their sovereignty, the ICC faces an uphill battle in obtaining jurisdiction over the crimes of forcible displacement in Colombia, unless there is a self-referral or the Security Council takes action.

4. Departure-Oriented Versus Arrival-Oriented Displacement

One distinction that can be used to classify displacements is based upon the mental state, or intention, of the perpetrators of the displacement. For example, the aim of the perpetrators may be to simply remove a group of people from a location, while not caring in particular about their ultimate destination: the salient point is to get rid of them in order to steal their land, to get rid of a group of people considered to be undesirable, or simply to exact revenge upon the group. In each case, however, the destination is not of importance, but rather the eventual absence of the group of people whence they were before. This type of displacement can be referred to as a "departure-oriented displacement". Another type of displacement is focused upon the intent of the perpetrators to move a group of people to a particular location. In these circumstances, it is not the origin of the displaced persons that characterises the crime, but rather the place whither they are moved. People can be rounded up from a variety of locations

93 *Faltan recursos y funcionarios*, El Espectador (10 Jan. 2011).

94 Kälin stated that he was "disturbed by reports that many of the demobilized were being allocated lands that had been illegally seized from displaced persons." Kälin Report on IDPs, ¶ 57.

95 Kälin Report on IDPs, ¶ 70 ("In the case of the indigenous groups and Afro-Colombian communities, the Representative was disturbed by the fact that it would seem that their lands are being increasingly encroached upon by the various armed groups or the military, as was the case in Curvaradó or in San José del Guaviare ….").

96 The Prosecutor led an investigatory mission in August 2008. *See* Fourteenth Diplomatic Briefing of the International Criminal Court (discussing "other potential situations" in need of the ICC's attention).

97 *See* 17th Diplomatic Briefing, Statement by Luis Moreno – Ocampo, Prosecutor of the International Criminal Court (4 Nov. 2009), http://www.icc-cpi.int/menus/icc/reports%20on%20activities/court%20reports%20and%20statements/seventeenth%20diplomatic%20briefing.

and transferred then to a particular place for a particular purpose. This type of displacement can be referred to as an "arrival-oriented displacement".

In Colombia, forcible displacement is primarily departure-oriented. The armed actors in Colombia seek to dispossess individuals of their land. The ultimate goal of the actors is to appropriate land, and the dispossession of individuals from their land is the method by which appropriation is carried out. The final destination of the displaced is of no importance to the actors in Colombia's armed conflict. In comparison, during the slave trade which was conducted from the early 1500s to 1870, approximately 12 million human beings were displaced from Africa to the Americas, with approximately two million dying during the dreaded "Middle Passage". This is an example of arrival-oriented displacement, at least from the perspective of the European slave-traders. The goal was to sell the slaves to plantations in the Caribbean and North and South America. Regardless of whether the perpetrators of forcible displacement are engaging in departure- or arrival-oriented displacement, the result is the same: the victims are forced from their homes.

Since its inception, the field of international criminal law has struggled with defining the crime of forcible displacement. But the Colombian situation, and other contemporary situations of forcible displacement, can defy classification. At the same time, however, the crime of forcible displacement must be broken down into elements in order to be prosecuted. Ultimately, the challenge is to fashion the legal elements of the crime of forcible dispalcement in a sufficiently flexible manner so that these elements can faithfully and rationally be applied to a variety of real-world situations, and thus not hinder the development of either the law or the successful prosecution of perpetrators.

***

The Colombian situation is a dramatic illustration of the deficiencies of the current systems in place for the prevention and prosecution of forcible displacement. The conflict in Colombia is paradigmatic of the complex and painful realities of modern warfare. It demonstrates the conundrum with which the international community finds itself faced when attempting to confront a crime that poses enormous conceptual and practical challenges to prosecutors and to the current international legal framework.

An assessment of the Colombian government's willingness and ability to prevent forcible displacement and prosecute responsible parties is not a straightforward matter; it may be that the Colombian government is simply unable to gain control over the conflict, which impedes it from preventing forcible displacement or effectively prosecuting perpetrators of forcible displacement. The High Commissioner for Human Rights summed up the situation succinctly when she stated:

> The scope of organized violence committed by these groups, their substantial economic power, capacity to corrupt authorities and State institutions, links

> with local authorities and local networks of influence, their impact on social actors and the alarming levels of violence against civilians make them a daunting challenge to the rule of law.[98]

In such a case, where the forcible displacement of millions of people cannot be prevented or lessened by national authorities, what is to be done? If nothing else, the Colombian experience provides some possible lessons. First, without enforcement mechanisms, the current international legal system is unable to prevent displacement or to fulfill the needs of the displaced. Under the *status quo*, violations of the current human rights treaties and international humanitarian law treaties generally do not lead to consequences for the offending states, unless other states—for example, through the UN Security Council—consider that a situation has become so urgent that it may warrant an exception to the international legal order's default position that sovereignty is to be respected. Unlike in the case of genocide, where the ability of other states to call on organs of the United Nations to intervene is explicitly identified in the Genocide Convention, there is no corresponding legal instrument that identifies the ability of states to call for intervention in cases of forcible displacement.

Courts such as the Inter-American Court have attempted to hold states accountable for human rights atrocities, including forcible displacement, but they are only part of the solution. Without a mechanism to enforce the judgement, states like Colombia can disregard those parts with which it does not wish to comply or with which it cannot comply. Regional human rights courts may not be the best placed to supervise or monitor the prosecution of those responsible for atrocities. This is certainly indicated by the Mapiripán and El Aro/La Granja cases, where the Colombian government did not comply with the Court's direction to prosecute the individuals responsible for the human rights violations at issue. Because the Inter-American human rights system is not structurally set up to assist with the domestic prosecution of perpetrators of human rights abuses or even to monitor prosecution in-depth, the Inter-American Court had little recourse in response to Colombia's lack of action.

The second lesson to be gleaned from the Colombia experience is that the ICC, while integral to the current international criminal law system, faces challenges in obtaining jurisdiction over individuals and in prosecuting those individuals, which cannot be overcome without assistance from other instruments that reinforce its jurisdiction. As it stands now, the ICC may never obtain jurisdiction over a case such as that of Colombia, where admittedly inadequate domestic attempts to prosecute those responsible for human rights atrocities have been sufficient to block the Court's jurisdiction. Moreover, the ICC does not have the resources—or perhaps even the institutional competence—to effectively monitor the many situations of forcible displacement that take place across the globe today. The ICC Prosecutor thus far has only been able to visit Colombia twice and even then has not been focused solely upon forcible displacement. It

98 2010 High Commissioner for Human Rights Report, ¶ 64.

would behoove the international community to have a body monitoring forcible displacement that could at the very least provide recommendations to the ICC regarding specific individuals and situations that bear closer consideration by the Prosecutor. A striking example was accomplished by the UN Security Council itself in February 2011, when it identified in a sanctions resolution specific persons from the Libyan regime whose assets were to be frozen and referred the Libyan situation to the ICC.[99]

The final lesson of the Colombia experience is that the formalistic construction of the crime of forcible displacement must be updated and modernised so that a consistent definition of the crime applies to all domestic and international fora and reflects the realities of contemporary warfare. A modern construction of the crime of forcible displacement must incorporate flexible standards and take into account forms of displacement that do not necessarily fit into the paradigmatic example of forced displacement, whereby displacement is part of an organised campaign, carried out pursuant to orders of a perpetrator. As seen in the Colombian context, the factual opposite of this example, whereby displacement is carried out "drop by drop" and by way of generalised violence, can be equally harmful to victims of displacement. And perhaps the most significant lesson to be learned from Colombia is that intra-state transfers must not take a "back seat" to cross-border transfers; both intra-state and cross-border transfers must be subject to the same criminal elements, as is argued in chapter four. It is clear from the displacement in Colombia that intra-state transfers can have consequences for the victims that are equally as disastrous as transfers across an international boundary, and thus the perpetrator of an intra-border transfer is no less culpable than the perpetrator of a cross-border transfer. The international community must therefore begin the process of reconceptualising and unifying the crime of forcible displacement in order encourage its effective prevention and prosecution.

The situation in Colombia has been so bad for so long that the international community may have lost its will to take meaningful, remedial action. The situation in Colombia approaches levels that may even be described as chronic, institutionalised forcible displacement. Thus far, the domestic, regional, and international legal instruments in place have not been implemented in a manner that prevents the continued displacement. The development of a new international legal instrument affirmatively prohibiting the crime could be a means by which to refocus the attention of the international community upon the situation in Colombia—and elsewhere—so that states and civil society can rededicate themselves to the prevention of the forcible displacement of innocent people from their homes.

99 Security Council Resolution 1970, S/RES/1970 (26 Feb. 2011).

Chapter Eight

A Proposal for an International Convention to Prevent and Punish Forcible Displacement

The greater danger for most of us is not that our aim is too high and we miss it, but that it is too low and we reach it.[1]

Throughout the chapters of this book, we have endeavoured to identify deficiencies in the current international regime governing forcible displacement.

First, we have discussed the limitations of the classifications and legal distinctions that have emerged in the various streams of law addressing forcible displacement. These limitations are particularly evident in the international conventions that address forcible displacement and in jurisprudence emerging from the international tribunals, where judicially constructed legal doctrines have been applied to highly-complex and variable scenarios of forcible displacement. A stark example of this is found in the ICTY's distinction between intra- and extra-border transfers, which would not square well with the current situation in Colombia. The ICTY is not the only entity to have made this distinction, but the ideological divide between internally and externally displaced persons is one that has developed for political reasons related to states' protection of their sovereignty and has led to a disparity of treatment that cannot be justified in law.

Forcible displacement, as conceptualised in most international instruments, also does not take into account forms of human dislocation that do not fit neatly within the human rights and international humanitarian law paradigm. The primary example in this category would be development-induced displacement, which can constitute a human rights violation and, like other displacements, can lead to the impoverishment and dispersal of communities. Viewed in this light, it seems contrary to reason to exclude development-induced displacement from the list of state and individual responsibilities recognised by international law.

Second, we have attempted to identify the lack of an effective enforcement mechanism to ensure that states comply with their obligations to prohibit forcible displacement. Genocide is viewed as necessitating an individual convention, and torture has an international convention as well, along with an enforcement mechanism apart from the one provided for in the ICCPR. Without entering into a hierarchy of crimes, which would be unjustified and pointless, it is submitted that individuals, whether acting at the behest of a state or not, have caused a massive amount of human suffering by forcibly displacing their fellow human beings and that this problem warrants an universally-recognised instrument that uniformly deals with the problem of forcible displacement, including by means of

1 Michelangelo.

a specific enforcement regime. With no such centralised instrument or enforcement scheme, we are left with a fragmented system that often lacks the cohesion, authority, and resources to adequately prevent or punish the crime of forcible displacement. The case of Colombia is a potent demonstration of the failure of the current system.

Third, there can be an inattention to the *prevention* of forcible displacement. This *lacuna* is of concern because, although punishing those who commit the crime of forcible displacement is an indispensable element of long-term deterrence of future commissions of the crime, active and determined efforts to prevent displacement before it occurs must be a priority on the agenda of the international community. The African Union has taken an important step in filling this void, with the adoption of the Kampala Convention, the first binding international legal instrument to address the prevention of displacement. While this action is laudable, it remains to be seen whether this regional instrument will have an impact upon the prevention of forcible displacement; and, even if it does, such an impact may be restricted to Africa.

In short, the current legal framework for responding to displacement needs to be improved, and improvement must take place expeditiously.

1. Recent Developments in International Institutions Regarding Forcible Displacement

There are important developments in motion to address forcible displacement. For example, the United Nations High Commissioner for Refugees has recently reaffirmed his commitment to the important precepts of the Refugee Convention, by maintaining that, even in the wake of recent increases by states in respect of securitisation of asylum practices and the economic burden of supporting significant populations of refugees on their territory, the basic principles set forth in the Refugee Convention still apply. The Convention provides the basic, agreed-upon legal standards for the protection of refugees, such as the non-return (*nonrefoulement*) of a person where he or she would face persecution. It provides a political framework within which states may cooperate on a regional and international level in order to coordinate their efforts to ease the suffering of refugees or to facilitate their integration into a new society, ensuring equitable burden-sharing.[2] Moreover, the states parties to the Refugee Convention reaffirmed their commitment to the Convention in the Declaration of States Parties to the 1951 Convention Relating to the Status of Refugees and/or Its 1967 Protocol, which was adopted at the Ministerial Meeting in December 2001. According to this Declaration, the Convention still stands as the cornerstone of the international protection regime for refugees. States' reaffirmation of the Refugee Convention is an important and welcome development, but more needs to be done to prevent people from becoming refugees in the first place.

2 UNHCR, *The State of the World's Refugees 2006: Human Displacement in the New Millennium* (20 April 2006), http://www.unhcr.org/4a4dc1a89.html.

International criminal law has begun to reawaken an interest in the problem of forcible displacement, but is structurally unable to be a *direct* method of preventing forcible displacement The recent, great strides in the realm of international criminal justice during the final decade of the 20th century, especially at the United Nations International Criminal Tribunal for the former Yugoslavia, have advanced the concept that individuals can be held responsible for their actions or inactions when they result in the forcible displacement of people, but the deterrent effect of criminal law has always been a speculative enterprise. Moreover, there is no consistent, agreed jurisprudential framework for the elements of the crime of forcible displacement, although the international tribunals have developed the law in this area to a significant degree. A common factual scenario in one court should attract the same liability in another court, rather than the legal definition of forcible displacement differing depending upon the forum; and, this holds true for domestic courts that are prosecuting forcible displacement as an international crime, for domestic courts are where the lion's share of the work must be done in order for impunity for atrocity crimes to be eradicated.

The ICC's development of the law in this area will be an important event to watch in the years to come, and the ICC has the potential to have the "last word" on the legal definition of the crime. The work of the ICC will have the potential of centralising and harmonising the approach to prosecuting the crime, which would put possible perpetrators on notice of exactly what behaviour is prohibited, which could in turn contribute to the prevention of the crime in practice and foster a culture of compliance on an operational level. These developments in international criminal law are an integral part of the solution to the problem of forcible displacement.

2. The Next "First Step" in Comprehensively Addressing Forcible Displacement

The above observations lead to the final conclusion of this book: it is necessary and timely for the international community to adopt an international instrument that provides a unified legal regime to govern forcible displacement that is flexible enough to encompass the crime in its many conformations. Such an instrument would supplement the current legal framework, by identifying specific state obligations to prevent forcible displacement and to punish perpetrators. A shift to state responsibility for forcible displacement is not a new idea. Nearly a quarter of a century ago, Professor Jack Garvey observed that "mass exodus is a matter of international legal responsibility, not just a violation of human rights ideals that states can denigrate on the basis of national sovereignty."[3]

Mass displacement is indeed a matter of international responsibility: not only do states have a responsibility to their own citizens, but they also have a responsibility to their neighbouring states to prevent refugee flows, which can

3 *See* Jack I. Garvey, *Toward a Reformulation of International Refugee Law*, 26 Harv. Int'l L.J. 483, 496 (1985).

create regional and international instability. This responsibility should translate into a binding system that requires states to proactively prevent forcible displacement before it occurs and that provides for involvement by United Nations entities in cases of noncompliance, as is already the case for noncompliance under the Genocide Convention.

The greatest challenge to framing the forcible displacement debate as one of state responsibility, however, is the question of state sovereignty. According to Roberta Cohen, "[t]he main reason no internationally-binding instrument on IDPs has been introduced is … because states have not been ready to adopt a treaty on anything so sensitive to their own claim to sovereignty as internal displacement."[4] The question of state sovereignty has also deepened the political schism between states receiving displaced persons and states producing displaced persons. In the case of proposals for a convention on internal displacement, the oft-repeated state sovereignty argument is that states producing internally-displaced persons will balk at the prospect of signing onto any binding instrument that further erodes their sovereignty by allowing for the international community to intervene in "internal matters". Yet, there have recently been efforts to shift the emphasis of state sovereignty away from the notion of non-interference and to instead recast the principle in terms of state responsibility.[5] This view advances the position that states cannot shield themselves with the principle of sovereignty if they do not meet their own international obligations, including obligations to their own citizens.[6] After all, states that are responsible for creating situations of displacement affect other states when the displaced seek refuge across international borders,[7] which is inevitably the case for millions of displaced persons, even those who are initially displaced internally and then cross an international boundary.

Given the *lacunae* in the current international legal regime, particularly with regard to the prevention of displacement, and with the notions of both state sovereignty and state responsibility in mind, the authors propose a convention

4 Roberta Cohen, *Response to Hathaway*, 20 J. Refugee Stud. 370, 373 (2007).

5 Thomas G. Weiss, *Internal Exiles: What Next for Internally Displaced Persons?* 24 Third World Quarterly 429, 442 (June 2003).

6 *See* Francis M. Deng et al., Sovereignty as Responsibility: Conflict Management in Africa 15 (1996).

7 A number of scholars have pointed out that states that allow or facilitate mass forcible displacement across borders lose their right to claim sovereignty because of their lack of respect for the sovereignty of the states that will have to address the situation of incoming displaced persons. *See, e.g.*, Christian Tomuschat, *State Responsibility and the Country of Origin*, *in* The Problem of Refugees in the Light of Contemporary International Law Issues 71-72 (Vera Gowlland-Debbas, ed., 1996) (explaining that "[i]f [a state] pushes large groups of its own citizens out of its territory, fully knowing that the victims of such arbitrariness have no right of entry to another country but will eventually have to be admitted somewhere else on purely humanitarian grounds, it deliberately affects the sovereign rights of its neighbours to decide whom they choose to admit to their territories").

that would engage state responsibility for a variety of illegal displacements of persons, while protecting the sovereignty of a state by promoting *state-sponsored* prosecution of individuals and corporations responsible for violating the prohibition on forcible displacement. At the same time, a state's noncompliance with its obligations to prevent forcible displacement and to prosecute those responsible could result in a referral to organs of the United Nations, including the Security Council. Such a convention would be the next "first step" towards effectively addressing the epidemic problem of forcible displacement. The principles embodied in the convention would be the ones that have been explored in this book, as derived from our long, bloody experience with the crime and from more recent developments during the 20th century, such as treaty law and the jurisprudence of international tribunals.

To this end, we submit the following proposed convention. The text of the convention is set forth in bold, with explanatory comments interspersed throughout the articles. The text of the proposed convention is also contained in an appendix, without the commentary.

Proposed International Convention on the Prevention and Punishment of the Crime of Forcible Displacement

The States Parties,

Considering that every person has the right to remain undisturbed in one's home or community,

Commentary: The positive right to freedom of movement and the right to remain in one's home are enshrined in a number of human rights instruments, all of which have been widely ratified. Such instruments include the International Covenant on Civil and Political Rights,[8] the International Convention on the Elimination of All Forms of Racial Discrimination,[9] and the Universal Declaration of Human Rights.[10] The positive right to freedom of movement and the right to choose one's residence necessarily imply the right to remain in one's

8 ICCPR, art. 12(1) (providing that "everyone lawfully within the territory of a State shall, within that territory, have the right to liberty of movement and freedom to choose his residence").

9 International Convention on the Elimination of All Forms of Racial Discrimination, art. 5(d)(i), (iii), (v), 21 Dec. 1965, 660 U.N.T.S. 195 ("... States Parties undertake to prohibit and to eliminate racial discrimination in all its forms and to guarantee the right of everyone, without distinction as to race, colour, or national or ethnic origin, to equality before the law, notably in the enjoyment of the following rights: ... (i) The right to freedom of movement and residence within the border of the State.").

10 UDHR, art. 13 (declaring that "everyone has the right to freedom of movement and residence within the borders of each State").

home, and the right to live within a community of one's choice.[11] See chapter three.

Considering that the violation of this right is a crime under international law,

Commentary: The criminalisation of forcible displacement is by now well-entrenched in international law. Geneva Convention IV contains one of the first explicit prohibitions on forcible displacement.[12] It also stipulates that unlawful deportation or transfer is a war crime and a grave breach of the Geneva Conventions.[13] Article 17 of Additional Protocol II, applicable in situations of internal armed conflict, prohibits and criminalises forcible displacement of civilians.[14]

In addition to the Geneva Conventions, the Statutes of all the *ad hoc* tribunals criminalise forcible displacement. Article 5(d) of the ICTY Statute explicitly recognises deportation as a crime against humanity, and Chambers have held that deportation and forcible transfer are both acts that amount to persecution, a crime against humanity, under Article 5(h) of the Statute,[15] and that fall within the residual "other inhumane acts" category of crimes against humanity, under Article 5(i) of the Statute.[16] Article 2(g) of the ICTY Statute identifies the unlawful deportation or transfer of a civilian as an act that is punishable as a grave breach of the Geneva Conventions. See chapter four.

---

11 *See* Report of the Representative of the Secretary-General, Mr. Francis Deng, submitted pursuant to Commission on Human Rights resolution 1997/39, Economic and Social Council, Doc. E/CN.4/1998/53/Add.1, 11 February 1998 ("[T]he eviction or displacement of persons is unlawful if it is based on grounds not permissible under international law. This aspect of the right not to be arbitrarily displaced implicitly derives from the rights to freedom of movement and residence, to the inviolability of the home and to housing.").

12 Geneva Convention Relative to the Protection of Civilian Persons in Time of War, 12 Aug. 1949, 6 U.S.T. 3516, 75 U.N.T.S. 287 [Geneva Convention IV], art. 49 (prohibiting "individual or mass forcible transfers, as well as deportations of protected persons from occupied territory to the territory of the Occupying Power or to that of any other country, occupied or not").

13 *Id.* art. 147.

14 Protocol Additional to the Geneva Conventions of 12 August 1949, and Relating to the Protection of Victims of Non-International Armed Conflicts, 8 June 1977, 16 I.L.M. 1442 [Additional Protocol II], art. 17(1).

15 *See Prosecutor v. Krnojelac*, Case No. IT-97-25-A, Judgement, 17 September 2003, ¶ 222.

16 *See Prosecutor v. Blagojević & Jokić*, Case No. IT-02-60-T, Judgement, 17 January 2005, ¶¶ 623-32; *Prosecutor v. Brđanin*, Case No. IT-99-36-T, Judgement, 1 September 2004, ¶ 539; *Prosecutor v. Krstić*, Case No. IT-98-33-T, Judgement, 2 August 2001, ¶ 519.

Recognising that, at all periods of history, forcible displacement has inflicted great losses upon humanity, and

Commentary: As Special Rapporteurs Al-Khasawneh and Hatano have noted, "population transfer has prevailed as an instrument of State-craft in every age in recorded history,"[17] dispersing cultures and destroying communities from time immemorial. Chapter two of this book considers historical and contemporary examples of forcible displacement, ranging across the globe. The examples examined in that chapter demonstrate that the motivations behind forcible displacement and the manner in which displacement is perpetrated have existed for centuries.

Being convinced that, in order to prevent and punish the crime of forcible displacement, international cooperation is required,

Commentary: States have the primary duty of prosecuting individuals responsible for perpetrating the crime of forced displacement. While the Refugee Convention is a key legal instrument for addressing the needs of certain types of persons who have been displaced, it is not a preventive document, and rather seeks to bind states to protect individuals *after* they have been displaced, as opposed to before the fact. Nor does the Refugee Convention address punishment of the perpetrators of forcible displacement. This Convention fills these *lacunae* by identifying the state obligation to prevent forcible displacement from occurring and to punish it if it does occur. The need for state prevention of displacement has been stressed by numerous UN officials.[18]

17 *See* The Human Rights Dimensions of Population Transfer, Including the Implantation of Settlers, Preliminary Report prepared by A.S. Al-Khasawneh & R. Hatano, Commission on Human Rights, Sub-Commission on Prevention of Discrimination and Protection of Minorities, Forty-fifth session (E/CN.4/Sub.2/1993/172 (6 Jul. 1993).

18 Report of the Representative of the Secretary-General, Francis Deng, Submitted Pursuant to Commission on Human Rights Resolution 1997/39, Economic and Social Council, Doc. E/CN.4/1998/53/Add.1, 11 February 1998 ("State responsibility in the context of displacement is relevant to prevention, as much as to the protection and assistance of those already displaced, and the search for lasting solutions.").

Hereby agree as hereinafter provided:

PART 1 – Definitions

Article 1

The States Parties confirm that forcible displacement, whether committed in time of peace or in time of war, is a crime under international law which they undertake to prevent and to punish.

Commentary: Although forcible displacement is prohibited in international humanitarian law, it is not universally settled that forcible displacement is a crime in peace time under human rights law. This has hindered the protection of displaced persons and disadvantaged the international community in its efforts to address forcible displacement. Francis Deng has noted that "[t]he lack of a comprehensive *de lege lata* rule in international human rights law on the forced movement of persons has resulted in an unclear understanding as to its status in international law .... It has also resulted in the matter not featuring much in the deliberations of the United Nations human rights treaty bodies."[19] This provision clarifies that forcible displacement is a crime when it is committed not only in the context of an armed conflict, but also where there is not an ongoing armed conflict. Both state responsibility and individual criminal responsibility therefore attach to forcible displacements, regardless of the existence of an armed conflict.

Article 2

1. **In the present Convention, forcible displacement means the removal of one or more persons to another location by expulsion or other coercive acts, from an area in which that person or those persons is/are lawfully present, without grounds permitted under international law.**
2. **Forcible displacement shall be considered a crime when it is committed during an international or internal armed conflict and during times of peace.**
3. **Forcible displacement may be prosecuted as a crime against humanity, a war crime, or an underlying act of genocide.**

Commentary: The elements of forcible displacement employed by the proposed convention make use of the definition of forcible displacement from the modern international tribunals.[20] See chapter four.

---

19 *Id.* at Part IV, ¶ 2.

20 At the ICC, the elements of deportation or forcible transfer of population as a crime against humanity under Article 7(1)(d) of the Rome Statute of the International Criminal Court, 2187 U.N.T.S. 90, *entered into force* 1 July 2002 [Rome Statute], are: "1. The perpetrator deported or forcibly transferred, without grounds permit-

The definition of forcible displacement provided here does not distinguish between cross-border transfers and intra-border transfers, and the prosecution of both internal displacement and displacement across international borders require proof of the same elements. Moreover, the prosecution should not be required to prove that the *mens rea* of the perpetrator is to permanently displace individuals.

This definition is also formulated to encompass a broad range of displacements; however, it purposefully avoids listing the types of displacement it is intended to cover. This is so that the Convention will not be under-inclusive. It also renders the Convention palatable to states that are reluctant to undertake obligations that they view as overly expansive, such as the obligation to refrain, where possible, from displacing persons for reasons relating to development. However, the text anticipates that, over time, practice will develop around the Convention leading to a broad construction of this provision, including, for example, its application to development-induced displacement, as well as other types of displacement that may arise in the future.

---

ted under international law, one or more persons to another State or location, by expulsion or other coercive acts. 2. Such person or persons were lawfully present in the area from which they were so deported or transferred. 3. The perpetrator was aware of the factual circumstances that established the lawfulness of such presence. 4. The conduct was committed as part of a widespread or systematic attack directed against a civilian population. 5. The perpetrator knew that the conduct was part of or intended the conduct to be part of a widespread or systematic attack directed against a civilian population." Elements of Crimes, Article 7(1)(d). The elements of unlawful deportation or transfer as a grave breach of the Geneva Conventions of 12 August 1949 (a war crime) under Article 8(2)(a)(vii) of the Rome Statute are: "The perpetrator deported or transferred one or more persons to another State or to another location. 2. Such person or persons were protected under one or more of the Geneva Conventions of 1949. 3. The perpetrator was aware of the factual circumstances that established that protected status. 4. The conduct took place in the context of and was associated with an international armed conflict. 5. The perpetrator was aware of factual circumstances that established the existence of an armed conflict." Elements of Crimes, Article 8(2)(a)(vii). The elements of ordering the displacement of the civilian population for reasons related to the conflict, unless the security of the civilians involved or imperative military reasons so demand, a serious violation of the laws and customs applicable in armed conflicts not of an international character (a war crime) under Article 8(2)(e)(viii) of the Rome Statute are: "1. The perpetrator ordered a displacement of a civilian population. 2. Such order was not justified by the security of the civilians involved or by military necessity. 3. The perpetrator was in a position to effect such displacement by giving such order. 4. The conduct took place in the context of and was associated with an armed conflict not of an international character. 5. The perpetrator was aware of factual circumstances that established the existence of an armed conflict." Elements of Crimes, Article 8(2)(e)(viii). *See also* ICTY Statute, articles 5(d), 2(g).

PART 2 – Individual Criminal Responsibility and State Responsibility

Article 3

The States Parties undertake to enact, in accordance with their respective domestic laws, the necessary legislation to give effect to the provisions of the present Convention and, in particular, to provide effective penalties for persons guilty of forcible displacement.

Commentary: This article acknowledges that states have a duty to prevent and punish the crime of forcible displacement on a domestic level. As such, states undertake to prosecute individuals responsible for forcible displacement in their own courts and to implement laws for the domestic prosecution of individuals that are consistent with the Convention. In this respect, the provisions of the Convention are similar to the Genocide Convention, which requires states "to enact, in accordance with their respective Constitutions, the necessary legislation to give effect to the provisions of the present Convention, and, in particular, to provide effective penalties for persons guilty of genocide."[21]

Article 4

Persons charged with forcible displacement shall be tried by a competent tribunal of the relevant State or by such international penal tribunals as may have jurisdiction over the commission of the crime.

Commentary: This article acknowledges that there may be instances when states are unable to domestically prosecute the crime of forcible displacement, in which case the international community is to ensure that the perpetrator is tried in an appropriate international court. This article is consistent with the principle of complementarity, which is employed by the Rome Statute.

Article VI of the Genocide Convention requires that those charged with genocide be tried either in a competent tribunal of the state in the territory where the act occurred or in an international penal tribunal.[22]

Article 5

Persons committing forcible displacement shall be punished, whether they are constitutionally responsible rulers, public officials, or private individuals.

Commentary: This article clarifies that criminal liability attaches regardless of a person's official capacity. It is modelled after Article IV of the Genocide

21 Genocide Convention, Dec. 9, 1948, 78 U.N.T.S. 277, art. 5.

22 *Id.* art. 6.

Convention and also reflects the statutes of the modern international criminal tribunals and the post-World War II courts.[23]

Article 6

The States Parties undertake to implement, in accordance with their respective domestic laws, all necessary and appropriate measures to prevent the commission of forcible displacement upon their territory or within their control.

Commentary: The measures referred to in this article involve both legislative measures, as well as practical, operational measures. This article is purposefully drafted in a broad manner because the measures that states are willing to undertake as binding measures will vary and a consensus will need to be achieved as to the interpretation of this article. It will be useful for states to look to both the Guiding Principles on Internal Displacement as well as the Kampala Convention for guidance.

The Colombian experience, discussed in chapter seven, offers additional insight into the types of preventive duties that states must undertake in order to combat the practice of forcible displacement. For example, comprehensive domestic legislation is necessary to prevent forcible displacement, but such legislation must also be implemented in a state's operational activities. Operational measures would include, for example, early warning systems to identify situations that could potentially result in displacement and effective training of military and police personnel in the rules of engagement.

PART 3 – Settlement of Disputes

Article 7

Any State Party may call upon the competent organs of the United Nations to take such action under the Charter of the United Nations as it considers appropriate for the prevention of forcible displacement.

Commentary: This article is modelled after Article VIII of the Genocide Convention. It is a necessary provision to ensure that states implement their

23 Charter for the International Military Tribunal, art. 7 ("The official position of defendants, whether as Heads of State or responsible officials in Government Departments, shall not be considered as freeing them from responsibility or mitigating punishment."); ICTY Statute, art. 7(2) ("The official position of any accused person, whether as Head of State or Government or as a responsible Government official, shall not relieve such person of criminal responsibility nor mitigate punishment."); ICTR Statute, art. 6(2) ("The official position of any accused person, whether as Head of state or government or as a responsible government official, shall not relieve such person of criminal responsibility nor mitigate punishment.").

obligations under human rights and international humanitarian law with respect to forcible displacement. The organ of the United Nations that would presumably be consulted most frequently under this provision is the Security Council, which has in the past played an important role in addressing situations of mass displacement, including in its resolutions concerning Iraq and the former Yugoslavia, both discussed in chapter three.

However, this article provides states parties with a choice of which organ of the United Nations to which they would resort, which is in-line with the *travaux préparatoires* of the Genocide Convention. In discussions relating to a provision of the Genocide Convention that is similar to the above article, it was debated whether or not to limit the article to calling upon the Security Council. Although the *travaux préparatoires* of the Genocide Convention reveal that various states envisaged that the Security Council would primarily be called upon, those states that wished to have resort to several options within the United Nations system prevailed in the debate. Among the primary reasons for the prevailing position were the arguments that organs other than the Security Council, such as the General Assembly, represent all states and use a simple majority voting procedure, therefore eradicating the possibility that a few states could prevent necessary collective action with their veto powers.[24]

Article 8

Disputes between the States Parties relating to the interpretation, application, or fulfilment of the present Convention, including those relating to the responsibility of a State for forcible displacement, shall be submitted to the International Court of Justice at the request of any of the parties to the dispute.

Commentary: This article is similar to Article IX of the Genocide Convention, which also refers disputes concerning interpretation and application of the Convention to the International Court of Justice.

PART 4 – Reporting

Article 9

1. **The States Parties shall submit to the Human Rights Council, through the Secretary-General of the United Nations, reports on the measures they have taken to give effect to their undertakings under this Convention, within one year after the entry into force of this Convention for the State Party concerned. Thereafter the States Parties shall submit supplementary reports every four years on any new measures taken, and such other reports as the Human Rights Council may request.**

---

24 Secretarial Draft E/AC.25/W.1/Add.4, *in* Hirad Abtahi & Philippa Webb, The Genocide Convention: The Travaux Préparatoires, Volume I 1006 (2008).

2. **Each report shall be considered by the Human Rights Council, which may make such comments or suggestions on the report as it considers appropriate, and shall forward these to the State Party concerned. That State Party may respond with any observations it chooses to the Human Rights Council.**

Commentary: As many commentators have pointed out, there is no monitoring mechanism for the Refugee Convention, a stark contrast to the UN human rights treaties.[25] The reason for this is no doubt due to the fact that states in the past have associated refugee protection with a challenge to their sovereignty; yet, the failure to include a monitoring body in the Refugee Convention has led to circumvention of obligations under the Refugee Convention and has detracted from the Convention's binding character. In contrast, the UN human rights treaties, such as the Convention Against Torture and Other Cruel, Inhuman or Degrading Treatment or Punishment, have monitoring bodies that routinely evaluate state compliance with the treaty.

A monitoring body to assess state compliance with the Convention on the Prevention and Punishment of the Crime of Forcible Displacement is integral to the effectiveness of the Convention. Such a monitoring body would have the capacity in particular to refer state violations of the Convention directly to a relevant organ of the United Nations, such as the Security Council, as is provided for in the following article.

Article 10

1. **If the Human Rights Council receives reliable information which appears to it to contain well-founded indications that forcible displacement has been, is being, or is about to be committed in the territory of a State Party, it may invite that State Party to cooperate in the examination of the information and to submit observations with regard to the information concerned.**
2. **The Human Rights Council may, if it decides that this it is warranted, designate one or more of its members to make an inquiry into the situation and to report to the Human Rights Council on an urgent basis.**
3. **After examining the findings of its member or members submitted in accordance with subparagraph 2, the Human Rights Council shall transmit these findings to the State Party concerned, together with any comments or recommendations which seem appropriate in view of the situation.**

---

25 *See, e.g.*, Deborah Anker, *Boundaries in the Field of Human Rights: Refugee Law, Gender, and the Human Rights Paradigm*, 15 Harv. Hum. Rts. J. 133, 135 (2002) ("[T]here is no regularized monitoring of states' compliance with their obligation to provide surrogate protection, although the United Nations High Commissioner for Refugees (UNHCR) serves an important supervisory function. No refugee-specific, international institutions hear interstate complaints or individual communications.").

4. **After having heard a State Party on a particular situation, the Human Rights Council may transmit the results of its investigations, along with any comments or recommendations, to a competent organ of the United Nations or to another appropriate entity so that such action as that organ or entity considers appropriate for the prevention of forcible displacement may be undertaken.**

Commentary: Much of the language of this article resembles that of Articles 19 and 20 of the Convention Against Torture and Other Cruel, Inhuman or Degrading Treatment or Punishment, which requires states parties to undertake to cooperate in any investigation initiated by its monitoring treaty body, the Committee Against Torture.

This article provides the Human Rights Council with the authority to monitor situations of forcible displacement in the territory of states parties. The primary role of the Human Rights Council is to assist states parties in developing and implementing domestic solutions to incidents of forcible displacement. Nevertheless, there will be situations in which purely domestic resolution is not possible, in which case organs of the United Nations or other international entities will need to become involved. In the event that involvement at an international level is necessary, this article permits the Human Rights Council to transmit both the reports it receives from states parties—as well as the results of any of the Council's investigations into allegations that forcible displacement has been, is being, or is about to be carried out in a state—to other competent international institutions or organs of the United Nations. This promotes cooperation and information-sharing between international institutions. Thus, for example, the results of an investigation of the Human Rights Council into a situation of forcible displacement could be transmitted to the International Criminal Court, supplementing that Court's information and corresponding ability to prosecute perpetrators of forcible displacement. The results could also be transmitted to the Security Council, which could then act under Chapter VII of the UN Charter to stop the displacement or even prevent the forcible displacement before it occurs.

PART 5 – Execution of the Convention, Accession, Amendment, and Notification

Article 11

1. **The present Convention is open for signature by any State Member of the United Nations or member of any of its specialised agencies, by any State Party to the Statute of the International Court of Justice, and by any other State which has been invited by the General Assembly of the United Nations to become a Party to the present Convention.**
2. **The present Convention is subject to ratification. Instruments of ratification shall be deposited with the Secretary-General of the United Nations.**

3. The present Convention shall be open to accession by any State referred to in subparagraph 1 of this article.
4. Accession shall be effected by the deposit of an instrument of accession with the Secretary-General of the United Nations.
5. The Secretary-General of the United Nations shall inform all States which have signed this Convention or acceded to it of the deposit of each instrument of ratification or accession.

Article 12

1. The present Convention shall enter into force three months after the date of the deposit with the Secretary-General of the United Nations of the thirty-fifth instrument of ratification or instrument of accession.
2. For each State ratifying the present Convention or acceding to it after the deposit of the thirty-fifth instrument of ratification or instrument of accession, the present Convention shall enter into force three months after the date of the deposit of its own instrument of ratification or instrument of accession.

Article 13

The provisions of the present Convention shall extend to all parts of federal States without any limitations or exceptions.

Article 14

1. Any State Party to the present Convention may propose an amendment and file it with the Secretary-General of the United Nations. The Secretary-General of the United Nations shall thereupon communicate any proposed amendments to the States Parties to the present Convention with a request that they notify him whether they favour a conference of States Parties for the purpose of considering and voting upon the proposals.
2. In the event that at least one third of the States Parties favours such a conference, the Secretary-General shall convene the conference under the auspices of the United Nations. Any amendment adopted by a majority of the States Parties present and voting at the conference shall be submitted to the General Assembly of the United Nations for approval.
3. Amendments shall come into force when they have been approved by the General Assembly of the United Nations and accepted by a two-thirds majority of the States Parties to the present Convention in accordance with their respective constitutional processes. When amendments come into force, they shall be binding upon those States Parties which have accepted them, other States Parties still being bound by the provisions of the present Convention and any earlier amendment which they have accepted.

Article 15

The Secretary-General of the United Nations shall inform all States which have signed the present Convention or acceded to it of the following particulars: signatures, ratifications, and accessions under article 11; the date of the entry into force of the present Convention under article 12; and the date of the entry into force of any amendments under article 14.

Article 16

1. **The present Convention, of which the Chinese, English, French, Russian, and Spanish texts are equally authentic, shall be deposited in the archives of the United Nations.**
2. **The Secretary-General of the United Nations shall transmit certified copies of the present Convention to all States which have signed the present Convention or acceded to it.**

Commentary: These clauses, which relate to execution, accession, amendment, and notification, have been modelled upon Part VI of the International Covenant on Civil and Political Rights, Articles 48-53.

3. Concluding Remark

This book has endeavoured to capture the grand, wicked phenomenon of humans forcibly displacing each other throughout their history on planet Earth. Any one book would not be able to catalogue comprehensively all the acts of displacement that have occurred. One reason for this is that much of the historical record in relation to displacements is located in documents; thus, displacements prior to the advent of writing are lost to the passage of time and the frailties of human memory, if they are not preserved reliably in the archaeological record or in oral histories. Even where a written or oral historical record does exist, it may not accurately record a displacement, especially if it is being compiled by a victorious party to a conflict or if its transmission has been tainted by some other agenda of the person creating the official account of the relevant events.

Another reason for the difficulty in cataloguing the forced migrations of people is the sheer scope of involuntary human movements. In this regard, it is helpful to have recourse to the Office of the United Nations High Commissioner for Refugees Statistical Online Population Database.[26] This impressive project demonstrates the breathtaking sweep of the problem of human forcible displacement, in cold hard statistics. At the end of 2008, there were 230,670 IDPs in Afghanistan; 94,093 refugees in Algeria; 603,251 IDPs in Azerbaijan; 7,257 refugees and 124,529 IDPs in Bosnia and Herzegovina; 81,037 refugees in Cameroon;

26 UNHCR, Statistical Online Population Database (19 March 2010), http://www.unhcr.org/pages/4a013eb06.html.

197,000 IDPs in the Central African Republic; 302,687 refugees and 166,718 IDPs in Chad; 3,000,000 IDPs in Columbia; 683,956 IDPs in Cote d'Ivoire; 1,460,102 IDPs in the DRC; 293,048 IDPs in Georgia; 2,647,251 IDPs in Iraq; 980,109 refugees in the Islamic Republic of Iran; 320,605 refugees and 404,000 IDPs in Kenya; 723,571 stateless persons in Myanmar; 800,000 stateless persons in Nepal; 765,720 refugees and 155,809 IDPs in Pakistan; 91,505 IDPs in the Russian Federation; 1,277,200 IDPs in Somalia; 504,800 IDPs in Sri Lanka; 1,201,040 IDPs in Sudan; 3,500,000 stateless persons in Thailand; 162,132 refugees and 853,000 IDPs in Uganda; and 140,169 refugees and 100,000 IDPs in Yemen. The list goes on … and on. In total, at the end of 2008, there were over 16,000,000 million refugees in the world, and over 26,000,000 IDPs. This is a population roughly the size of Canada. Some estimates are significantly larger. And this is only a snap shot of present day displacements. If one thinks of the thousands of years during which human beings have been displacing each other, one begins to grasp the enormity of the situation.

An aspect that has not been included in this book is displacement caused by global anthropomorphic climate changes.[27] For example, people are moving as arable land becomes more and more scarce due to desertification caused by the irresponsible use of our planet's fragile and finite resources. Another example of such pending crises are the millions of people inhabiting small island nations and coastal areas that will become submerged in the not so distant future because of the melting of the polar ice caps and the resulting rise in the oceans.[28] The vast scope of the environmental problems that humanity has collectively brought down upon itself are only beginning to sink into the minds of the public. The political, geographical, economic, and social changes that we will undergo as a species due to the changes in our environment will be *the issue* of our next generation and beyond. It may be that the displacements of our past will appear as nothing more than a rather tame dress rehearsal for those that lie ahead, as the competition for resources and space intensifies.

A final aspect of displacement caused by humans is not the displacement of our fellow humans, but rather the displacement of our fellow species upon the Earth. Such a thought may be considered somewhat unorthodox to some: forcible displacement of animals from their natural habitat? But such a notion is the moral and legal basis of endangered species acts in many countries of the world, which is a genus of a prohibition against displacing animals from their native habitats. Perhaps if we could learn to respect the rights of animals to remain in

27 UNHCR, *Climate Change, Natural Disasters and Human Displacement: A UNHCR Perspective* (23 October 2008), http://www.unhcr.org/refworld/type,RESEARCH,UNHCR,,492bb6b92,0.html.

28 *See, e.g.*, Shaina Stahl, *Unprotected Ground: The Plight of Vanishing Island Nations*, New York Int'l L. Rev., vol. 23, No. 1, at 1, 3 *et seq.* (Winter 2010) (discussing the legal implications of an estimated 25 million people who might be displaced when their forty-three island nations become submerged due to a relatively small rise in sea level caused by climate change).

their habitats, it may aid us in accepting the immorality of displacing each other. The objective of this book has been to analyse the actual, not theoretical, causes and effects of forcible displacement and to propose a new international instrument for how displacement can be prevented in the future. Perhaps—in some small way—such an instrument would contribute to deterring those who would seek to displace their neighbours. Someday, if we humans can stop mistreating each other, we might be able to start upon our long journey of treating with more compassion and respect the members of the other multitudinous species with whom we share the planet.

Appendix

Proposed International Convention on the Prevention and Punishment of the Crime of Forcible Displacement

The States Parties,

Considering that every person has the right to remain undisturbed in one's home or community,

Considering that the violation of this right is a crime under international law,

Recognising that, at all periods of history, forcible displacement has inflicted great losses upon humanity, and

Being convinced that, in order to prevent and punish the crime of forcible displacement, international cooperation is required,

Hereby agree as hereinafter provided:

PART 1 – Definitions

Article 1

The States Parties confirm that forcible displacement, whether committed in time of peace or in time of war, is a crime under international law which they undertake to prevent and to punish.

Article 2

1. In the present Convention, forcible displacement means the removal of one or more persons to another location by expulsion or other coercive acts, from an area in which that person or those persons is/are lawfully present, without grounds permitted under international law.

2. Forcible displacement shall be considered a crime when it is committed during an international or internal armed conflict and during times of peace.

3. Forcible displacement may be prosecuted as a crime against humanity, a war crime, or an underlying act of genocide.

PART 2 – Individual Criminal Responsibility and State Responsibility

Article 3

The States Parties undertake to enact, in accordance with their respective domestic laws, the necessary legislation to give effect to the provisions of the present Convention and, in particular, to provide effective penalties for persons guilty of forcible displacement.

Article 4

Persons charged with forcible displacement shall be tried by a competent tribunal of the relevant State or by such international penal tribunals as may have jurisdiction over the commission of the crime.

Article 5

Persons committing forcible displacement shall be punished, whether they are constitutionally responsible rulers, public officials, or private individuals.

Article 6

The States Parties undertake to implement, in accordance with their respective domestic laws, all necessary and appropriate measures to prevent the commission of forcible displacement upon their territory or within their control.

PART 3 – Settlement of Disputes

Article 7

Any State Party may call upon the competent organs of the United Nations to take such action under the Charter of the United Nations as it considers appropriate for the prevention of forcible displacement.

Article 8

Disputes between the States Parties relating to the interpretation, application, or fulfilment of the present Convention, including those relating to the responsibility of a State for forcible displacement, shall be submitted to the International Court of Justice at the request of any of the parties to the dispute.

PART 4 – Reporting

Article 9

1. The States Parties shall submit to the Human Rights Council, through the Secretary-General of the United Nations, reports on the measures they have taken to give effect to their undertakings under this Convention, within one year after the entry into force of this Convention for the State Party concerned. Thereafter the States Parties shall submit supplementary reports every four years on any new measures taken, and such other reports as the Human Rights Council may request.

2. Each report shall be considered by the Human Rights Council, which may make such comments or suggestions on the report as it considers appropriate, and shall forward these to the State Party concerned. That State Party may respond with any observations it chooses to the Human Rights Council.

Article 10

1. If the Human Rights Council receives reliable information which appears to it to contain well-founded indications that forcible displacement has been, is being, or is about to be committed in the territory of a State Party, it may invite that State Party to cooperate in the examination of the information and to submit observations with regard to the information concerned.

2. The Human Rights Council may, if it decides that this it is warranted, designate one or more of its members to make an inquiry into the situation and to report to the Human Rights Council on an urgent basis.

3. After examining the findings of its member or members submitted in accordance with subparagraph 2, the Human Rights Council shall transmit these findings to the State Party concerned, together with any comments or recommendations which seem appropriate in view of the situation.

4. After having heard a State Party on a particular situation, the Human Rights Council may transmit the results of its investigations, along with any comments or recommendations, to a competent organ of the United Nations or to another appropriate entity so that such action as that organ or entity considers appropriate for the prevention of forcible displacement may be undertaken.

PART 5 – Execution of the Convention, Accession, Amendment, and Notification

Article 11

1. The present Convention is open for signature by any State Member of the United Nations or member of any of its specialised agencies, by any State Party to the Statute of the International Court of Justice, and by any other State which has been invited by the General Assembly of the United Nations to become a Party to the present Convention.

2. The present Convention is subject to ratification. Instruments of ratification shall be deposited with the Secretary-General of the United Nations.

3. The present Convention shall be open to accession by any State referred to in subparagraph 1 of this article.

4. Accession shall be effected by the deposit of an instrument of accession with the Secretary-General of the United Nations.

5. The Secretary-General of the United Nations shall inform all States which have signed this Convention or acceded to it of the deposit of each instrument of ratification or accession.

Article 12

1. The present Convention shall enter into force three months after the date of the deposit with the Secretary-General of the United Nations of the thirty-fifth instrument of ratification or instrument of accession.

2. For each State ratifying the present Convention or acceding to it after the deposit of the thirty-fifth instrument of ratification or instrument of accession, the present Convention shall enter into force three months after the date of the deposit of its own instrument of ratification or instrument of accession.

Article 13

The provisions of the present Convention shall extend to all parts of federal States without any limitations or exceptions.

Article 14

1. Any State Party to the present Convention may propose an amendment and file it with the Secretary-General of the United Nations. The Secretary-

General of the United Nations shall thereupon communicate any proposed amendments to the States Parties to the present Convention with a request that they notify him whether they favour a conference of States Parties for the purpose of considering and voting upon the proposals.

2. In the event that at least one third of the States Parties favours such a conference, the Secretary-General shall convene the conference under the auspices of the United Nations. Any amendment adopted by a majority of the States Parties present and voting at the conference shall be submitted to the General Assembly of the United Nations for approval.

3. Amendments shall come into force when they have been approved by the General Assembly of the United Nations and accepted by a two-thirds majority of the States Parties to the present Convention in accordance with their respective constitutional processes. When amendments come into force, they shall be binding upon those States Parties which have accepted them, other States Parties still being bound by the provisions of the present Convention and any earlier amendment which they have accepted.

Article 15

The Secretary-General of the United Nations shall inform all States which have signed the present Convention or acceded to it of the following particulars: signatures, ratifications, and accessions under article 11; the date of the entry into force of the present Convention under article 12; and the date of the entry into force of any amendments under article 14.

Article 16

1. The present Convention, of which the Chinese, English, French, Russian, and Spanish texts are equally authentic, shall be deposited in the archives of the United Nations.

2. The Secretary-General of the United Nations shall transmit certified copies of the present Convention to all States which have signed the present Convention or acceded to it.

Index

F

G

H

I

K

L

M

N

O

P

R

S

T

U

W

Y

www.ingramcontent.com/pod-product-compliance
Lightning Source LLC
LaVergne TN
LVHW020652300926
849161LV00004B/918
* 9 7 8 9 0 0 4 2 2 0 5 4 6 *